KLANDESTINE

KLANDESTINE

How a Klan Lawyer and a Checkbook Journalist Helped
James Earl Ray Cover Up His Crime

PATE M^cMICHAEL

CHICAGO
REVIEW
PRESS

Copyright © 2015 by Pate McMichael
All rights reserved
Published by Chicago Review Press Incorporated
814 North Franklin Street
Chicago, IL 60610
ISBN 978-1-61373-070-6

Library of Congress Cataloging-in-Publication Data
McMichael, Pate.
  Klandestine : how a Klan lawyer and a checkbook journalist helped James
Earl Ray cover up his crime / by Pate McMichael.
    pages cm
  Summary: "This fast-paced history traces the escalating racial violence that
led to the assassination of Dr. Martin Luther King Jr., and then documents
how Klan lawyer Arthur J. Hanes and checkbook journalist William Bradford Huie aided the evolution of James Earl Ray's bogus alibi"—Provided by
publisher.
  Includes bibliographical references and index.
  ISBN 978-1-61373-070-6 (cloth)
  1. Ray, James Earl, 1928–1998. 2. King, Martin Luther, Jr., 1929–1968—
Assassination. 3. Ray, James Earl, 1928–1998—Friends and associates.
4. Hanes, Arthur J., 1916–1997. 5. Huie, William Bradford, 1910–1986.
6. Conspiracies—United States—History—20th century. 7. Ku Klux Klan
(1915–)—History—20th century. 8. Assassins—United States—Biography.
9. Lawyers—United States—Biography. 10. Journalists—United States—
Biography. I. Title. II. Title: Clandestine.

  HV6248.R39M325 2015
  364.152'4092—dc23
  [B]

                                        2014037543

Interior design: PerfecType, Nashville, TN

Printed in the United States of America
5 4 3 2 1

A 1968 Herblock Cartoon, © The Herb Block Foundation

CONTENTS

Preface..xi

Prologue.. 1

Part I: The Deal, 1968

1 A Pretty Fair Country Lawyer: London, June 1968.......................... 7

2 Extradition: London, June 27–July 17, 1968................................ 14

3 The Memphis Gag: Memphis, July 18–22, 1968 20

4 Giant Conspiracy: Memphis, July 23–31, 1968............................26

5 The Checkbook Journalist: Memphis, August 1968.......................33

Part II: Strange Bedfellows, 1954–1963

6 Little Mencken: Alabama, 1941–1954 39

7 Wolf Whistle: Money, Mississippi, 1954–1957 46

8 Birmingham's New Mayor: Birmingham, Alabama, 1961 52

9 No Summertime Soldier: Birmingham, 1962................................59

10 Project C: Birmingham, Spring 1963...64

11 A Rotten Harvest: Birmingham, Fall 1963.................................70

12 Mr. X: November 1963–June 1964...77

Part III: The Bloody Road to Selma, 1964–1965

13 A $25,000 Lie: Philadelphia, Mississippi,
   June–December 1964..87

14 Cattle Prods and Plaited Whips: Selma, Alabama,
   January–February 1965..94

15   Bloody Sunday: Selma, March 7, 1965...99

16   Baby Brother: Selma, March 25, 1965.................................... 104

17   The Klonsel's Stage: Hayneville, Alabama, April–May 1965 109

Part IV: Krossings in Klan Kountry, 1965-1966

18   I Was a Ku Klux: Hayneville, Alabama,
     May–September 1965 119

19   The Parable of Two Goats: Hayneville,
     October–December 1965 127

20   The Klokan: Los Angeles, January 1966.................................. 133

21   Klan Kourt: Washington, February 1966.................................. 139

22   The Escape: Missouri State Penitentiary, Jefferson City,
     March 1966 146

Part V: Stand Up for America, 1967-1968

23   Meet Me in California: Los Angeles, 1967 153

24   A Sick White Brother: Memphis, April 4, 1968.................... 157

25   Stoner's Visit: Memphis, June–September 1968.......................... 163

26   A Blond Latin: *Look*, October 1968 169

27   Election Night: Tuesday, November 5, 1968............................175

28   Pink Slip: Memphis, Tuesday, November 12, 1968 179

Part VI: Waiting for Raoul, 1969

29   Tramps: New Orleans, December 1968 189

30   The Bay of Hubris: Birmingham, January 1969.......................... 195

31   An Educated Bluff: Memphis, February 1969............................204

32   A Simple Story: Grand Jury Room, Shelby County
     Courthouse, February 3, 1969 208

33   Guilty, Not Racist: Memphis, February 1969 211

34   The Last Supper: Shelby County Courthouse,
     March 10, 1969..218

Part VII: Though It Hath No Tongue, 1969-1986

35   Bushman: *Look*, March 1969 225

36   The Bushy Knoll: Memphis, April–September 1969 228

37   Belated Justice: Birmingham, 1977 235

38   The Grapevine: St. Louis to Washington, 1978 240

39   Walking It Back: Hartselle, Alabama, 1977–1978 249

40   The Klan?: Washington, 1978 255

41   Full Circle: Alabama, 1980s 258

Epilogue: Memphis, 1993–1999 261

Acknowledgments 272

Notes 275

Selected Bibliography 310

Index 313

PREFACE

"A long line of unpunished killings." That's how Martin Luther King Jr. described the legacy of violence and injustice that defined the South's decades-long resistance to integration and civil rights. That King managed to survive as long as he did is an amazing feat. From 1954 until his death in 1968, the civil rights leader received hundreds of death threats, endured physical assaults in open public, and survived multiple bombings targeting him, his family, and his movement. Watching coverage of President John F. Kennedy's slaying in Dallas, King famously remarked that his own fate would be sealed in a similar fashion. That hour finally arrived four and a half years later, at 6:01 PM on April 4, 1968, in Memphis. While standing on the balcony of the Lorraine Motel, King was struck by a single bullet fired from an elevated and concealed position. Like Kennedy, he died in the line of duty.

King's murder served as a predictable capstone to an era of unspeakable racial violence. Yet unanswered questions surround the circumstances of his demise, and many still wonder whether justice was served. After all, only one man, an escaped convict from Missouri named James Earl Ray, has been punished for the crime. On the surface, Ray does not fit the caricature of a hangdog racist thirsty for blood. Media coverage has often portrayed him as hapless and apolitical, someone who must have been paid by clandestine forces. It's a narrative that Ray himself put in motion upon his June 1968 arrest in London, then continued from jail until his death in 1998.

This book argues that Ray pulled the trigger in Memphis. It documents the evolution of Ray's alibi from 1968 to 1999, the year Dr. King's own family declared him an innocent man. Despite widespread skepticism, authoritative accounts of the assassination, like Gerold Frank's *An American Death* (1974), Gerald Posner's *Killing the Dream* (1993), and Hampton Sides's *Hellhound on His Trail* (2009), have established a bedrock narrative linking Ray to King's murder through convincing evidence and primary source material. Each work establishes important pieces of Ray's racial motive, yet none makes an overarching argument that Ray was motivated by racial hatred. Frank's book is a well written and skillfully reported journalistic account, based largely on Federal Bureau of Investigation (FBI) reports and his own reporting of Ray's ill-fated Memphis trial. Posner's work is an encyclopedic dissection of the crime and the evidence. Using scores of primary source material, it does the most of the three to debunk Ray's alibi, particularly his invention of a conspiracy. Sides's book gives the FBI's masterful manhunt investigation its due, while also noting Ray's special interest in segregationist causes.

Klandestine benefits from those three works, as well as many others listed in the bibliography. All of the literature on the assassination, and much of the expanding literature on civil rights, provided important clues that made each chapter better. But the foundation of this book is built on the back of novel primary source discoveries gathered over an eight-year period through the Freedom of Information Act and the National Archives. A trove of newly released documents from the Shelby County Register of Deeds, as well as dusty files from a 1965 House Un-American Activities Committee investigation of the United Klans of America, provided precious sourcing that takes readers deep inside Ray's Memphis jail cell and Alabama's violent Klaverns. The author also exploited more than a dozen university archival collections to establish key factual assertions.

Klandestine puts Ray's racial motive into focus. It paints him as a wannabe Southerner, a die-hard segregationist, and a George Wallace fanatic who left behind a compelling trail of evidence, as well as a telling escape plan. *Klandestine* closes the book on the conspiracy that Ray and his defense team created in the fall of 1968. That's when the world first learned of an assassinations mastermind named Raoul, described by Ray as a blond Latin with Canadian citizenship. According to this bogus theory, Raoul, a mysterious seaman with deep connections to the criminal grapevine, framed Ray as part of a complicated New Orleans–based conspiracy.

Ray brought Raoul to life by forging a publishing partnership with two very strange bedfellows: a slick Klan lawyer named Arthur J. Hanes, the de facto "Klonsel" for the United Klans of America, and checkbook journalist William Bradford Huie, the darling of *Look* magazine and a longtime menace of the Klan. Before representing the Klan, Hanes served as the mayor of Birmingham from 1961 to 1963, infamously closing the city's parks rather than obeying federal orders to integrate. No one can dispute that Hanes's role was overshadowed by the outrageous behavior of his benefactor, Birmingham commissioner of public safety Eugene "Bull" Connor, but *Klandestine* is the first book to treat Hanes as more than an auxiliary source of intransigence during Birmingham's darkest hours. It shows that Hanes's bitter ouster as mayor led directly to his affiliation with the Klan and his eventual representation of Ray.

William Bradford Huie was everything that segregationists like Hanes and Connor despised. Huie made his fortune taking on the sacred cows of World War II and Jim Crow laws. His bestselling books and sensational magazine articles were testaments to his libertarian attitudes, particularly on race. While Hanes spoke at White Citizens' Council rallies, Huie traveled inside the Klan's killing dens to expose its most heinous crimes, such as the 1955 murder of young Emmett Till in Money, Mississippi; the 1957 castration of Judge Edward Aaron in Tarrant City, Alabama; the 1963 bombing of the Sixteenth Street Baptist Church in Birmingham; and the 1964 killing of three civil rights workers in Philadelphia, Mississippi. Armed with a satchel of cash, Huie brokered deals with killers in exchange for detailed admissions of guilt. Paying Klansmen, regardless of their reliability, to reveal racial conspiracies was what he called "the truth business." Indeed, much of what we know about Klan violence comes from Huie's reporting, but as *Klandestine* shows using previously undisclosed FBI files, some of Huie's most important factual assertions do not survive scrutiny. In short, Huie played fast and loose with the truth and in the process invented falsehoods that sullied the historical record. Nowhere is this more evident than in his writings on the King assassination.

Despite polar opposite views on race, Hanes and Huie found common cause in the lucrative world of conspiracy. As journalist Edward Jay Epstein showed in *Inquest*, a brilliant 1966 exposé of the Warren Commission, the public's obsession with conspiracy—exasperated by the government's attempt to squash "assassination rumors" to protect the "national interest"—instilled a collective schizophrenia that publishers, broadcasters, and producers soon turned into profits. The traumas of racial strife, foreign war, and political assassination paved a gilded road of riches for those callous enough to exploit a credulous public. Conspiracist Mark Lane, who became Ray's lawyer in 1977, first capitalized on this phenomenon in 1966 with his bestseller *Rush to Judgment*, an opportunistic exploitation of the Kennedy assassination that gave voice to the grassy knoll–multiple shooter theory. Others followed suit. As historian Gary Wills pointed out in *Jack Ruby* (1968), Dallas judge Joe B. Brown and defense attorney Melvin Belli both inked book deals while Ruby's conviction for Lee Harvey Oswald's murder awaited appeal.

Huie and Hanes thought they could make Memphis the new Dallas. They approached Ray while he was in British custody and struck a three-man deal with *Look* magazine and its publishing arm, Dell Publishing Company. *They Slew the Dreamer*, the project's original title, had all the trappings of a bestseller turned silver screen blockbuster. The first serial hit newsstands just days before the nation voted in a dead-heat presidential election and only a week before Ray's much anticipated "Trial of the Century." But something happened on the way to Hollywood. The deal suffered a major setback when Ray fired Hanes on the eve of the trial, then fell apart completely when he pled guilty to the crime in March 1969.

Despite the publishing deal's collapse, the conspiracy of Raoul survived. Part of the reason for its longevity can be explained by the mystery of Ray's eventual guilty plea. He took a nearly maximum sentence in lieu of the death penalty, which was highly unlikely anyway because King himself abhorred capital punishment. But the other reason for Raoul's longevity, as *Klandestine* reveals for the first time, is that Hanes and other important segregationists vigorously defended Ray's innocence after being fired. From 1969 until his death, Hanes gave interviews and inspiration to notorious peddlers like Mark Lane and William Pepper, claiming all the while that Ray was the victim of a black-militant conspiracy with ties to New Orleans and Cuba. Huie, by contrast, finally concluded that Hanes and Ray had played him like a fiddle. He spent the last years of his life trying to cover up his authorship of the Raoul conspiracy, telling everyone who'd listen that Ray was nothing but a two-bit, Wallace-loving racist.

In 1978, ten years after King's assassination, Congress revisited the FBI's investigation and shockingly concluded that Ray likely acted as part of a St. Louis–based plot involving a die-hard segregationist and big-time Wallace donor named John H. Sutherland. But, as *Klandestine* shows, the inquiry stopped short of trying to connect Sutherland's "plot" back to Birmingham, Hanes's hometown and the place where Ray bought his getaway car, a 1966 white Mustang, and the murder weapon, a Remington 760 Gamemaster rifle. Though Hanes and Huie both participated in the inquiry, Congress did not fully scrutinize Hanes's ties to the Klan nor Huie's inquiry into a Birmingham-based conspiracy.

Klandestine picks up where the most promising facts left off. The narrative begins with Ray's capture in London and the revelation of his mysterious publishing deal with Hanes and Huie. It then flashes back into a fast-paced narrative of escalating racial violence that almost made King's assassination inevitable. Told chronologically through Hanes's and Huie's perspectives, this unique vantage shows how a legacy of unpunished racial killings combined with fevered interest in political assassinations provided the perfect exigency to sell a reckless conspiracy to a suspicious and outraged nation.

PROLOGUE

The aftermath of the King assassination unleashed a bloody week of race rioting and lawlessness that ended with national guardsmen occupying the charred streets of Washington and Memphis. As the summer of 1968 approached, conservative presidential candidates like Richard Nixon and George Wallace ran on campaigns of "Law and Order," but on June 6, Robert Kennedy, the brother of a martyred president and himself a popular Democratic candidate in the dead-heat election, was assassinated. These devastating tragedies were as surreal as they were shameful.

Two days later, on June 8, British police captured the lead suspect in the King assassination at Heathrow Airport. Sixty-four days had passed since April 4, when a single bullet traveled 205 feet and 3 inches, striking Dr. King on the right side of his face and severing his spinal cord. Upon arrest, the suspect possessed a revolver and two copies of a fake Canadian passport under the alias Raymond George Sneyd. But the suspect's real name was James Earl Ray, and he was an American fugitive from the Missouri State Penitentiary. Until his arrest, the reporting of evidence against Ray went unregulated in the States. No American judge had yet been assigned to protect his Sixth Amendment right to a fair trial, so the American media—protected by the First Amendment—gained access to what would later become courtroom evidence, much of which linked Ray to a forlorn flophouse in Memphis where he allegedly fired the fatal shot with a rifle while standing in a bathtub. On television and in wanted posters, the FBI claimed that Ray escaped the penitentiary on April 23, 1967, and wandered aimlessly across North America before showing up in Memphis on April 3, 1968, the day before the assassination.

The media eagerly painted an unflattering portrait of Ray's midwestern upbringing. An exposé in the May 3, 1968, issue of *Life* titled "The Accused Killer Ray Alias Galt: The Revealing Story of a Mean Kid" reached more than eight million subscribers who learned the depressing details of his childhood in Alton, Illinois, and Ewing, Missouri. Taken as a whole, the article portrayed Ray as an indigent, racist "Hoosier" (St. Louis slang for redneck) with an inept, habitual tendency to commit petty crimes. It came replete with pictures of his miserable birthplace, his jailbird family, and his previous mug shots. Ray's third-grade class picture made the cover, and the editor's note, a gloating admission of journalistic zeal, spoke for itself. "We started with nothing but Ray's name, his brother's P.O. box number in a Chicago suburb, and a town, Alton, Illinois," the note read. "That was Friday afternoon. By Saturday night Woodbury [a reporter] had pulled county clerks out of bed to check on marriage license records, knocked on more than one hundred doors and talked to schoolteachers and bartenders and anyone one else who might have known about the Rays."

Time followed suit with a story in the June 21, 1968, issue called "Ray's Odd Odyssey," an overview of Ray's previous convictions for armed robbery and his mysterious activities after escaping prison in April 1967. "As a thief, James Earl Ray's specialty was botching his getaway," the article read. "After he escaped from the Missouri State Penitentiary in 1967, Ray's style changed; he seemed to have become a cum-laude graduate in criminality. Flush with unaccustomed cash and astute at espying loopholes in the law's vigilance, he rambled across the country using a collection of aliases."

Television and radio listeners soon learned isolated but intriguing details about Ray's yearlong escapade in cities like Los Angeles, Birmingham, Atlanta, and New Orleans. They heard about his never-ending stash of twenty-dollar bills, attributed by reporters Jack

Anderson and Drew Pearson to an unsolved bank robbery in Ray's birthplace of Alton, Illinois. The holdup occurred on the morning of July 13, 1967—three months after Ray's escape from prison and nine months before the assassination. Three culprits, believed to be Ray and his two brothers, got away with nearly $30,000 in cash. Ray's cut, if assumed to be $10,000, would help explain his itinerant lifestyle and significant purchases, such as the 1966 Mustang and the murder weapon.

But not everyone bought the holdup story. Growing public skepticism of government investigations put conspiracy in the air and magnified the state's burden of proof in future political assassinations. Meanwhile, opportunists like New Orleans district attorney Jim Garrison tried to link Ray's crime all the way back to President Kennedy's assassination, a mafia-funded conspiracy Garrison claimed to have solved in February 1967. In this context, candid citizens thought less about Ray's innocence and more about the prospect of a well-funded, multifaceted plot.

PART I

⟫ ⟫ ⟫ ⟪ ⟪ ⟪

The Deal, 1968

1

A Pretty Fair Country Lawyer
London, June 1968

James Earl Ray, the man accused of assassinating Martin Luther King Jr., was scheduled to be arraigned at Bow Street Magistrate's Court in London on June 10. The resultant media coverage intrigued a young British solicitor named Michael Eugene, who joined the crowd gathering outside for a view of the suspect's plea on the proxy charges of passport fraud and carrying an unlicensed firearm. None of the journalists on hand could ever recall being searched before entering the building, but everyone received a thorough pat-down to protect Ray from an attempt on his life. As the hearing began, Eugene watched as a battery of guards formed a shield around Ray and led him into the same courtroom where famous men like Charles Dickens, Oscar Wilde, and Casanova once stood before the bar of justice.

The arraignment proved anticlimactic, just another short scene in the court's historic tenure. In the course of one palpable minute, Ray pled not guilty, claiming against reason that he was a citizen of Canada with no permanent address. With little hesitation, British judge Frank Milton remanded him to custody until an extradition hearing could be held. The US government had already applied for additional warrants on the grounds that Ray was an escaped fugitive and a suspected murderer. When the arraignment was over, Eugene scurried off to work.

Later that morning, the phone rang. By 3:00 PM, Eugene was crossing the Thames bound for Brixton Prison, assigned by the court as the equivalent of an American public defender. A guard led him into an interrogation room, where a passive man in glasses sat in silence. Eugene called his client Ramon George Sneyd—the name on Ray's false passport and the only name he would provide to British police. Since his escape from prison in April 1967, Ray had used nearly a dozen aliases in a dozen cities and five countries. Eugene exchanged a greeting and explained his assignment. He was there to prepare a defense for the extradition hearing. The whole process could take as long as two months, should they choose to drag it out.

After all, Ray was arrested with a Canadian passport, not an American one. Proving Ray's US citizenship would not be enough to merit extradition. The American government must hire British barristers and transport its evidence abroad; legitimate reasons for wanting Ray returned to the States must be presented to the court. Eugene also explained Article VI of the Extradition Treaty of 1931, which forbids the British from extraditing a fugitive criminal to another country for prosecution of a political crime. Eugene believed that he could establish the political nature of the King assassination by pointing out America's troubled legacy of racism and the government's long-standing harassment of civil rights leaders.

Eugene outlined the process, then asked Ray for concerns. The American spoke with purpose. "Get in touch right away with my brother Jerry," he asserted calmly, "and also with Arthur Hanes. He's a lawyer in Birmingham, Alabama." In dropping Jerry's name, Ray was admitting his true identity to Eugene for the first time. As a May 1968 *Life* article on Ray's upbringing explained, Ray called the St. Louis area home, where his father, sister, and two jailbird brothers, Jack and Jerry, lived in two-state proximity. But this lawyer from Alabama was a complete mystery to Eugene. More disturbingly, Ray seemed adamant. "I know he'll represent me and look after my interests back in the States," the suspect claimed. "I saw Hanes a couple of times on television a few years ago when he was mayor of Birmingham."

Eugene left the prison and contacted the American embassy in Grosvenor Square. The diplomat fielding his call was disapproving. This Arthur Hanes, a politician turned trial attorney, has a bad reputation for taking racial cases. Ray should be advised to reconsider his choice of counsel. Taking the hint, Eugene approached his client about picking someone else. After all, Ray claimed to have only seen Hanes on television. Why would he want to make this more racial than it already was? With some apparent irony, or pretense, Ray agreed to consider two alternates: F. Lee Bailey and Melvin Belli, the Camaro and Mustang of American defense attorneys. Eugene agreed to reach out to all three.

But after Eugene left, Ray quickly penned a letter to "Mr. Hanes" dressed in six stamps depicting the queen. In all caps, he acknowledged the British charges of passport fraud, as well as "the Martin King case." Ray told Hanes that without a real lawyer in waiting he would be convicted "of whatever charge they file on me before I arrive" in Memphis. At the time of his writing, a bogus media report speculated that Ray had been "interviewed" by Fred Vinson Jr., head of the US Department of Justice's criminal division. Vinson was sitting on a bench during the arraignment, and when reporters approached him after the hearing, he confirmed having "seen" Ray. Vinson was being literal, but the remark fed a rumor that Ray might have confessed inside his cell. "The reason I wrote to you," Ray explained to Hanes, "is I read once where you handled a case similar to what I think may be filed on me."

On June 14, just before Ray's letter arrived at the Birmingham Bar Association, Eugene phoned the firm of Hanes & Hanes in downtown Birmingham. The law office was a suite in the Frank Nelson Building, a haven for the city's lawyers and die-hard segregationists, the very building where the United Klans of America—the largest umbrella of Klansmen in the nation—had been represented for many years. Hanes, a smooth-talking Southerner with an animated drawl, picked up. Eugene explained the circumstances of the call, as well as the letter that would soon arrive in the mail. Suspecting a prank but playing along, Hanes confirmed being the former mayor of Birmingham but claimed no knowledge of anyone named Sneyd or Ray. He listened carefully and promised to await the letter but also wanted to know if the man had the money to pay his fee. Eugene fumbled for an answer. "He gave me that indication, sir."

》》》 》》》 》》》 《《《 《《《 《《《

At 5:05 PM on the Sunday evening of June 16, the deputy director of the US Passport Office phoned a Washington FBI agent to check the background of a lawyer who was planning to visit London on short notice. The applicant, Arthur Jackson Hanes, needed papers ASAP but was told that no passports could be issued on a Sunday night. Should he appear in New York or Washington on Monday morning, he could acquire one immediately. The FBI agent jotted down some background information on Hanes, then typed up a memo: "Born 10-19-16, Alabama; profession: attorney, Birmingham, Alabama; it is noted that Hanes is a former Special Agent of the FBI who resigned 8-4-51."

The next morning, on June 17, Hanes called a press conference and announced his plans to leave for London on June 19 at 7 PM from Washington, DC. Outside the Frank Nelson Building, the world learned that Birmingham's former mayor would be representing the American charged in the King assassination. His remarks were carried on the radio and later appeared on the nightly news. To skeptics the story didn't make much sense. Why would Ray seek out an Alabama lawyer who was not even a member of the Tennessee bar? Hanes took similar questions as he made the trek from Birmingham to Atlanta to Washington to London. In what soon became a pattern, Hanes pleaded ignorance of his client's identity, as well as his intentions. "I've never heard of Ray, and I've never heard of any of the aliases used," Hanes said in Atlanta on June 18, before boarding a plane to Washington. "Also, I have never, as far as I know, seen any of the people depicted in any of the photographs or artists' drawings of anyone connected to this case. This man, whomever he may be, is unknown to me. I don't know who's in jail in London, and I'm not so sure that anybody in this country knows as of now."

As Hanes made his way to Washington, the legal attaché of the US embassy in London phoned the FBI for guidance. The treatment Hanes received abroad by the US government would reflect directly on President Lyndon Johnson's administration, which had enough on its plate with the Tet Offensive in Vietnam. The attaché wanted to know if Hanes should be met at the airport and extended certain courtesies, like a ride to his hotel. More immediately, the attaché wanted the FBI to provide some background on Hanes. The British, determined to protect Ray's rights and safety, were eager to know more about this Alabama attorney, so the FBI passed along the following information: "Hanes is a former Special Agent of the Bureau who entered on duty October 25, 1948, and resigned August 4, 1951, less than three years service. Subsequent to his Bureau service he was mayor of Birmingham and represented Klansmen defendants in the case involving the murder of Viola Liuzzo, the Michigan woman who was shot and killed on March 25, 1965, near Selma, Alabama."

More telling was the Birmingham FBI's assurances that it possessed "no information indicating that Hanes is or was a member of the Ku Klux Klan or is an official legal representative of the Klan." FBI director J. Edgar Hoover was not convinced. Hoover wanted the legal attaché in London to know one more thing about his former employee: Hanes is "absolutely no good. Have no contact with him."

>>> >>> >>> ‹‹‹ ‹‹‹ ‹‹‹

Dapper, confident, and well dressed, Hanes and his son, Art Jr., a twenty-six-year-old Princeton graduate, landed in London on June 20. The American embassy confirmed their afternoon arrival and subsequent registration at the four-star Royal Lancaster Hotel in Hyde Park. Hanes gave his first press conference in the lobby at 3:00 PM, in plenty of time for the morning papers. He described himself as a "pretty fair country lawyer." When asked if he would even be allowed to see his client while in London, Hanes shrugged. "I rather doubt it." Only a licensed barrister can practice law in the United Kingdom; his visit was for moral support.

The reporters were not satisfied. They demanded to know how Ray would pay Hanes's fee, his transatlantic flight, and his ritzy hotel bill. It just didn't seem to add up, but Hanes was unmoved, responding that he would not work pro bono. When a reporter called him a segregationist, Hanes suddenly got testy. "You don't label liberal lawyers 'integrationist.' This question doesn't enter into the case. My views on civil rights are too far afield here," he added. But the grilling only continued with more intensity. Reporters asked about Hanes's relationship with Dr. King, the victim. In a roundabout way, King was partly responsible for Hanes's 1963 ouster as mayor of Birmingham, but the attorney dismissed these inquiries with boilerplate: "I've seen him and I've met him. As far as I'm concerned his business was his business and mine was mine. I don't knock anyone's kick." What about the KKK? reporters asked. Haven't you represented Klansmen in the past? Hanes said he recalled "no knowledge of the Klan" because he personally does not "join right-wing groups or left-wing groups. Just the Lions Club and the PTA."

⟫⟫ ⟫⟫ ⟫⟫ ⟪⟪ ⟪⟪ ⟪⟪

Hoover read these news reports and entered into a conversation with US attorney general Ramsey Clark, who on April 27, less than a month after the assassination, had assured the American people that there was no evidence of a conspiracy. Hoover shared the sentiment but told Clark on July 20 that he wasn't entirely convinced.

> I commented that, of course, the lawyer who has gone over to represent Ray is a former FBI Agent; that he is no good and was the attorney in the Mrs. Viola Liuzzo case, but, of course, we got convictions in that, but this lawyer has always been strongly pro-Klan. I said he was Mayor of Birmingham, Alabama, at one time and at that time he was a strong supporter of 'Bull' Connor and I thought it significant that Ray should get a fellow who has certainly a strong smell of Klan about him.

I said he denies he is a Klansman or that he ever attended any of their meetings and he claims he does not know how Ray came to ask for him as his lawyer. I said Ray claims he read about him in the newspaper when he was in the penitentiary in Missouri. The Attorney General said he does not see how Ray would remember that. I agreed and told the Attorney General that the lawyer and his son, who is a partner, went over to England and we alerted our London Office to alert the British as to his background so they would know with whom they are dealing.

>>> >>> >>> <<< <<< <<<

The day after his London arrival, Hanes presented himself to Scotland Yard demanding an audience with Ray. A British official denied his request, informing Hanes that his "client" possessed less than 200 pounds. The money he'd just wasted scurrying abroad to conduct this publicity stunt would never be repaid, at least not by Ray. Hanes did not take umbrage. Writing on a business card, he scribbled a short message and asked that it be given to the prisoner. "Dear Mr. Sneyd," Hanes wrote, "We made an effort to see you but will see you immediately upon arrival in the USA."

As the note implied, extradition was inevitable, though not immediate. After four days in London and a little sightseeing, Hanes headed back to Birmingham to monitor the situation. The trip was legally futile, yet fruitful in the court of public opinion. Pictures of Ray's handsome American lawyer walking purposely through Trafalgar Square appeared in hundreds of American newspapers and ended, for good, the manhunt media narrative that had so demonized Ray as a habitual criminal. Perhaps just as important, the story of Hanes's involvement in the King assassination was given prominence in a news cycle that included the Tet Offensive in Vietnam, the assassination of Robert Kennedy, and the riveting third-party candidacy of former Alabama governor George C. Wallace.

2

Extradition
London, June 27–July 17, 1968

On the morning of June 27, the first day of Ray's extradition hearing, an attorney representing the state of Missouri appeared in Bow Street Court to claim its ward. Don't forget, Missouri reminded the court, Ray is an escaped convict who held up a Kroger grocery store in East St. Louis in 1959. He received twenty years as a habitual offender and served that sentence up until the moment he escaped from prison in Jefferson City in April 1967. Missouri wanted him back.

Next the state of Tennessee and the FBI presented evidence linking Ray to King's assassination. Hoover was not waiting until the trial; he sent over the smoking gun. FBI forensics expert George Bonebrake, who pulled a latent print off the murder weapon, presented three photographic charts tying Ray to the crime. Bonebrake's team had compared the print against those of fifty-three thousand known fugitives. It was a tiresome task, a hunch really, that required precious hours of trial and error. Working in a secret bureau outpost for twenty-four hours straight, the FBI matched the print to James Earl Ray on the 702nd card, the court learned.

The physical evidence was later supported by Scotland Yard detective chief superintendent Robert Butler, the British agent who interrogated Ray on June 8. Despite international warrants for his arrest, Ray was captured with two Canadian passports and a revolver. So that day in court, Butler recalled the moment when Ray heard his given name spoken for the first time in many months. The suspect dropped his head and blurted out "Oh God" and "I feel so trapped," Butler testified.

The hearings continued until July 2. Eugene planned to make a final plea for asylum, and he warned Ray not to speak regardless of the outcome. English courts only recognize barristers, he explained. A defendant's words would be ignored and viewed as a sign of disrespect. As the court came to order, Eugene demurred to the evidence presented by the US government and claimed that King's murder was a "political crime," a conspiracy to which Mr. Sneyd was an obvious patsy. Under bilateral treaty obligations, no citizen of either country can be extradited for a political crime, Eugene pleaded.

At noon, the judge called a recess, promising to return at 2:00 PM with a decision. As people shuffled into the street, the clerk suddenly shouted for everyone to sit down because Ray wished to address the court. Eugene was aghast. He watched in disbelief as his client, who was chewing gum, stood up like a child caught in cowardice. Ray had been fuming since Butler's testimony a few days earlier, and he stood up to tell the judge that he never uttered those ridiculous lines, "I feel so trapped" and "Oh God." His little speech devolved into a rant against the "liberal press," whom he felt would take unattributed quotes and use them against him by not "taking into totality all of the circumstances." Curiously enough, Ray said nothing about Bonebrake or the latent fingerprint. Nor did he deny being James Earl Ray. Later that afternoon, his petition for asylum was denied, but under British law, he had two weeks to appeal.

》》》 》》》 》》》 《《《 《《《 《《《

After hearing the news, Hanes planned another trip to London for July 4, and this time he would meet with Ray face-to-face. What Hanes hoped to prove baffled the FBI. Flying between Washington and London was so expensive that the Department of Justice had debated keeping a handful of necessary personnel abroad rather than fly them back and forth. For Hanes to spend hundreds of dollars just for a face-to-face with his client struck Hoover as suspicious.

Guards were present when Ray and Hanes talked for the first time on July 5 inside Wandsworth, the maximum-security prison in southwest London where Ray had been transferred. Trading notes and whispering through a wire screen, they spoke privately for thirty minutes, and the conversation was not recorded. When Hanes emerged, he praised the prison's security as "austere and severe," a subliminal contrast to the way Dallas police handled Lee Harvey Oswald's incarceration. "There have been people hurt in other cases like this and I didn't like that at all," Hanes said.

The mystery of Hanes's trip also piqued the media's interest. The press followed him back to the hotel, where Hanes smoked and drank and took questions in a shiny, dark suit. The conversation soon returned to money. The idea that a family of ex-cons and alcoholics could pay for Hanes's defense was utterly ridiculous, a complete farce. The American press had established that Ray's relatives in Missouri lived in utter poverty and plain ignorance. "He ain't going to pay me with love, I can tell you that," Hanes joked. But as the questions persisted, his nonchalance turned to anger. "His face reddening," one account read, "the attorney almost shouted at the British reporters. 'I'm not on trial. Bear that in mind. The source of any money is not relevant to the case.'" Flustered and indignant, Hanes suddenly promised a not guilty plea, calling Ray a patsy in a "conspiracy masterminded by black instead of white extremist groups."

That sudden outburst, as unscripted as it seemed, owed its ancestry to a disturbing, decades-long segregationist campaign to cover up racial violence as black-on-black crime. Perhaps more to the point, Hanes's comments laid the foundation of a conspiracy that Ray would soon latch onto for the rest of his life. Hanes did not deliver the comment in a sarcastic or flippant way. He seemed entirely convinced. "I am beginning to build a case, to organize a defense. He gave me names and other leads to follow up back in the United States, and I am building a file," Hanes added.

Ray and Hanes met for a second time on July 6, this time for nearly an hour. Hanes returned to the States the next day, but his parting advice was for Ray to waive his appeal because only guilty men fight extradition. Taking the hint, Ray ended the fiction of Raymond George Sneyd for good on July 15 when the *Chicago Daily News* published a letter from London signed by one "Lord R.G. Sneyd." It was addressed to Ray's brother, Jack, who leaked it to the papers. "That's probably his idea of a joke," Jack told the *News*. In the letter, Ray asked his family for $600 to pay Art Hanes's expenses. "I could appeal my extradition hearing," the note read, "but I am getting tired of listening to these liars, so I might close it up about Tuesday."

〉〉〉 〉〉〉 〉〉〉 〈〈〈 〈〈〈 〈〈〈

Word that Ray might be ready to go home put the FBI on a war footing. His removal from London had to be orchestrated very carefully indeed. Moving prisoners abroad presents an expensive security risk, and for that reason, Hoover and Clark decided that Ray should be flown home in a military, not civilian, jet. He should also be accompanied by trusted federal agents, and while en route to Memphis, Ray could choose to remain silent—or not. Regardless, it would be an opportunity to take his statement and ask him about his choice of representation.

Having worked under Hoover, Hanes knew what to expect. On July 11, he requested that his client not be interviewed by "any member" of the Justice Department before, during, or after the extradition flight. He also requested permission to accompany Ray on the plane because his client had "fear for his personal safety while in the custody of the Justice Department." Hanes knew all too well that Hoover wanted to avoid a state trial. Despite a significant amount of hard evidence against Ray, the possibility of an acquittal was quite real. All-white juries in state courts all over the Deep South had earned a bad reputation for freeing violent racists. Many trials had been rigged, witnesses had been intimidated, and smoking guns had been eagerly ignored. Hanes enjoyed that line of work, so when asked if he would seek a change of venue when Ray returned to Tennessee, he almost laughed. "No sir, I will not. I feel that the people of Memphis and the people of Tennessee are fair-minded and just," he told the Associated Press. "Like most Americans, I feel that once they are presented the evidence and the testimony, coupled with the law the judge will charge them with, they will give a fair and just verdict."

The FBI's extradition plan became more complicated on July 16, when Hoover learned that Hanes was headed to London for the third time in less than a month "for the purpose of getting on the plane to return" with his client. The report came two days after Hoover received intelligence that Hanes had recently met with the Imperial Wizard of the United Klans of America, a giant umbrella of Klaverns extending across the Deep South and into the Midwest. An informant claimed that the meeting occurred in Birmingham and concerned Hanes's possible representation of Klansmen who would likely be enjoined from protesting school integration in Crenshaw County, Alabama. The informant's report called for redactions when disseminated outside of Hoover's office. "We have been advised REDACTED that on 7/14/68, Robert K. Shelton, Imperial Wizard of the United Klans of America Inc., had a meeting at Birmingham, Alabama, with Arthur Hanes, attorney for James Earl Ray," the report read.

Now Hoover's skepticism of Hanes turned into outright contempt. He told Attorney General Clark to anticipate some negative media coverage when Hanes was forbidden from riding on the plane. "He will probably try to put on a shyster act," the director warned. For that reason the FBI did not want "Ray sitting around waiting for the arrival of the plane." Instead, the government should have the jet ready to go, leaving Hanes on an empty runway with a choir of clicking cameras. Hoover eventually got his way. In a written response, Clark told Hanes that he was making "a very unusual request," adding, "From your prior experience in the Federal Bureau of Investigation, I am sure you can understand why this request cannot be honored."

As Hoover waited for the presidential warrant for Ray's extradition to be signed, he made it known to anyone who would listen that Hanes was not "honorable," nor a "high-class person." He would definitely not be allowed onboard. And to eliminate accusations of a false confession, Hoover and Clark forbade agents from speaking to Ray while in transit. Hoover also assured Clark that the sheriff in Memphis would "keep his mouth shut" and prepare the cellblock with bulletproof material. Once the plane hit the ground in Memphis, armored cars would carry Ray to a special cell in the Shelby County Criminal Courts Building. The police in those cars would become Ray's permanent guards for the duration of the trial. Clark could be assured, Hoover wrote, that none of Ray's Tennessee guards was subject to "Klan infiltration."

On July 17, Hanes showed up at the US embassy in London demanding to speak with the consul general about boarding the plane. When his bid ultimately failed, Hanes held a press conference with Ray's British attorney, Michael Eugene, to denounce the federal government's trickery and "the unprecedented, libelous press and television campaign" in the US media to portray Ray as a "convicted murderer, a monster." Before boarding a return flight home, Hanes told the British press that Ray was innocent. "We want him back in Memphis to prove this as soon as possible," he declared.

3

The Memphis Gag
Memphis, July 18-22, 1968

On the Thursday night of July 18, James Earl Ray crossed the Atlantic Ocean inside an air force behemoth. To ensure his safety, the C-135, which can hold more than one hundred passengers, made a round-trip flight from Washington with a three-person military flight crew. Ray was handcuffed to his seat in the company of four FBI agents. The first leg of Operation Landing, as it was called, ended at Millington Naval Air Station in Memphis at 3:36 AM on July 19.

The second leg began at 3:45 AM. Shelby County sheriff William Morris, who maintained contact with the pilot during the last two hours of the flight, stripped and searched Ray while reading him his Miranda rights. Ray had to be transported across Memphis, and Sheriff Morris was taking no chances. He deployed two decoys for overzealous journalists and would-be assassins, putting them in motion while guards carefully prepared Ray for transport. After a brief physical, Ray put on a plaid shirt, bulletproof vest, and "armored trousering." Wearing handcuffs, he was lifted inside a sixty-one-ton silver-and-blue armored car previously used to deter civil rights marchers in Jackson, Mississippi. Sheriff Morris and a Memphis physician rode with Ray while a convoy of motorcycles and cruisers escorted the vehicle into town at high speeds.

Operation Landing went racing up to the Shelby County Criminal Courts Building, a fortress on Washington Avenue, at 4:29 AM. Airspace was blocked off and snipers were positioned atop adjacent buildings. Helmeted deputies with riot guns lined the perimeter while Ray was frantically led inside the north door of the jail. Confused by the decoys and general chaos, journalists waiting outside the cordon remained at bay. Before they could figure out what happened, Ray was inside getting fingerprinted, photographed, and videotaped. Within seconds, he was escorted to a maximum-security cellblock on the third floor that was 100 percent impregnable. Block A, better known as the "Tank," consisted of six individual cells through which Ray would alternate on a daily basis. A bullpen-like common area divided the cellblock with a shower located at the far end. It stood out like a film set, surrounded by fluorescent lights, surveillance cameras, and a security desk. Ray's every private action was now the stuff of public record. All told, Sheriff Morris spent more than $10,000 making Ray's accommodations as secure as humanly possible.

A security desk surrounded the exits, and pairs of guards, working in three eight-hour shifts, held watch twenty-four hours a day. Each time Ray's cell door opened, a red light flickered on the sheriff's desk, and the guards, after being searched, presented special tokens to enter or leave the block. Ray's food was prepared by prison trustees under surveillance, then placed into a steel lockbox with three shelves and a cup holder. Only the deputy behind the bulletproof glass could give out the key.

》》》 》》》 》》》 《《《 《《《 《《《

Ray's first meal as a ward of the state of Tennessee consisted of spaghetti, salad, white bread, Jell-O, and iced tea. The Memphis physician who accompanied Sheriff Morris during Ray's transfer, Dr. McCarthy DeMere, then delivered a clean bill of health despite Ray's refusal to give a blood sample. Shortly before midnight, as Ray tried to sleep in the brightly lit cell, his attorney landed in New York. Six police escorts followed Hanes to a Manhattan hotel for the night, and the next morning, on July 20, he boarded a commercial flight to Memphis. As the plane prepared to land, the pilot ordered Hanes to remain seated upon arrival. When the cabin finally cleared, ten police officers came aboard. "I don't want to alarm you," one officer said to Hanes, "but we believe an attempt may be made on your life."

Police escorted Hanes inside Ray's cell at 11 AM. Barricaded by a steel-plated door, white iron bars, and a window of bulletproof glass, Ray's attorney announced himself through a microphone, prompting a green light to flash. Guards then led him to a small room with a sign that read NO GUNS ALLOWED. There he received a pat-down, before boarding an elevator to the third floor. Hanes spent two hours with Ray that Saturday and returned frequently over the following days.

The two men developed a bizarre routine for privacy. It consisted of Ray leaving his cell (with permission) and walking to the community shower. Then Hanes would turn on the shower and lie down near the drain to evade the sheriff's elaborate surveillance. In that posture, they talked for hours on end—about exactly what, Morris or Hoover never knew. When Hanes left that first day, Ray stayed up watching television and talking to his guards. Before going to bed he asked for a pen and paper to write a few letters, and at 10 PM guards delivered the following items: "one pocket comb, one ball point pen, one crossword puzzle book, one *Field & Stream* magazine, one pad of writing paper, and twenty envelopes, one [Memphis] *Press-Scimitar* paper, one clear plastic shower curtain, one card table and four chairs."

Like a mad novelist pinned to a deadline, Ray started writing at a furious pace. He wrote into the night, letters and notes first, then a more complicated document, in thousand-word increments, complete with diagrams and maps. Under Hanes's careful guidance, Ray was plotting out the conspiracy that led him to Memphis on the eve of King's assassination.

〉〉〉 〉〉〉 〉〉〉 〈〈〈 〈〈〈 〈〈〈

Hanes remained under police protection until the arraignment. On the morning of Monday, July 22, guards escorted him from his

Mississippi River suite at the Holiday Inn Rivermont through the tense, riot-defaced streets of Memphis. He arrived shortly before 10:00 AM and found the court on lockdown; every visitor, including the judge, passed through a metal detector, received a pat-down, and provided fingerprints. Next they were photographed, videotaped, and voice-recorded. Those steps completed, everyone—no exceptions—received a ticket to enter the windowless courtroom.

Hanes and son, dressed in tailored lines and French cuffs, cleared security at 10:00 AM. They entered a dark-paneled court filled with journalists from all over the world chatting in the press box. Ray suddenly arrived too, looking rehabilitated in a suit cut by Hanes's Birmingham tailor. He was no longer the ignorant criminal from the underbelly of the Midwest, nor the scruffy, vanquished man in a bulletproof girdle. Sheriff Morris seated him next to his attorneys. The arraignment lasted less than ten minutes. The Tennessee attorney general's office presented charges of murder in the first degree and its intention to pursue the death penalty. Hanes asked for a reading of the indictment, which the clerk articulated in a loud voice.

> The grand jurors of the state of Tennessee, duly elected, empanelled, sworn and charged to inquire in and for the body of the County of Shelby, in the state aforesaid, upon their oath, present that, James Earl Ray, alias 'Eric Starvo Galt,' alias 'John Willard,' alias 'Harvey Lowmeyer,' late of the County aforesaid, to-wit on the 4th day of April, A.D. 1968, before the finding of this indictment, in the County aforesaid, did unlawfully, feloniously, willfully, deliberately, premeditatedly, and of his malice aforethought kill and murder Martin Luther King, Jr.

Judge W. Preston Battle, a short, heavy-jowled man of sixty, called for the plea. "Not guilty, Your Honor," Hanes announced.

》》》 》》》 》》》 《《《 《《《 《《《

Despite his less than imposing stature, Judge Battle was described by some of his colleagues as MacArthuran, an allusion to the ousted but popular five-star military general Douglas MacArthur. Before becoming president of the Tennessee Criminal Courts Division,

Battle served as a tough state prosecutor, putting criminals away with hard evidence and little sympathy. As a judge, he built a reputation as a strict jurist who tolerated no grandstanding or hand-wringing. Battle hoped to redeem the image of his beloved city, much as he'd redeemed his own reputation years earlier by kicking a bad drinking problem. King's murder and the subsequent riots had shamed Memphis unfairly, Battle believed, but what happened in Dallas after Kennedy's murder would not happen in Memphis. The defendant would get a fair trial, come hell or high water. If it took the suspension of certain inalienable rights, like the First Amendment, Battle couldn't care less. His job was to defend Memphis's reputation and protect Ray's Sixth Amendment rights.

Battle's office was a floor below Ray's cell. On his desk sat a symbol of his new burden: a well-worn copy of *Sheppard v. Maxwell*, a seminal US Supreme Court opinion from 1966. Just two years earlier, Judge Earl Warren's court forever changed the relationship between judge and journalist. The *Sheppard* decision put the burden of striking a nearly impossible compromise between the First and Sixth Amendments, the right of the press versus the defendant's right to a fair trial, directly on the shoulders of the judge. Too much prejudicial pretrial publicity, the legal term used in the *Sheppard* opinion, can make conducting a fair trial impossible under American law. In other words, if Battle let the media run roughshod, Ray's probable conviction might be overturned on appeal.

Outside Battle's chambers, a media circus had begun to stir. Conspiracy was in the air, and Battle knew that Hanes would go beyond the pale to free his man. So he put down the Greek classics he loved to read and picked up the newspaper. To avoid being reversed, Battle would have to monitor the press with great diligence, then punish those who stepped out of line. He would also have to issue a stringent gag order. Virtually anyone involved in the trial, from the lawyers and the clerks to the jurors and the jailers, would be forbidden from making extrajudicial statements to the press, which should also be enjoined. Wearing "Ben Franklin spectacles," Battle carefully, meticulously, composed his words:

No cameras, photographic equipment, television, radio, or sound equipment, including tape recorders, will be permitted in the Criminal Courts building, or upon the alleyways, parking lots, yards or grounds immediately surrounding said buildings. No photographs will be taken of the jury, nor will they be televised. No sketches will be made in the Criminal Courts building.

All lawyers participating in this case . . . are forbidden to take part in interviews for publicity and from making extra-judicial statements about this case as are prejudicial to a fair trial from an impartial jury from this date until such time as a verdict is returned in this case in open court.

The prior restraint, a legal term for censorship, was printed, bound, and handed out to everyone involved in the trial. It proved so notorious that court employees simply went mute. Reporters looking to answer basic questions, like the procedure for picking a jury or the male-to-female ratio of the county's jury rolls, could no longer find a sympathetic face. What remained unclear, however, was the reach of Battle's jurisdiction outside Memphis, as well as its authority over the federal government and the defendant, both of whom would continue to fight for public opinion in the media.

4

Giant Conspiracy
Memphis, July 23–31, 1968

Having recently lost police protection, Art Hanes called the FBI on July 23 to report death threats at his Birmingham office and residence. They began, Hanes said, after he announced his representation of Ray. Now his wife, his secretary, and his African American maid had become targets. Each caller was different; some stayed on the line in silence while others threatened murder, and while they seemed local in nature, Hanes suggested they were likely sponsored by Communists. The existence of these threats, whether real or not, gave Hanes another opportunity to inject into the media a narrative of conspiracy, a sinister plot that he claimed involved black militants with Communist affiliations.

The next day, July 24, the Birmingham FBI received another call from Hanes, who "advised that in the near future he intends to talk to the Director" about something of "grave national concern." Hanes refused to elaborate, just noting, cryptically, that the "thrust" of the King assassination "came from the left." As the report noted, "Hanes indicated he owes a duty to his client, however, he considers himself an American first and believes the Bureau should not let up in its efforts. He did not elaborate nor expand on these statements and in response to questions indicated that he would at some future date furnish additional information to the Director."

Hoover had seen this trap before and refused the bait. Hanes could scream "I'm an American first" and "My life's in danger!" all he wanted, but Hoover was not moved. Cooperating with Ray's lawyer without Ray's permission would only provide ammunition to appeal a guilty verdict. "In the event Hanes attempts to establish contact with the Director," instructions from Washington made clear, "he will not be afforded this opportunity. Hanes will be advised that he should furnish any information that he has to the [Special Agent in Charge] at Birmingham."

Hanes did not wait on the FBI to act on his advice. Despite Battle's gag order, he quickly took his case into the court of public opinion. And so did Hoover. The director felt sure that Ray pulled the trigger, even as his agents worked tirelessly to track down an array of conspiracy leads. In the history of the FBI, there had never been a dragnet quite like it. Hoover was so proud of his agents that he secretly forged a partnership with *Reader's Digest* to produce a story called "The Greatest Manhunt in Law-Enforcement History," which hit newsstands during the last week of July 1968, almost two weeks after Battle's gag order took effect. Though there would never be an official admission of FBI collusion, Hoover's own files show that *Reader's Digest* submitted the article for the FBI to make "any changes," which included "two additional references to the participation of Director Hoover and Associate Director [Clyde] Tolson."

The idea for the article came from *Washington Star* journalist Jeremiah O'Leary, one of Hoover's "special correspondents." In 1960, O'Leary used FBI photographs in a story called "The FBI Wants This Man." It led directly to the killer of Adolph Coors III, heir to the lucrative Coors Brewing dynasty. To help find Ray, O'Leary wanted access to investigative reports and to unknown details that might help crack the case, but Hoover initially turned down the offer. The thought of a journalist taking credit for solving this historic crime taxed his limited humility. After Ray's capture, when only the Bureau could take full credit, he changed his mind. An internal FBI memo framed the partnership as a public service "in light of the many unfactual and speculating-type articles which have been published regarding this case by others."

Cooperating with *Reader's Digest* showed little regard for the state of Tennessee's effort to convict Ray of murder, much less the defendant's Sixth Amendment rights. More disturbingly, certain passages in the article revealed Hoover's hand to a careful reader because no one in the media could possibly have acquired internal FBI files on King's murder without Hoover's permission. "The FBI had to find a shortcut," one very suspect passage read. "From all it had learned, Hoover reasoned that the wanted man might be not only a criminal but also an escaped convict. So he ordered identification experts to pick out all the cards bearing fingerprints of fugitives." A suspenseful scene then took readers inside the Bureau's forensic laboratory, a black box where journalists had previously never been allowed to venture during an active investigation. O'Leary described agents flipping through more than fifty-three thousand fingerprint cards, and then dramatized the moment when Hoover's intuition paid off. "A supervisor asked, 'Who is No. 405, 942G?' The almost instant answer: 'James Earl Ray, born March 10, 1928, Alton, Ill. We have 19 separate cards on him. He's a born loser.' "

One enlightened subscriber of *Reader's Digest*—one out of seventeen million—wrote to the FBI to complain. On July 28, the brave soul, a Mr. Hill from California, directed his concerns to Hoover personally. "I was appalled at the amount of evidence against the suspect that is revealed in this article," the letter read. "This certainly does not seem in keeping with the tight security usually practiced by your bureau. I am as anxious as any American citizen to see that the likes of this suspect are brought to a speedy justice. In view of the fact that this man has not even been brought to trial, it would seem to me that this article and the information in it referring to the FBI would be termed very prejudicial."

Mr. Hill received a quick, some might say curt, reply from a concerned Hoover, who wanted "to assure you that the FBI did not participate in the preparation of the article by Jeremiah O'Leary which appears in the August, 1968, issue of 'The Reader's Digest.'" A copy of this letter, when placed into the bulky assassination file, included a notation stating that Mr. Hill "is not identifiable" in Bureau files, the suspicion being that Mr. Hill might be an enemy of the state or a run-of-the-mill Communist. As for the dangerous disclosure of courtroom evidence, the FBI shrugged it off as just a minor hypocrisy. "O'Leary's article consists primarily of previously published material, together with information furnished by the Canadians and British," a notation in Hoover's reply read.

〉〉〉 〉〉〉 〉〉〉 〈〈〈 〈〈〈 〈〈〈

The media battle to frame the assassination as the product of a conspiracy or the lucky work of a lone gunman continued to escalate despite Battle's gag order. On the same day Mr. Hill wrote to Hoover, the papers reported details of an impromptu July 27 news conference that Hanes had given at the Memphis airport. Puffing impatiently on a cigarette, Ray's attorney blatantly ignored Battle's gag order and told the media that his client was just a patsy in a much larger plot. "In my judgment Ramsey Clark is 100 percent wrong. This is a giant conspiracy and my client is being used," Hanes said.

Reporters pushed for more. People were seething for the cold, dark truth, something juicy and fresh, something they could believe. Hanes knew better than to say more—knew better, yet he did the opposite. "It doesn't take a Phi Beta Kappa key to realize there is an international Communist conspiracy," Hanes blurted out. "They will do everything in their power to see that we don't walk into that courtroom. . . . Gentlemen, I've got my neck way out on this one." Hanes then drew parallels to what he believed was a governmental effort to frame Ray as a lone wolf. "When Kennedy was killed in Dallas, the government asked the press to play down Oswald's Communist affiliation because it would harm relations with Communist countries," Hanes said, "and the American press rolled over and played dead just to be near the throne."

Hanes returned to Memphis on July 29 and dropped off a copy of *Reader's Digest* to Ray's cell at 11:20 AM. Together, they studied the accusations and ranted in disgust while a guard took notes of what should have been a private conversation. "The *Reader's Digest* contains an article about Ray which was unfavorable to him and he seemed a little upset over this," the guard wrote. "After Mr. Hanes left, Ray was stripped, searched, everything OK. Ray was given one *Press-Scimitar* and one Coca-Cola." That same day, the papers reported that Hanes had tried to enter the courthouse with a concealed weapon. This obvious publicity stunt, meant to give validity to Hanes's continued vocalization of a Communist plot, worked because Memphis was saturated with journalists who simply could not resist parallels, however flawed, to Jack Ruby's execution of Oswald. "I had a gun on me," Hanes admitted to a reporter. "As soon as I walked into the building I displayed it and my briefcase, just as anybody else would. Hell, I wasn't trying to smuggle the thing in. That's ludicrous. The sheriff knows the true facts of the matter."

Sheriff Morris confirmed Hanes's version of events, but an anonymous official in the courthouse described it differently to the *Memphis Press-Scimitar*. "One source told this newspaper that the pistol was discovered when deputies searched Hanes," the story read. "'It really shook up the whole place.'" Hanes flatly denied that account. "I didn't forget I had the gun. That's ridiculous. The first thing I did was to take my coat off and give them [the guards] the gun," he said. "It's true that I'm not used to carrying guns. I have never carried one except when I was with the FBI, and in World War II when I was a PT boat skipper."

Tennessee attorney general Phil Canale, the man prosecuting Hanes's client, did not find the idea so crazy. Even though Hanes later submitted his Alabama gun permit, Canale cited a state law banning any civilian from carrying a concealed weapon. "Neither Mr. Hanes nor any other citizen has a right to go armed in Tennessee. It is a violation of the law," his statement read. "We are going to look into this situation." After all, Hanes had flown in from Birmingham, and one thoughtful journalist called the FBI to ask about the federal legalities of carrying a concealed weapon on an airplane. Hoover's boys knew better than to entangle themselves in Hanes's ploy: "No formal complaint against Hanes has been received by the Memphis division, therefore, Memphis does not intend to take any further action in regard to possible violation of federal law by Hanes in regard to loaded weapon."

>>> >>> >>> <<< <<< <<<

The gag order was clearly not working. Judge Battle, angered by Hanes's statements, developed a quick remedy. He formed a committee of eight distinguished Memphis lawyers that would monitor press coverage with consistency and investigate potential violations of the gag order with zeal. This "contempt committee" issued its first report on July 30 and swiftly concluded that Hanes was in violation of the gag order for saying "the shooting of Dr. Martin Luther King Jr. involves a communist conspiracy" and for claiming "he, his family and servants are being threatened by 'them.'" Hanes was also out of line for describing his client's twenty-four-hour surveillance as cruel and unusual treatment. "It's like something out of *1984*," Hanes told one newspaper, referencing the dystopia created by novelist George Orwell.

The contempt committee didn't stop with Hanes. The report also singled out Sheriff Morris for lamenting the burdensome costs of keeping Ray under surveillance and for countering Hanes's rhetoric about "inhuman" conditions. Despite the constant glare of lights, Morris assured reporters that Ray was getting eight hours of sleep with no signs of depression. Another violator was US attorney general Ramsey Clark, whose words were "in probable violation of the principles set out in *Sheppard v. Maxwell*." During a recent trip to Memphis, Clark repeated what he'd said just hours after King's slaying, namely that there was "no evidence" of a conspiracy in the assassination. Judge Battle responded in a fair way. First, he admitted imperfections with the gag order. Second, he clarified five imprecise provisions. Last, he put no one in jail. The three violators were given a stern warning and told that next time would be different. Reporters called Hanes in Birmingham to ask if he still stood by his conspiracy allegations. Having gotten Battle's drift, Hanes refused to comment. "Just my name, rank, and serial number," he replied.

The thought of Hanes getting locked up for contempt amused Ray, who continued to write out his story while feasting on "wieners stuffed with cheese." To aid his recollections, Hanes dropped off a dictionary, a New Testament, and two date books. As guards noted on July 31, Ray showed no interest in the Bible but thought the world of Hanes's antics: "After supper he watched the evening news and laughed about the possibility of his lawyer getting a cell next to his because of the contempt of court charges. Ray watched TV or listened to the radio until 10:00 PM. During this time, he was in very high spirits, laughing and joking about which cell his attorney would be placed in."

5

The Checkbook Journalist
Memphis, August 1968

If Battle expected Hanes to be grateful for the reprieve, he received a very rude awakening on the afternoon of August 24. A short, handsome man with a cue-ball head showed up in his chambers holding a publishing contract signed by Ray and Hanes before Battle was even assigned to the case. The visitor was William Bradford Huie, an international bestselling author, magazine checkbook journalist, and motion picture screenwriter. When Hanes visited Ray in Wandsworth on July 5, Battle learned, the attorney hand delivered Huie's straightforward proposition. "I'm interested in dealing with you," the note read. "I'm told that you read, so perhaps you have read some of my books or magazine stories. My latest books, *Three Lives for Mississippi* and *The Klansman*, are about murder planned and done by groups of men to try to prevent racial change. Both these books are being filmed. I want to find the truth about how the murder of Dr. King was planned and done. I want to publish this truth, then film it."

The deal, completely unknown to the FBI, explained the mystery of Hanes's three flights to London. Using Huie's pile of cash, Hanes took the contract abroad, where Ray signed off inside Wandsworth, then again upon his extradition to Memphis. The royalties, Huie explained, would be divided three ways. He would take 40 percent, with Hanes and Ray splitting the rest. Hanes had already received a $10,000 retainer from Huie, and Ray's handwritten memoir, delivered piecemeal to Huie by Hanes, would soon form the basis of two exclusive magazine articles worth $10,000 apiece. Battle could not believe his ears. Huie said the articles would hit newsstands during the week of the trial. The deal called for a $45,000 advance upon acceptance of the book manuscript, which was tentatively titled *They Slew the Dreamer*. The contracts showed that *Look* approved the deal back on July 11. Huie hoped to sell the movie rights for a much larger sum in due time.

As outrageous as it must have seemed to Battle, Huie then asked permission to enter Ray's cell. He wanted to question Ray about his motive while also securing some exclusive pictures for *Look*. Battle dismissed the request unequivocally and threatened Huie with contempt for creating this scheme to go around the gag order. Undeterred, Huie then approached the FBI with an offer to trade Ray's writings for exclusive photographs. Upon learning of this preposterous offer, Hoover requested permission from the Justice Department to call Huie before a grand jury. If Ray had provided a journalist with evidence of a conspiracy, the FBI felt justified in getting that information by any means possible.

Despite Battle's best effort to abide by *Sheppard v. Maxwell*, Ray now had him in a catch-22. The publishing contract, at its core, simply provided the defendant with a means to acquire competent counsel. As Huie explained, Ray was giving up all of his royalties to Hanes in exchange for representation, so if Battle tried to stop the *Look* articles, Ray could claim Huie as part of his defense team. Under that logic, Ray's memoir fell under the domain of attorney-client privilege. If that tack didn't work, Huie could fight any subpoena on First Amendment grounds, as Justice Department lawyers later pointed out in denying Hoover's grand jury request.

The Associated Press cornered Huie outside Battle's chambers and broke the story on August 25. It shocked the country to learn that the man accused of assassinating Martin Luther King Jr. had effectively received a $10,000 bonus, but Huie offered no apologies.

"I don't particularly like paying somebody for his story," he said, "but often there is no other way at getting the truth." In deference to Judge Battle's gag order, Huie promised that no stories would be published until a jury was sequestered. Convicting someone of murder does not require establishing a conspiracy, Huie reminded his critics, and unless Ray turned state's evidence, no details of the nefarious plot would emerge during the trial.

The day after Battle's meeting with Huie, August 26, Hanes poured fuel on the fire by filing a hypocritical motion to dismiss the murder charges against Ray because "pervasive and widespread" news coverage had taken away what the Constitution guarantees to all defendants: the presumption of innocence. The motion cited radio, television, newspaper, and magazine reports, coverage that "so canonized and so depicted the victim of the crime" that "widespread outrage and hatred have been generated" against the accused. Ray made sure his lawyers included a specific reference to *Life*'s "Mean Kid" cover story, a pervasive libel the defense believed made it impossible for Ray to receive a fair trial "in the United States."

》》》 》》》 》》》 《《《 《《《 《《《

The story of Ray's deal with Huie and Hanes was overshadowed by violent unrest at the 1968 Democratic National Convention in Chicago. Bloody images of police beating back unruly protesters played right into Hanes's theory of the assassination. To many on the hard right, including Ray, Chicago provided more evidence of a resilient Communist conspiracy infecting the entire nation. On August 27, guards noted Ray's glee: "At 2:00 PM, he watched the news on TV concerning the Democratic Convention and a report about sixteen newsmen being injured by the Chicago police and made the statement that he wished all the newsmen would get hurt or arrested."

Ray usually watched ABC's *The F.B.I.*, a dramatic piece of pro-Hoover propaganda, but increasingly, coverage of the election captured his attention. He was particularly interested in Wallace's promising third-party campaign to deny Nixon, the Republican nominee, and Humphrey, the Democratic nominee, a majority of electoral votes. The FBI had acquired intelligence on Ray's habits from Sheriff Morris, and this clandestine operation—which was unconstitutional—provided Hoover with additional details about the publishing deal, as well as something much more disturbing. In late August, Ray quietly approached another Klan attorney to help him file libel claims against the liberal media. That lawyer was J. B. Stoner, figurehead of the National States Rights Party (NSRP), a neo-Nazi organization with direct ties to Birmingham's most violent Klavern, Eastview 13. Stoner, an admitted bomb maker and lifelong Klansman, had long been suspected of blowing up African American churches and Jewish temples across the Deep South.

Stoner's involvement in the defense of Martin Luther King Jr.'s killer added another layer of intrigue to Ray's crime. But the public, upon learning of this connection in October, had no way to access the classified intelligence linking Hanes and Stoner, the Klan's top trial lawyers, to some of the most heinous violence of the civil rights era. As the fog of the election took over, even the journalists who'd covered the race beat ignored the critical roles that Hanes and Stoner, not to mention Huie, played in the bloody war for racial change. Only by establishing that context can one put Ray's motive in the dramatic relief it deserves. Only then does the devilish ruse that soon emerged in *Look* reveal its origin in the Klan's playbook for white-washing racial killings.

PART II

»» »» »» ««« ««« «««

Strange Bedfellows,
1954–1963

6

Little Mencken
Alabama, 1941-1954

The November 1941 issue of *American Mercury* carried a short story entitled "The South Kills Another Negro." Penned by a young Alabaman writer, the lead was a flattering imitation of the learned disillusionment and feigned apathy that made legendary *Mercury* editor H. L. Mencken immortal. "Whenever I try to feel that I am an honest and self-assured supporter of the American Dream," Mencken read in the story, "Roosevelt Wilson perches on my shoulder, laughs sardonically, and reminds me that I am just another lousy compromiser. . . . Think of him as a black, burr-headed creature who felt no superiority to a hound dog."

Mencken's newest disciple was a thirty-one-year-old journalist named William Bradford Huie, a Phi Beta Kappa with an English degree from the University of Alabama. After graduation, Huie took a job as a reporter in Birmingham, much as Mencken had done in Baltimore. Four years at the *Birmingham Post* gave the privileged, young college graduate a window into an indifferent world. During the Great Depression, Huie earned fourteen dollars and fifty cents per week "covering all the rape cases and labor wars and every damn thing else older men didn't want to do." He saw runs on banks and poor people running out of food, entire families standing in bread lines.

That desperation taught him the limits of religion, charity, and government, but it was the subject of race that became his obsession. Huie could not get over the trial of an African American man who was falsely accused of raping a white woman. His name was Roosevelt Collins—not Wilson—and Alabama executed him in 1937 for a crime he did not commit. "You would have been proud of Roosevelt in the death house. He was scared, but there were no hysterics," Huie wrote, fictionalizing Collins's execution. "For a second the frail form quivered in the chair, and then the sovereign State of Alabama exploded 2,300 hundred volts of lightning. They buried him in the prison plot for unclaimed bodies."

It took years of reflection for Huie to complete the story of Roosevelt Collins's execution. What struck Mencken was the courage to confront the guilt he felt over race, the willingness to indict himself and his own people for their hypocrisy, and the nerve to do it all with a limited amount of sentimentality. "I wish I could tell you that the case of Roosevelt Wilson perched on my shoulder like a raven and that I never rested until I had freed him from his cell and thrown him back into the faces of the Pontius Pilate," another line read. "I wish I could tell you that I made a brave speech to the editor of my paper; that I flung my job in his face; and that I fought for Roosevelt's freedom with pamphlets printed on a hand press. But none of these things happened." Mencken was so taken with the article that he sent the young writer a private note: you will "go on to write more, but none finer."

Huie's editors actually refused to publish the true story of Collins's execution. Unlike in the short story, Huie actually did quit. He and *Post* editor Hubert Baughn resigned to start a literary magazine with a conservative conscience. This anti-union pulp, *Alabama: The News Magazine of the Deep South*, read like a libertarian polemic, much like the *Mercury*. Birmingham's "Big Mules," the city's titans of industry and protectors of the status quo, kept it afloat financially, but in kind, they too put pressure on Huie to tame the threat of libel. So once again, he decided to walk away. He and Baughn already knew that the business could support only one man. Baughn was older, supporting both wife and child, so Huie defected to California. He was happy to go. Covering society from a partisan viewpoint was no longer healthy for his writing career. He had "turned fascist" and spent too much time "hating [President] Roosevelt's guts." He'd exerted too much effort trying to throw "communists" out of the country. This led him to take refuge in Los Angeles, where he decompressed by "doing nothing but traveling around, warming bar stools, sleeping in the sun, arguing with everybody I met, trying to figure out what-the-hell, and selling an occasional piece to some editor."

Bumming around Hollywood as a part-time screenwriter, Huie was able to witness the seamless way that paperback novels were turned into big-budget films, an experience that immediately provided a business model for his writing career. In early 1942, Huie published his first novel, *Mud on the Stars*, a meandering, heavily autobiographical coming-of-age story. Some of the content, like "The South Kills Another Negro," had been previously published, but critics seemed to share Mencken's admiration. "If we're ever going to understand the South, we'll have to get our facts from men like Huie," the *Saturday Review* praised. Several dreams suddenly came true for the bestselling author. Sales of *Mud on the Stars* made him nouveau riche, the *Mercury* hired him as an associate editor, and Hollywood optioned the book for a movie that eventually became *Wild River* (1960).

Living in New York and officially on the *Mercury's* masthead, Huie secured endless writing assignments in important publications such as the *Saturday Evening Post*, the *New York Herald Tribune*, *Colliers*, *Coronet*, *Cosmopolitan*, *Cavalier*, and *Look*. Handsome and charismatic, he accepted invitations to the best parties with the biggest stars and exercised his sudden celebrity in more ways than one. Though married since 1934 to his high-school sweetheart, Ruth, Huie soon began a passionate tryst with Hollywood siren Gloria Swanson, Senator Joseph Kennedy's mistress.

Those salad days in New York were postponed by the world's violent unraveling. One month after "The South Kills Another Negro" ran in the *Mercury*, Japanese planes attacked Pearl Harbor. Huie resigned his dream job and enlisted in the US Navy to serve as a press agent for Vice Admiral Ben Moreell of the Seabees, a newly formed construction battalion made up of civil engineers and craftsmen. The Seabees built the infrastructure of the Pacific War. They constructed barracks, docks, and roads, as well as airstrips, landing crafts, and command centers.

Huie's job was to tell their story while hopping from island to island. In the summer of 1944, he released a book, *Can Do! The Story of the Seabees*. It came out just as the famous invasion of Europe began. On June 6, Huie landed on the beaches of Normandy with a film crew. He was supposed to produce a documentary called *The Navy at Normandy*, but the intense fighting left him cowering on the beach as the invasion forces met deadly resistance. The camera equipment was ruined and no documentary emerged, but Lieutenant Huie survived the historic invasion and lived to write about it. Later that year, Huie was discharged but chose to stay on as a well-paid foreign correspondent for private media companies. He tagged along with the Seabees as they built their way to Okinawa. When the Japanese finally surrendered, Huie returned to New York having served on every American front while earning more than $100,000 in royalties during the war. The navy even let him keep the money.

Back in Manhattan, Huie's drive to write and his taste for money grew insatiable. The subjects of war, sex, and greed dominated his incessant prose. In each new work, hammered out in months rather than years, Huie dramatized taboo subjects that drew in readers by the millions. In 1951, he published *The Revolt of Mamie Stover*, the story of a Mississippi prostitute turned rebellious war profiteer. This provocative novel sold millions of copies, and Hollywood bought the dramatic rights. Actor Jane Russell, the Republican version of Marilyn Monroe, played the infamous Mamie Stover in the film.

Huie could not get enough money. He supplemented his writing wealth with lavish speaking fees and media retainers. During the Korean War, he co-moderated *Longines Chronicles*, an hour-long talk show that featured interviews with prominent politicians. Three nights a week, Huie politely interrogated the century's most powerful leaders, men like senators John F. Kennedy and Joseph R. McCarthy.

With grace and courage, Huie asked tough, penetrating questions in a charming Southern drawl that women loved. But not all of his career gambits worked out so smoothly. In 1950, Huie purchased the *Mercury* and tried to reestablish Mencken's original vision as editor. It would be "Tory," he said, quoting Mencken, "but civilized Tory." He branded the magazine for a new conservative movement, hiring young William F. Buckley Jr. as an assistant editor.

After two years under Huie's ownership, the *Mercury* was still bleeding cash, and Huie was desperate for an investor. Word soon spread that he planned to accept financial backing from J. Russell Maguire, a known anti-Semite and racist who manufactured the tommy gun. When the news leaked, Huie's top editors quit immediately, and his friends in the media questioned his scruples, viewing it almost like a publicity stunt gone wrong. The way Huie responded revealed a deep flaw in his character, a blind spot that would have a long-term effect on his journalism. "Money to me is impersonal," he claimed. "If suddenly I heard Adolf Hitler was alive in South America and wanted to give a million dollars to the *American Mercury*, I would go down and get it." Huie eventually cut his losses and sold out to Maguire, who repurposed the great magazine into a racist, uncivilized rag. In 1956, the *Mercury* hired a new writer named George Lincoln Rockwell, founder of the American Nazi Party.

»» »» »» «« «« ««

Huie's stint with the *Mercury* was just a temporary setback. In 1954, he published an enduring work of investigative journalism called *The Execution of Private Slovik: The Hitherto Secret Story of the Only American Soldier Since 1864 to be Shot for Desertion*. The book was a frontal assault on the credibility of President Dwight Eisenhower, chief allied commander during the war. Huie somehow learned of a secret burial plot in France that contained the unmarked remains of US soldiers executed on Eisenhower's orders. With this information, Huie approached a high-ranking army colonel in Washington, DC, for the specific burial plot number so he could take pictures, and during a long meeting in the colonel's office, Huie spotted a top-secret key on the desk that functioned like a graveyard directory. It was just sitting there, Huie later claimed, so when the colonel left the room, he scribbled down all the names and corresponding locations, for which he worried the military would later order him to appear for a "court martial."

Private Eddie Slovik's name was on the key. And despite Eisenhower's persistent effort to censor the story, Huie finally established that America's thirty-fourth president personally ordered the execution of Slovik for desertion and cowardice. Of the ninety-six Americans given capital punishment during the war, all but one committed either a violent crime or engaged in treason. All except Slovik. Huie proved that the private from Detroit was killed for cowardice, a charge leveled against hundreds of soldiers not executed. The story was so explosive that Eisenhower pressured Huie's publisher not to release the book, and the Department of Defense neutralized any possibility of an imminent movie deal by securing the dramatic rights. Still, the effort was mostly futile. *The Execution of Private Slovik* proved to be a trailblazing success and eventually a made-for-television movie in 1974.

>>> >>> >>> <<< <<< <<<

Huie's ability to vocalize injustice led him into a partnership with *Mercury* contributor Zora Neale Hurston, a writer and journalist from the Alabama Black Belt. Hurston called Huie from Florida one day in 1954 with a request. As an African American woman with little influence and fewer rights, Hurston wanted Huie's help with a story about Ruby McCollum, a thirty-seven-year-old African American housewife. In 1952, McCollum had been convicted of murdering Dr. Clifford Leroy Adams, a white, respected state senator. Some folks in Live Oak, Florida, believed he "was gonna be governor, sure." McCollum's motive? Prosecutors claimed that Ruby simply didn't want to pay her medical bills; that's why she killed Dr. Adams.

The first trial was in Suwannee County and McCollum was easily convicted. Hurston covered it for the *Pittsburgh Courier* and listened in disbelief as Ruby took the stand and described her affair with Dr. Adams. As Huie soon learned, the woman's fourth child belonged to the white doctor, as did the fifth child, the one in her belly. She killed Adams because he would not allow her to have an abortion. That was just the beginning. Rumors also circulated that Ruby's husband, a rich, African American gambler, was a partner with the doctor in a local gambling syndicate, an apparatus so corrupt that if it were exposed, it would implicate the entire power structure of Live Oak.

Hurston and other African American journalists wanted to hear Ruby's side of the story, but a stubborn white judge—who may or may not have been complicit in the gambling racket—would not allow it. Hurston thought a white journalist might receive different treatment, so Huie headed south in March 1954. Despite Huie's fame and knack for publicity, Judge Hal W. Adams refused to yield. Denied access, Huie took on an assignment with *Ebony* and exposed the judge as an honorary pallbearer at Dr. Adams's funeral. The corruption and hypocrisy in Live Oak, not to mention the bizarre plot twists, quickly evolved into a book project that successfully freed Ruby from death row. An appellate court took up her appeal and ordered a new trial. Before it began, Huie helped Ruby get declared insane, so she would not have to stand trial again. She was sent away to a mental institution where she would live for the next twenty years.

In the process of "freeing" McCollum, Huie found himself in contempt of court for allegedly trying to sway a psychiatrist to declare McCollum insane. Fuming over Huie's clever antics and personal attacks, Judge Adams leveled a $750 fine for Huie's bail. "You shoveled out a mess of filth and stuff of scandalous nature against a man who was dead and couldn't defend himself," the judge vented in open court. Huie spent the weekend in jail rather than pay the fine. Back in New York, where in 1956 he published *Ruby McCollum: Woman in the Suwannee Jail,* Huie became a fugitive when the Florida supreme court upheld Judge Adams's ruling and ordered Huie to six months in jail. The outrageous sentence garnered precious publicity that fueled sales of the book, though none in Florida. Like its author, the book was banned.

7

Wolf Whistle
Money, Mississippi, 1954-1957

Huie returned to the subject of race at a pivotal moment. A judge from Mississippi named Tom Brady famously dubbed May 17, 1954, "Black Monday." On that day, the US Supreme Court outlawed two hundred years of injustice with a seminal opinion: "Segregation of white and Negro children in the public schools of a State solely on the basis of race, pursuant to state laws permitting or requiring such segregation, denies to Negro children the equal protection of the laws guaranteed by the Fourteenth Amendment—even though the physical facilities and other 'tangible' factors of white and Negro schools may be equal."

The ordered mixing of black and white students shocked the white South into resistance. Brady and a group of Mississippi lawyers, judges, and businessmen quickly organized the "White Citizens' Council," a government in exile, complete with policymakers. One of its proposals was to endow a forty-ninth state where the nation's entire "Negro" population would be forcibly relocated. Other propositions included abolishing public schools and indoctrinating children about the "facts of ethnology" and "communism." Council members vowed not to seek violence, but the hate expressed in White Citizens' Council propaganda earned it an appropriate nickname, "Uptown Klan."

By the summer of 1955, a year after the *Brown v. Board of Education* decision, Klansmen in Mississippi had already assassinated black leaders like the Reverend George W. Lee of Belzoni for encouraging people to vote. In this environment, a fourteen-year-old boy named Emmett Till came to the dusty crossroads of Money, Mississippi. He was there to pick cotton and play with his cousins for the summer, and three days into the trip, he walked inside Bryant's Grocery and Meat Market to purchase bubble gum. A young white woman, Carolyn Bryant, was working the register because her husband, owner Roy Bryant, was not around. When Carolyn followed the boys outside headed for her car, Emmett let out a "wolf whistle."

Four days later, on August 28, Emmett slept in a small cabin with his cousins when a loud knock awoke them at 2:30 AM. Till's relatives opened the door to find Bryant and his half brother, J. W. Milam, demanding to speak to the boy who whistled at Carolyn. Emmett's great aunt begged them to just whip the boy and go back home, but they paid her no mind. Emmett was kidnapped and taken away into the night. No one saw him again until fishermen dredged his corpse out of the Tallahatchie River on August 31 with a seventy-pound cotton gin fan wrapped around his neck and a bullet hole in his temple. Three days later his mother held an open-casket funeral in Chicago, exposing her son's disfigured remains, an indelible symbol of racial barbarity, to press photographers.

The governor of Mississippi expressed outrage over the killing. A grand jury in Tallahatchie County returned indictments against Bryant and Milam, who were arrested without bail. By late September 1955, across the river in the county seat of Sumner, national press packed into the courthouse for a five-day trial that commenced on the nineteenth. Any hope that the people of Mississippi would bring justice to the killers died the day of deliberations. An all-white, all-male jury freed Bryant and Milam in sixty-seven minutes. The joke in Mississippi went like this: "Crazy nigger stole the fan out of a cotton gin and tried to swim the river with it chained around his neck."

》》》 》》》 》》》 《《《 《《《 《《《

When news of an acquittal in the Till murder broke, Huie was in New York vowing to fight extradition to Florida, where a warrant had been issued for his "on sight" arrest. It was a risky time to head back South, but Huie had a profitable idea. Four months after the Bryant and Milam acquittal, he reached out to the killers' attorney, John Whitten, and asked whether they might be persuaded to tell the truth. What did they have to lose? Under the Fifth Amendment of the Constitution, they could never be tried again for the murder of Emmett Till. The attorney was intrigued. He set up a meeting one evening after work, and Huie drove west from Alabama, pulling off the road several times to vomit along the way from nerves. He knew the meeting could very well be a trap, but he kept going, arriving in Sumner that afternoon and nonchalantly strutting into the attorney's office. Bryant and Milam were already there, and Huie followed them back to the library, where he offered each man $4,000 cash for the right to portray them as the killers of Emmett Till. All they had to do was sign a contract and tell the absolute truth.

Both men agreed. Over the next few days, Huie dug up some of the details of the senseless crime. He listened as Bryant and Milam joked about not wanting to kill the boy until he showed them a picture of a white girl from Chicago. Angered by Emmett's insolence, they pistol-whipped him until his skull cracked, before executing him with a .45-caliber revolver. To hide the body, they tied the gin fan around Till's corpse and threw it into the river. Huie wrote the story quickly and returned on a sultry Friday night with *Look*'s libel lawyer. The young Fordham graduate possessed contracts and a satchel of cash. Bryant and Milam read, signed, and initialed every page while Huie and the lawyer sipped whiskey and admired Bryant's young wife, a real-life femme fatale.

"The Shocking Story of Approved Murder in Mississippi" appeared in *Look* on January 24, 1956. It was the killers' confession in their own words. Nothing like it had ever been done, and it became an international sensation overnight, despite the fact that Huie never interviewed the victim's family members. The story contained numerous factual errors, such as what happened outside Bryant's Grocery, but publishers as far away as Italy paid Huie record fees to reprint the article. Not everyone in the journalism community believed the story. The two killers denied every word, publicly, and Huie's critics accused him of taking license with the truth. Some editors still remembered his first exposé, the one targeting the South's most sacred tradition: college football. A national magazine had retracted the story with this mea culpa: "Collier's, in apologizing [to the University of Alabama], said it had been unable to verify some allegations of the article, which criticized the University's academic policies as related to athletics."

As a journalist, Huie's biggest sin was to make up important facts regarding conversations that happened outside the grocery and during the night of the killing. He incorrectly claimed that African Americans could purchase items at Bryant's Grocery on credit, and he claimed that Milam's wife, Juanita, was in the back of the store on the day Till whistled at Carolyn Bryant. But overall, Huie's critics spoke too loudly, and his inaccuracies became part of the factual record. Huie attacked his doubters to keep the story alive, threatening one vitriolic Alabama columnist with litigation. "Admit that you've gone off half-cocked, and apologize. Otherwise, I'll see you in court," Huie lambasted.

≫≫ ≫≫ ≫≫ ≪≪ ≪≪ ≪≪

Something brought Huie back to Alabama after the Till case. Some people said his wife, Ruth, hated New York. Others thought he left to care for his mother, Lois, whom he credited for his success because she "flogged the hell out of me." Whatever the real reason, Huie returned just as a young African American preacher won a key battle in the movement for racial change. The Montgomery Bus Boycott of 1955–1956 was Martin Luther King Jr.'s audition on the national stage, and Huie was an early fan. On multiple Sundays, as blacks in Montgomery carpooled to avoid segregated public transportation, Huie made the trek from Hartselle to Dexter Avenue Baptist Church in Montgomery to hear those passionate sermons, delivered by a young man with a deep intellect. Huie reached out to Dr. King, and they formed an unpublicized friendship.

The change that King was effecting made bloodshed in Alabama inevitable, Huie understood. Most likely, the violence would continue in Birmingham, where Alabama's most committed Klansmen lived. The world's most segregated city, plagued by the dynamiting of black churches, had already assumed the nom de guerre "Bombingham." After the *Brown* decision, posses of white rednecks reconstituted Klaverns across that apartheid city. The radical ones were led by Asa Earl Carter, founder of the Original Ku Klux Klan of the Confederacy. In early 1957, six men from Carter's Klan stormed the Birmingham Municipal Auditorium. They rushed the stage hoping to kidnap singer Nat King Cole, a native of Montgomery. Cole was knocked to the ground after taking one on the chin, but police foiled the kidnapping. A segregated audience coaxed the singer back on stage with a ten-minute ovation in lieu of an apology.

Later that year, Carter's mercenaries struck again. They headed out of the city proper, stopping on the outskirts of Birmingham to purchase razors and turpentine. They patrolled several black neighborhoods, making their way to Tarrant City. It was late in the evening when they spotted a random African American man walking down a desolate road in the company of a female friend. His name was Judge Edward Aaron. He was thirty-four years old and weighed one hundred forty-eight pounds. The Klansmen grabbed him off the street and drove him back to Carter's lair, a cinderblock farmhouse down a dirt road. Aaron was forced to crawl blindfolded while Carter's men beat him with a crowbar. In that slaughterhouse, he was held to the ground, stripped of his clothes, and restrained. What happened next was unforgivable. Bart Floyd—a member in good standing of the North Alabama Citizens Council—took out a razor and sliced away Aaron's scrotum. Another Klansman held out a cup to collect the testicles while Aaron was doused in turpentine. Carter's men then carted the mutilated victim back to their vehicle and dropped him in a nearby ditch to die.

The media called it a "ritual castration." Huie read how two of the Klansmen vomited at the scene and turned themselves in the next morning. Miraculously, Aaron survived the night by hiding in a creek, and an emergency surgery saved his life. The district attorney serving Birmingham convinced the two cowards to turn state's evidence and testify against Floyd. At the trial, women were asked to leave the courtroom so Aaron could show the all-male jury his impotence. Carter's men were convicted and put away on twenty-year sentences.

The outcome surprised Huie and provided false hope that the South could move on, or least step forward. "In 1957, on learning of the Aaron atrocity, the people were capable of profound indignation against the Klan," Huie claimed. "In those pre-Wallace days the people of Alabama were still capable of racial humanity." During this same period, Huie reflected on the war and wrote two of his best works, *The Americanization of Emily* in 1959 and *The Outsider and Other Stories* in 1961. *Emily* fictionalized Huie's D-Day experiences, while *Outsider* told the shameful story of Ira Hayes, the Pima Indian flag raiser at Iwo Jima who later died of alcoholism. Both books soon became Hollywood productions, earning Huie more money than he could spend.

8

Birmingham's New Mayor
Birmingham, Alabama, 1961

In November 1961, Arthur Jackson Hanes became the mayor of a city that made "race mixing" a criminal offense. Segregation laws were codified. You could go to jail for not enforcing them in a private business. The previous spring, Harrison Salisbury of the *New York Times* paid a visit to Birmingham and put it this way: "Every channel of communication, every medium of mutual interest, every reasoned approach, every inch of middle ground has been fragmented by the emotional dynamite of racism, reinforced by the whip, the razor, the gun, the bomb, the torch, the club, the knife, the mob, the police, and many branches of the state's apparatus." Under no circumstances were black people to entertain on the same airwaves as whites. They could not swim in the same pools, play at the same golf courses, worship in the same churches, or drink in the same bars. Hanes was elected to leave it that way. His constituency rallied behind the campaign slogan "Never."

Such a hard-line stance baffled the liberals who knew Jimmy Oscar Hanes, the mayor's father. The elder Hanes was a beloved evangelist and a revival genius, a kind, flamboyant pastor who traveled a Methodist circuit spreading God's word. He worked out of tents "winning souls," amassing rallies as far west as the deserts of

West Texas and as far east as the mining communities of West Virginia. He penned two books on the subject of revivals, and his moderate views on race seeped through the page. "A colored minister attended one of my tent meetings daily," a line from *Aggressive Evangelism* read. "One day he said: 'All these brother ministers, white and colored, ought to come and hear this man preach. When this meeting is over I intend to take his ideas, and with my ability I ought to be able to do something.'"

Hanes's son Arthur was born in 1916. The boy grew up in a modest home on North Forty-Fourth Street, with five sisters and two brothers. When he was eight years old, he started his first full-time job. He rode an oversized bicycle under the bar to jerk sodas at a downtown drugstore. Standing on a box to reach the counter, he worked twelve-hour shifts, six days a week. That work ethic matched his athletic prowess. In high school he played football for Woodlawn High School, racking up hundreds of yards rushing. It earned him an athletic scholarship to Birmingham-Southern College, where he played halfback in the fall and captained the baseball team in the spring. "Chicken" Hanes, as teammates inexplicably dubbed him, joined the Theta Kappa Nu fraternity and worked full-time in a bowling alley. He married his wife, Eleanor, as a sophomore, and after graduation took a job as an athletic coach in Shelby County, Alabama. For two and a half years, he earned eighty-five dollars per week and loved the job. But it wasn't enough money for a man looking to start a family, so for the first time in his life, Hanes left the state he so dearly loved for an opportunity in civil service.

Hanes joined the US Border Patrol in El Paso. Manning a post on the Santa Fe Bridge, his job for three years was to keep illegal immigrants out of Texas. His superiors admired his zeal for the job and his no-nonsense ethic. On paper, he was a model agent, though several coworkers described him as "hot-tempered" and "argumentative." Another claimed that "on a few occasions he rough handled members of the general public." Hanes became a father the day James Doolittle struck the Japanese Home Islands. Art Jr. was born in El

Paso five months after Pearl Harbor, leaving Hanes little time to bask in the bliss of fatherhood.

Hanes joined the navy as an ensign and volunteered to command a patrol torpedo vessel, or PT boat, in the South Pacific. His vessel, PT-525, was placed in service April 3, 1944, and taken out on October 29, 1945. Hanes's combat role exacted the highest degree of danger. Under constant threat of an enemy air assault, Hanes's job was to shoot, torpedo, or mortar Japanese ships across the Pacific Theater. On October 25, 1944, Captain Hanes was in the sick bay when his men and his boat ferried Douglas MacArthur back to the Philippines, fulfilling the general's pledge to "return." Missing that historic moment was crushing, but weeks later, history came calling once more. Hanes found himself in the greatest naval contest in history, the Battle of Leyte Gulf. He proved his valor during the Battle of Surigao Strait, a horrifying night engagement that included six battleships, twenty-eight destroyers, and thirty-nine PT boats. Hanes's PT-525 was one of the first six to ambush Admiral Nishimura's Southern Force in the sightless night, as the Japanese took the bait and turned north into the trap set by the Americans.

On November 9, PT-525 struck again. Just off the Camotes Sea in the Philippines, Captain Hanes helped attack a convoy of two thousand Japanese infantry, severely damaging two frigates, *Okinawa* and *Shimushu*. During the Battle of Ormoc Bay, the enemy came to know the speedy, wooden-hulled terrors that Hanes piloted as "Devil Boats." PT-525, having helped liberate the Philippines, kept fighting throughout the winter. In preparation for the invasion of Borneo, Hanes's boat strafed the beaches of Tarakan, and on the night of April 30, 1945, finished off a damaged Japanese lugger that sank to the bottom of the ocean. Proud, tested, and patriotic, Lieutenant Hanes was discharged from the navy a war hero.

He decommissioned in November 1945 and returned to Alabama. Using the G.I. Bill, he earned a law degree from the University of Alabama in Tuscaloosa. It was the late blooming of a deep love for the Constitution, law-making, and political theater. During the final year of law school, he ran for president of the Jefferson County Commission, the utilities and taxing arm of the city of Birmingham. In a five-man race he finished second. The defeat forced him out of Alabama for a second time. His war experience and education made him a natural fit for the FBI, so in 1949, after surviving the rigorous demands of the academy, he took an oath to "defend the Constitution of the United States against all enemies, foreign and domestic" as a newly minted G-man. He started off in Chicago, earning $4,800 a year. After seven months, he transferred to the Washington field office, a highly respected assignment fighting Communism and public corruption. It was the type of job that could lead an agent into headquarters. But months into the task, Hanes quit, citing the need for more money. Superiors "brought to his attention the critical international situation" and convinced him to stick it out for a year, but during the summer of 1951, Hanes finally resigned.

Money may or may not have been his motivation. It became known later that Hanes applied to work for the Central Intelligence Agency (CIA), which was only four years old at the time. After the war, it morphed into a den of spies dedicated to stopping the spread of Communism. The Korean War was just beginning when Hanes put in his application, and he told anyone who would listen that the Soviets were a godless menace. In later years, he openly expressed frustration that the FBI wasn't doing all it could do to stop the fleecing of American secrets from Soviet spies in the United States.

The CIA kept a record of his application, but Hanes ultimately settled for a unique national-security opportunity back home in Birmingham. Hayes Aircraft, a start-up military contractor making everything from fighter jets to ballistic missiles, was hiring. Hanes started off in sales before quickly climbing the corporate ladder. In nine years on the job, his role evolved into an executive position protecting classified information and intellectual property. The money was good. It got him accepted into society life. He became a mason, Sunday school teacher, church steward, member of the American Legion, president of the Birmingham Softball Association, and representative of the Red Cross.

Taking on leadership positions only increased his ambition for political office. If he couldn't fight Communism abroad, he could do it at home. To Hanes that meant defending segregation in the face of federal orders to integrate. He became an early and outspoken member of the White Citizens' Council. Now, more than ever, Birmingham needed someone to protect her borders from Soviet agents like Martin Luther King Jr. In 1961, Hanes quit his job to run for mayor.

》》》 》》》 》》》 《《《 《《《 《《《

For decades, Birmingham's city government consisted of three elected positions: mayor, public safety commissioner, and public works commissioner. Eugene "Bull" Connor, an important figure in Alabama's "Southern" Democratic Party, dominated the three-man council as head of public safety, and in January 1961 he sought reelection in what would be his sixth term as Birmingham's general. Connor's political power got him an invite to President John F. Kennedy's January inauguration, where he stayed at the same Washington hotel as Hayes Aircraft president Lew Jeffers, another Birmingham invitee. On the morning of Kennedy's swearing in, Connor called Jeffers to his room in the Mayflower Hotel to discuss a serious matter, face-to-face. Like all segregationists, Connor was worried what would become of Birmingham in the following months. The seven-year-old *Brown* decision made it inevitable that federal authorities—now led by a young, liberal Catholic from Boston—would try to force integration on Birmingham. Federal judges were already running roughshod over Southern segregation ordinances.

That's where Jeffers, Hanes's boss, came in. Connor wanted his blessing to run Hanes as a stand-in for mayor in the three-member city commission. He wanted someone who would stand up to Communists and say "Never" to niggers, while deferring to Connor on nearly every other important matter. In short, Connor wanted a respectable-looking, smooth-talking yes-man. It wasn't the first time he'd called on Hanes. On a previous appointment, Jeffers's employee served as president of the Board of Education, a key role in Birmingham's defiance of federal orders to integrate.

That historic morning in Washington, Jeffers agreed to give up Hanes, the man who protected his company's secrets. Upon hearing the news, Hanes started campaigning immediately and found the spotlight intoxicating, campaigning across the city in a 1953 four-door Packard sedan. On the stump, he preached two sermons: segregation and patriotism. "Nobody has ever heard me apologize for my town or its citizens," Hanes said repeatedly. In the general election that May, Connor won his sixth term handily, but Hanes finished second in the race for mayor, losing by fewer than seventeen hundred votes. The narrow margin forced a runoff with his opponent, fellow segregationist Tom King. To pull even, Hanes needed to take the focus off policy issues. He needed to put Tom King on the defensive.

The opportunity came on Mother's Day, when two interstate buses carrying Freedom Riders crossed into Alabama. The Greyhound bus, the one that stopped in Anniston, was firebombed and stoned by a mob of bloodthirsty Klansmen. The blacks on board might have died had it not been for an undercover state trooper who cocked his pistol and evacuated the charred transport just in time. The second bus, a Trailways, pulled into the Birmingham depot without police escorts. Connor had known about the Freedom Riders' pending arrival for weeks. Rather than blanket the depot with security, he gave most of his force the day off and knowingly allowed members of the United Klans of America inside. Carrying bats, chains, and brass knuckles, the Klan was given fifteen minutes to teach the "outside agitators" a bloody lesson.

The Mother's Day Riot, as it became known, was a savage assault of unarmed citizens. News photographers, who were also being beaten, came away with no pictures because Klansmen destroyed their cameras. However, photojournalist Tommy Langston, who suffered several broken ribs, later discovered that the film in his shattered camera had not been exposed. The next morning, that ugly, unspeakable scene disgraced the nation when it appeared in newspapers across the country. But in parts of white Birmingham, it had the opposite effect. The riot created a siege mentality. People blamed the federal government for allowing it to happen and "foreign media" for sensationalizing the story. Seeing their city tarnished in segments like CBS's "Who Speaks for Birmingham?" united the hard-liners.

Hanes seized the moment. He jump-started a political action committee called "Keep Birmingham White." He purchased verbose ads that labeled his opponent as part of the Negro "bloc vote." Losing all the black districts during the general election meant that Hanes could now boast about it. "Up until a few months ago, Tom King lived in Washington, DC, the cesspool of integration in the US," one campaign ad read. "We are sincere in our belief that Tom King is an NAACP-Washington dominated candidate and a man who will make any kind of deal to the point of trading with Negro votes to gain the office of mayor."

Hanes and Connor's dirtiest trick was to hire an African American man with an outstretched hand to approach Tom King outside City Hall. The stranger waited until King took the bait, then one of Connor's cronies snapped the picture. With the city in a racist fever, this photo of an interracial handshake, depicted in campaign ads with the caption "Keep Birmingham White," got Hanes back in the game. On the eve of the runoff, he turned that momentum into fire and brimstone. "You may be assured that if my opponent is elected tomorrow that this will be hailed as the fall of the South's greatest segregation stronghold," Hanes warned.

Birmingham voted the next morning. Hanes won by four thousand votes.

9

No Summertime Soldier
Birmingham, 1962

Hanes did not take office until November. City industrialists viewed the summer lull as a cooling-off period, a time to focus more on economic growth and less on segregation. The *Birmingham News* wanted Hanes to bring conciliation, immediately: "A divided city cannot make the progress that Birmingham must make if all citizens are to have a happy, prosperous life with a strong economy, adequate jobs, and with an understanding among its people that will prevent disorder such as was deliberately provoked here Sunday, May 14. . . . The responsibility for a great united city is now chiefly in his hands." On the surface, Hanes seemed open to that argument. He was forty-four years old, the father of two boys and the son of a moderate minister. He earnestly wanted to grow the city's economy by attracting more industry and expanding the tax base. People who knew his father expected him, despite the hard-line campaign pledges, to stand up to Connor and make race a secondary issue.

But a federal court order spoiled those hopes before Hanes even took office. In October 1962, Judge Hobart Grooms ruled Section 859 of the Birmingham code—the segregation ordinances—unconstitutional, citing federal precedents like *Brown v. Board of Education*. Judge Grooms, a longtime Birmingham lawyer, gave Birmingham until January 15, 1962, to integrate public facilities. For the state that birthed the Confederacy, this federal ultimatum created a secessionist stir. Hanes was forced to pick a side and he took the hard line, voting with Connor and Public Works commissioner Jabo Waggoner to padlock the parks rather than integrate. It happened immediately. Within hours, hundreds of NO TRESPASSING signs were hammered into the grounds of sixty-seven parks, eleven community centers, and four golf courses. Longtime city employees were fired, and much of the city's green space was put up for sale.

Two weeks before Christmas, Hanes called a public meeting to hear complaints. More than a hundred people packed into City Hall on a rainy night to speak their peace. An older white resident appealed to Hanes's background and education, his intellect and composure. "You're realistic, Mayor," she said, "and you must know that integration is coming ultimately whether we like it or not." Hanes sat at a long three-man bench smoking a cigarette. The phrase CITIES ARE WHAT MEN MAKE THEM was branded above the doors of the wood-paneled chamber. "That's your opinion, madam," he replied.

Hanes said the election gave him a mandate to stop the "onslaught from federalism, communism, and integration." He believed the city stood along the invisible front of two undecided wars: the Cold War and the Civil War. There was no turning back. "I don't think any of you want a nigger mayor or a nigger police chief," Hanes warned. "But I tell you, that's what'll happen if we play dead on this park integration. They can come in here and tell us which church to go to . . . worse yet, abolish churches." One supporter asked whether Hanes would also close the public schools. Like the parks, the schools were required to integrate. Wasn't it just a matter of time? Angered by the idea, Hanes put his resolve on the record. "If they integrate, it will be at gunpoint," he swore. "I'm not a summertime soldier. I don't give up when the enemy shows up."

That swagger and bravado infuriated Birmingham's halfhearted segregationists and closet liberals. Together, they formed a "Citizens Committee," announcing their opposition in a full-page newspaper ad called "A Plea for Courage and Common Sense." The petition contained more than one thousand signatures and pointed out that Hanes campaigned to expand recreational facilities, not close them. Birmingham should take the high road by letting the parks integrate peacefully. "We are gravely concerned at the spirit of antagonism recently present in our community," the petition read. "No solution to the problems we face can be found in threats, charges, and counter-charges."

⟫⟫ ⟫⟫ ⟫⟫ ⟪⟪ ⟪⟪ ⟪⟪

In February 1962, Mayor Hanes received another petition, from a different faction, postmarked from the city's Southside jail. A political prisoner named Fred Shuttlesworth, minister of the Bethel Baptist Church, sent Hanes a request that read, "As citizens of this city, we hereby respectfully request that facilities at City Hall be desegregated and open to all the public upon the same and exact basis." During the past seven years, Shuttlesworth had risked his life, daily, trying to force integration in Birmingham. After the *Brown* decision, he and his wife, Ruby, tried to admit their daughters into a whites-only public school. At the schoolhouse gate, Klansmen beat Fred into a pulp with brass knuckles. Ruby, who was stabbed, survived in part because Fred got everyone back into the car and drove to the hospital. That brand of fearless daring was costing Shuttlesworth his congregation. He had to constantly remind his supporters, as he reminded Hanes with the petition, that his destiny was to "kill segregation or be killed by it."

Hanes read Shuttlesworth's note on television. "This letter acknowledges receipt of your ridiculous so-called petition, and to let you know that action is being taken immediately." The mayor then balled it up and tossed Shuttlesworth's petition into the wastebasket. "My advice to you is to do the best job you can on KP duty while confined in City Jail, and I will do my best to do my duty in running the mayor's office," Hanes continued. "Ordinarily, I do not carry on correspondence with jailbirds; however, inasmuch as you insist upon being extraordinary people, I shall treat you as extraordinary jailbirds."

Discontent continued to spread behind Hanes and Connor's backs. White businessmen began negotiating with black leaders like

Shuttlesworth to discuss the token integration of downtown water fountains, bathrooms, and elevators. Black citizens wanted more, so a boycott of certain white business began the first of March led by students at Miles College, a historically black institution in West Birmingham. "Wear Your Old Clothes for Freedom" was their slogan. The city's newspapers mostly ignored the boycott, but even without publicity, the students doggedly held rallies and lookouts canvassed the city, shaming those who shopped in white stores. White businesses soon felt the financial jolt, and pressure soon mounted for Mayor Hanes to take action.

On April 3, the city commission responded. It voted unanimously to withhold $18,000 in surplus food to more than twenty thousand of the city's poorest black families. The draconian measure attracted national attention, and Mayor Hanes's statement, written in the tone of an irritated slave-owner, appeared in the *New York Times*: "The city of Birmingham, in cutting off its contributions to the surplus food program, is demonstrating to the Negro community who their true friends and benefactors are. If the Negroes are going to heed the irresponsible and militant advice of the NAACP and CORE leaders, then I say, let these leaders feed them, because in excess of ninety percent of the recipients of the free food handouts are Negroes."

Any frustrations the young mayor might have harbored about finding a middle way on integration were not put in the public record. Hanes found no dignity in dissent. The president of Miles College, Lucius Pitts, learned about Hanes the hard way. In April 1962, Hanes and Pitts discussed the college's March of Dimes campaign, a fund-raiser that would allow the small liberal arts college to purchase enough books to meet an accreditation standard. Despite the ongoing boycott started by Miles students, Hanes gave his word to grant a permit for the march if Connor turned it down. It made logical sense. Miles received no money from the state or city, yet supplied half of Birmingham's public school teachers for black students. To let the college collapse because of a lack of funding would hurt everyone. When the day of the march arrived, Connor played his usual role. He denied Miles's application, putting it on Hanes to keep his word. Instead, the mayor crawfished, telling Pitts that Connor's decision was final. A disgusted Pitts released the following statement on April 7: "If the good people in Birmingham and the people of this land of the free and home of the brave take this kind of action by the City Officials lying down, what hope is there for those of us, who by accident of birth are Negroes, who want to make a contribution to a great country in a time like this."

Meanwhile, the boycott proved unrelenting. Some businesses finally capitulated, allowing whites and blacks to use the same elevators, restrooms, and water fountains for the first time. Segregation in Birmingham was on the ropes, but Mayor Hanes had no intention of backing down.

>>> >>> >>> <<< <<< <<<

For some time, the airport, which received federal money, was the city's most visible integrated facility. During the fall of 1962, as Hanes's segregation agenda foundered, the mayor found himself in the airport's bathroom. It was an awkward experience, standing at the urinal next to a short African American man with a thin moustache. The man was well dressed and from out of town. In the national press, he was slurring the mayor's city as "a community of violence and fear." Hanes gave the man a quick glance, but they exchanged no words.

It was Martin Luther King Jr. He'd come to Birmingham to issue an "ultimatum." While in that dangerous city, a member of the American Nazi Party punched King in the face. Not easily deterred by violence, King vowed to bring the main event of the civil rights movement to the Magic City. The boycott of Birmingham was just an opening bell.

10

Project C
Birmingham, Spring 1963

The fight almost didn't come at all. A group of five hundred moderate young lawyers and city industrialists, calling themselves Citizens for Progress, wanted to give voters an opportunity to change the structure of city government. If successful, the referendum would eliminate the current mayor's job but expand the role of mayor in a future government. With some defiance, Hanes promised to call a vote should enough signatures emerge. The effort would fail, he believed, thus confirming his mandate.

It required seven thousand signatures. On August 28, 1962, Citizens for Progress collected eleven thousand by showing up outside an election for state representatives. Hanes had set his own trap. And once again, despite giving his word, the mayor balked. The issue was forced into the courts, and Citizens for Progress won. A Birmingham probate judge ordered the referendum to be held on November 6. To Hanes, Connor, and Waggoner, the prospect of losing power after only one year in office was maddening. In desperation, they tried to rig the jury. They bribed city employees with a 10 percent raise in exchange for their votes. "Do we get the raise regardless of how the election comes out next Tuesday?" one fireman asked. "Absolutely not," Hanes replied. "You don't get your raises unless we are here to give it to you." This exchange was surreptitiously taped and provided to the Citizens for Progress. It was edited down and produced into a radio spot. The mayor's "Absolutely not" played on a loop in the days before the referendum. It was followed by an imperative: "Stop corruption in City Hall. Vote Mayor-Council."

The referendum passed by fewer than eight hundred votes. The new election for mayor, called for March 5, 1963, would not even have Hanes's name on the ballot. He was simply too unpopular to run for his current job.

>>> >>> >>> <<< <<< <<<

The election to bolster the role of mayor in Birmingham's city government pitted Bull Connor against a more moderate segregationist, Albert Boutwell. Tornadoes ripped through the city the day of the election, and Connor lost by more than three thousand votes. Just like that, the hard-liners were out of power. But instead of conceding defeat, the ousted city commissioners—Hanes, Connor, and Waggoner—filed a lawsuit. This litigation would keep them in power until a ruling could be handed down. If successful, the appeal would nullify the referendum and the election; it would allow Hanes and Connor, as they explained in ads announcing the lawsuit, to serve until 1965. "It is our purpose to cooperate in seeing that our rights and those of the persons demanding our ouster are decided by the Supreme Court with the least inconvenience and delay possible to Birmingham and its citizens and ourselves," the ads read.

The irony for Birmingham was cruel. Had Connor and Hanes just walked away, King's civil rights operation in Birmingham might have failed. Like Birmingham's city commissioners, the young preacher wasted the better part of 1962 in a stalemate. He spent more than twelve months in Albany, Georgia, trying to desegregate an entire city using nonviolent techniques. It backfired because Albany's police chief, Laurie Pritchett, gave his officers strict orders to avoid brutality that might attract media coverage. Albany police arrested more than one thousand black citizens, including King, but concerted white restraint, in the face of mass protests, poisoned the urgency of the movement. Without disturbing pictures or tales of cruelty, King could not generate the outrage needed to stir change.

By the time Hanes and Connor were voted out of office, King had been in Birmingham for weeks preparing demonstrations that would look something like a general strike. The purpose was to attract media attention and incite the white resistance to commit violence. King called it Project C—the C was for confrontation. It began the first week of April, and Connor played his usual role, threatening to "sic the dogs" on demonstrators and to "fill the jails." Riding along in Connor's tank one afternoon, Mayor Hanes referred to the protesters as a "Congolese mob" and called King a "witchdoctor." He told reporters, "This is Communism in its purest form. These people are nothing but Communist agitators." He repeated the same warning on NBC's *Today* show.

King was arrested on Good Friday with forty-nine other demonstrators. While incarcerated, he penned "A Letter from a Birmingham Jail," arguing that the scourge of white violence can be ignored by men of faith no longer. "There have been more unsolved bombings of Negro homes and churches in Birmingham than in any other city in the nation." The passionate plea was also an act of desperation. Project C had stalled just like the protests in Albany. Not enough people were taking to the streets because they feared going to jail, losing their jobs, or getting killed.

This desperate hour called for questionable measures, and one of King's lieutenants, James Bevel, put his finger on the radical solution: we need children. Alerted by radio broadcasts, black students as young as six years old reported to the Sixteenth Street Baptist Church for a party on the first Thursday of May 1963. As they packed into the temple, King asked them to accept a dangerous mission. "If you take part in the marches today," he preached, "you are going to jail but for a good cause."

When the sermon was over, the children ran out toward the city's parks. In a loud chorus they chanted "Freedom, Freedom, Freedom" and sang "We Shall Overcome." They soon encountered a police roadblock flanked by fire hoses. A minority of the children became unruly, throwing rocks as if to hasten their inevitable arrest. That's when Connor, who maintained control of the police, took the bait. He arrested hundreds of children, bussing them to the city jail and holding them in overcrowded cells. "Today was 'D-Day' in Birmingham," King told the Associated Press. "Tomorrow will be Double D-Day.'"

More than five thousand men, women, and children flooded the streets the following afternoon of May 3, the majority marching and chanting peacefully. But a minority was at work, hurling the occasional bottle, brick, or rock toward Connor's barricades, hoping his men would crack under the strain. It finally happened on Seventeenth Street, when someone tossed a brick toward firemen holding a high-pressure hose. An AP photographer named Bill Hudson captured the moment that beast came to life, pelting children in the face and knocking women to the ground. Some lost clothes, some lost hair, some lost teeth. Occupying the high points, a group of four hundred white spectators cheered. Hudson also snapped another iconic image that same day across the street from Jockey Boy Restaurant. It depicted a Birmingham police officer holding a black demonstrator by the sweater while a German shepherd police dog lunged toward his stomach.

Those still images dominated the evening news and morning papers. To a candid reader it said: dogs are more human than blacks in Birmingham. President John F. Kennedy worried that children might be killed exercising their First Amendment rights. He called Birmingham "an ugly situation," but his brother, Attorney General Bobby Kennedy, said it better: "An injured, maimed, or dead child is a price that none of us can afford to pay." After months of secret negotiations, Burke Marshall, the Justice Department's top adviser on civil rights matters, brokered a truce. The Senior Citizens' Committee, an integrated mix of black and white citizens, had been working for a solution since August 1962. Its secret members included Hanes's former boss, Lew Jeffers of Hayes Aircraft. The deal was reached on Friday, May 10. It called for desegregating lunch counters in downtown stores, employing black workers across the economy, and releasing black demonstrators from the city jail. All across Birmingham, black citizens celebrated their first real victory en masse.

Hanes and Connor felt betrayed. This surrender to lawlessness and rioting, they claimed, amounted to a usurpation of legitimate authority. Hanes called it a "capitulation by certain weak-kneed white people under threats of violence by the rabble-rousing Negro, King." They demanded the names of those on the secret committee, which were released a week later. The next day, on Saturday night, Imperial Wizard Bobby Shelton of United Klans of America burned King in effigy atop twenty-five-foot-tall crosses in Bessemer's Moose Park. Two hundred Klansmen listened to a mysterious "Man in Red," who made some bold claims. "If so much as one drop of Nigger blood gets in your baby's cereal, the baby will surely die in one year." A more sophisticated gentleman promised revenge. "We know who the men are who are selling out our country. The KBI [Klan Bureau of Investigation] has learned their names."

As soon as the Klan rally ended, the bombings started. The first two blew off the front of King's brother's house in Birmingham. Another one struck Room 30 at the Gaston Motel, which happened to be King's resident war parlor, a symbol of his presence in the city. Though King had left town earlier in the day, the bombing was, for all intents and purposes, the first racially motivated attempt on his life since 1956. Witnesses said the crude device was hurled from a moving vehicle that appeared to have a police escort. What happened next played right into Hanes's hands. A twenty-five-hundred-person riot engulfed twenty-eight blocks of the city, causing more than a million dollars in property damage and injuring fifty civilians. The mob destroyed police cruisers, burned black homes, and looted black-owned businesses. Many of the rioters were drunk, and some shouted threats to "kill Bull Connor." President Kennedy was forced to federalize the National Guard.

Hanes used the opportunity to question King's commitment to nonviolence. It was a charge that many, including the FBI, would continue to level against King until the end of his life. As flames engulfed surrounding buildings, the ousted mayor arrived on scene, where newsmen and bystanders stood behind police barricades. "Martin Luther King is a revolutionary. This nigger has got the blessing of the Attorney General and the White House," Hanes shouted. "I hope that every drop of blood that's spilled he tastes in his throat, and I hope he chokes on it." If an FBI field report was correct, Hanes then headed straight for a meeting "to be sponsored by the Klan or attended by Klan members."

Five days after the riot, the Supreme Court of Alabama upheld the referendum and subsequent election that cost Hanes his job. Minutes after the order was handed down, reporters stopped by City Hall to find him cleaning out his office. Defiant, bitter, and unemployed, Hanes pouted. "If I were a Negro, of course, I could go into federal court and claim that my civil rights have been violated."

11

A Rotten Harvest
Birmingham, Fall 1963

Hanes was voted out just as Alabama elected its forty-fifth governor. Judge George Corley Wallace, a boxer from Barbour County, vowed throughout the gubernatorial campaign of 1962 to "Stand Up for Alabama." Four years earlier, in 1958, he'd lost the race because he failed to play up race rhetoric. This time was different. His fiery, hate-filled speeches against "niggers" and "communists" drove rural whites to the polls in record numbers. The Wallace mandate was built on the back of bigotry and fear. To make it official, the fighting little governor tapped Klansman Asa Earl Carter to write his inaugural address. Carter was the former grand dragon of Birmingham's Original Knights of the Confederacy, and his followers bore responsibility for castrating Judge Aaron in Tarrant City. Later, in January 1957, Carter had shot two members of his own Klavern and mysteriously beat the rap.

Now, in January 1963, a rehabilitated Carter worked inside a suite at the Jefferson Davis Hotel in Montgomery, smoking and typing through the night. He was drafting Wallace's inaugural address, carving his thesis out of an old Klan motto, both an ultimatum and a call to arms. When Wallace reviewed the speech, he loved the passion and the anger. It was warlike and biblical, defiant and poetic. Everything

Carter wrote seemed to reach the white common man. It reflected his frustrations, his insecurities, and his anger. With little revision, Wallace delivered the speech on the cold morning of January 14, 1963. In the spirit of Confederate idol Jefferson Davis, he announced the state's perpetual defiance of federal law. "In the name of the greatest people that have ever trod this earth, I draw the line in the dust and toss the gauntlet before the feet of tyranny," he promised, "and I say segregation now, segregation tomorrow, segregation forever!"

Wallace meant it. His first challenge as governor was to navigate the situation in Birmingham. As Hanes and Connor fought to keep the city white, Wallace applauded their efforts and vowed to fight orders to integrate state institutions with the same vehemence. When US attorney general Bobby Kennedy came to Montgomery to remind the governor of the *Brown* decision, Wallace lectured the president's brother on the Southern way of life. Bobby Kennedy reminded Wallace that the University of Alabama, not to mention every other public institution in the state, would have to integrate just like the city of Birmingham. African Americans in Alabama must be given their civil rights, the attorney general warned, predicting lawlessness and violence if Wallace continued to inflame the situation.

Wallace stuck to his guns. He blasted the compromise that led to Birmingham's ultimate integration, then allowed the Alabama State Troopers, led by Wallace's Barbour County friend Colonel Al Lingo, head of Alabama's Public Safety Division, to withdraw from the city just in time for the Klan to bomb King's suite at the Gaston Motel. A state investigator later admitted having evidence that such an attack was imminent. And when riots broke out over the bombings, Wallace's troopers suddenly returned to the streets. Colonel Lingo, who was known as "hell on niggers," attacked the rioters despite the Birmingham Police's request to stand down. Reporters on the scene cringed at the repeated thuds of indiscriminate clubbing.

One month later, in June, Wallace literally stood in the schoolhouse door rather than integrate the University of Alabama. He orchestrated the entire scene for television, to the point of placing tape on the stage so he would know where to stand. During a live, cut-in national broadcast, Wallace lectured President Kennedy and denounced the tyrannical actions of the "central government." Kennedy quickly rebutted the governor's actions in a moving address from the Oval Office, then federalized Wallace's guard. Kennedy's poise under pressure led to a peaceful integration of Alabama's flagship university.

On July 15, Wallace took his show to Washington to testify before a Senate committee. He was there to oppose a civil rights bill gaining momentum on the Hill. Pundits already assumed that he would make a trial run for president in 1964, so it came as no surprise when he chastised Congress for "fawning and pawing over such people as Martin Luther King and his pro-Communist friends and associates." Few took Wallace's bombast seriously, but later that summer, out of the public limelight, the governor secretly recommended that the Alabama Legislature hire a member of the Klan Bureau of Investigation (KBI) to infiltrate civil rights organizations across Alabama. On the Legislature's orders, this secret investigator crossed state lines to gather intelligence during King's March on Washington. Using a state-owned camera, the agent sought to acquire damaging images of miscegenation or drunkenness that could be used as antipropaganda.

On August 28, King's historic address singled out Wallace for trying to go around the *Brown* decision. Speaking at the steps of the Lincoln Memorial to an overflowing crowd, King touched the soul of the nation: "I have a dream that one day the state of Alabama, whose governor's lips are presently dripping with the words of interposition and nullification, will be transformed into a situation where little black boys and black girls will be able to join hands with little white boys and white girls and walk together as sisters and brothers."

Wallace supporters were furious over the criticism of their governor on national television. Within forty-eight hours, Hanes, now a hot item on the White Citizens' Council lecture circuit, countered King's "dream" rhetoric with a much darker message. One thousand people showed up to the Sage Avenue Armory in Mobile to hear him speak to a new chapter. He stoked the crowd into a paranoid frenzy, a cocktail of apocalypse and revolt. "With missile bases in Cuba, Mobile is two minutes away from annihilation which can happen at any time," Hanes yelled into the microphone. "They say the Civil War was fought one hundred years ago but I tell you that the Civil War is just starting!" That sultry night on the Gulf Coast, Hanes dialed up the rhetoric one more notch, referring to Bobby Kennedy as "the chief perpetrator of organized militant moves in the United States."

It was at least Hanes's second White Citizens' Council address of the summer. In late July he had spoken in Tarrant City, the site of Judge Aaron's castration, and declared that "anyway you look at it the white race is superior to the black race." He believed the Supreme Court was abetting "a Negro revolution in the United States." These Communist infiltrators, Hanes told the sweaty crowd in Tarrant, are sitting back while the nation falls "like ripe fruit from a tree." On August 23, Hanes spoke for two hours at a Klan rally at the Graysville armory "against a backdrop of Confederate flags." The headline, HANES LASHES OUT AGAIN, showed the depth of his anger. "I'm not a member of the John Birch Society," Hanes swore, "but I am a friend of any right wing organization." The *New York Times* described him as the leader of "resistance forces" working alongside "extremists" elements like the Klan and a neo-Nazi outfit called the National States Rights Party (NSRP). The following night, August 24, Hanes rallied the Klan in McCalla, Alabama, to tell "white voters" about "how Birmingham is fast becoming the Washington, DC, of the South."

》》 》》 》》 《《 《《 《《

Wallace's sin was to embolden extremists at a time when many white Alabamians felt under siege. During the first week of September 1963, the governor doubled down, with deadly consequences. A new school year was on the horizon, and black students planned to integrate white public schools in Birmingham, Tuskegee, and Mobile. Wallace made it clear that he would do everything in his power to stop it. The night before the Tuskegee integration, he spoke at a ten-thousand-man rally in Birmingham's Ensley Park, sharing the stage with a plethora of Klansmen, before issuing an executive order the following morning to close the school. "We will never surrender!" Wallace vowed.

In Birmingham, the situation spiraled out of control as the first day of classes approached. Klansmen had already firebombed the house of Arthur Shores, a prominent civil rights attorney instrumental in defending those arrested in the Project C demonstrations. Now Shores was helping black citizens willing to register their children at all-white schools. The moderates who saved Birmingham in the spring of 1963 blamed Wallace, not Shores, for the escalation. Editorials titled VIOLENCE MUST NOT HAVE ITS WAY and DON'T LET WALLACE SEIZE THE SCHOOLS ran in both Birmingham papers. One went so far as to accuse the state's chief executive of federal-like tyranny: "The governor has no legal leg on which to stand. He may receive the acclaim of crowds which do not think of the seriousness of what is happening—a state government's unlawful intrusion into local affairs. But the governor plows a bitter field. All our people will reap a rotten harvest as one man seeks more and more power in this state."

Birmingham's new segregationist mayor, Albert Boutwell, refused to become the next Art Hanes. On September 4, he unhappily allowed the schools to integrate and ordered police to guard the entrances. That morning, Fred Shuttlesworth escorted his children into Graymont Elementary nine years after his first ill-fated attempt. One hundred protesters waved Confederate flags, played tug-of-war with a police line, and screamed obscenities at young African American children. Another caravan of white terrorists arrived throwing rocks and tried to storm the school, but Birmingham police, under new leadership since Connor's ouster, drew their guns and cracked down hard.

The payback was typical. On the Thursday night of September 5, Shores's house was bombed again, and this time his wife sustained minor injuries. Another black riot broke out, and Wallace used it to his advantage, demanding that the Birmingham Board of Education close the schools in the name of public safety. The board complied, until a panel of judges quickly ordered Wallace and his state troopers to stand down. Wallace replaced the troopers with the Alabama National Guard, which left President Kennedy with no option but to federalize his troops once again. Thereafter, the integration of Birmingham's public schools began as a trickle. For several days, black students attended white institutions with only a limited amount of confrontation and violence.

That Saturday night, September 7, Wallace was honored at a fund-raiser inside the Emerald Room of the Redmont Hotel. Members of the NSRP, the Nazi group, sat in a place of honor below the speaker's platform devouring a five-dollar dinner entree. A federal grand jury would soon indict them for trying to storm Graymont Elementary, for throwing rocks at children, and for obstructing the civil rights of black citizens. The honor of introducing Wallace that night went to Hanes, who spoke in front of a backdrop of Confederate flags and bunting. The crowd cheered as Wallace took the stage, shook Hanes's hand, and pointed to a figure in the crowd. "I'm happy to see my friend Bull Connor," Wallace announced, to rebel yells and catcalls.

To his credit, Wallace asked Birmingham's most notorious racists to "keep the peace" and to let Lingo's state troopers do the work. He seemed a little uneasy, as if he knew that a bad storm was gathering. When Wallace finally sat down, the crowd sang "Dixie."

》》》 》》》 》》》 《《《 《《《 《《《

Birmingham's rotten harvest arrived at 10:22 AM on Sunday, September 15. Nineteen sticks of dynamite exploded outside the Sixteenth Street Baptist Church—the staging ground for King's Project C demonstrations. The thunderclap could be heard six blocks away, over hundreds of shattering windows. The explosion tore a hole into a granite wall and sent showers of stone and mortar into the bottom floors atop four young girls: Addie Mae Collins, Cynthia Wesley, Carole Robertson, and Denise McNair. They died together, preparing for a Sunday school lesson called "The Love That Forgives."

Alarms sounded inside the nation's newswire bureaus: FOUR LITTLE GIRLS KILLED IN BIRMINGHAM. It was just five days since the integration of three all-white public schools. The church quickly became a ruin, and for days and weeks thereafter, people who entered that violated hall of worship could not ignore what some called a malediction. A single stained-glass window survived the explosion. It portrayed a barefooted Jesus, wearing red and pink robes, holding a shepherd's crook and leading God's children through the door of heaven. There was just one noticeable blemish. The face of Christ was blown away by the tremor.

Visibly shaken, Wallace immediately called on his state troopers to track down the killers and bring them to justice. Hanes, a preacher's son, released this statement on that afternoon of shame: "The untimely death of innocent children is a sad pall over Birmingham. This latest bombing is the most dastardly in a series designed by a conspiracy dedicated to the idea of destroying a great and proud city. . . . Birmingham is a great city of great people and there is room for all to live and work together. A way must be found."

King spoke at the funeral. It was held at a neighboring parish on Sixth Street. While the nation seethed for justice, King delivered a message of peace. "The innocent blood of these little girls may well serve as a redemptive force that will bring new light to this dark city," King preached. "The Holy Scripture says, 'A little child shall lead them.' The death of these little children may lead our whole Southland from the low road of man's inhumanity to man to the high road of peace and brotherhood."

12

Mr. X
November 1963–June 1964

The church bombing was a defining moment in the war for racial change. William Bradford Huie immediately reached out to the grieving kin of Denise McNair, one of the four children killed in the bombing. Her story, "The Death of an Innocent," ran in *Look* laid out with an image of Denise hugging a white doll. The picture was taken by her father, Chris, who worked as a professional photographer. Her mother, Maxine, was a public school teacher, and both parents graduated from Booker T. Washington's Tuskegee Institute. They considered themselves quiet supporters of the civil rights movement, as did McNair's grandfather, who ran a dry cleaner's across the street from the church. On the day of the bombing, the old man pulled his baby girl from the rubble. A piece of rock was still in her skull. "I'm glad I found her," he told Huie. "It seems right to find your own at such a time."

Huie walked readers through the eleven-year-old's short life in a segregated city. She died two months shy of her twelfth birthday. She played piano, loved to dance, and admired entertainer Jerry Lewis. At school, she drew scenes of black and white children playing in concert, but the insults of segregation she found perplexing. She could not buy a hot dog at the five-and-dime. She could not invite her white friends home to play. During the Project C demonstrations, she begged to join her older friends on the streets, to stare down the fire hoses and police dogs, but her parents refused on account of her age. She loved Dr. King, her hero, and now she had died, in a purple dress, for the movement. She was, as King put it, one of the "martyred heroines of a holy crusade for freedom and human dignity."

As for the killers, Huie predicted they would never be caught. Too many people could have done it. "I don't think the murderer will ever be identified," he wrote. "For whenever authority shares the fears of a murderer, and condemns only his violent effort to relieve his fears, the murderer is seldom identified, almost never convicted."

》》》 》》》 》》》 《《《 《《《 《《《

Few believed the case would be solved, even as the FBI descended upon Birmingham. Hoover vowed to investigate with zeal, putting a team of eleven men on the case, ordering polygraphs of key suspects, and telling President Kennedy that he would mount a manhunt not seen in America since the arrest of John Dillinger. Field offices from across the country filed reports on potential suspects and probable leads. The Birmingham Police investigated aggressively. City detectives infiltrated the city's Klaverns and used informants to begin building a case.

But before any traction could be gained, Wallace and the Alabama State Troopers sabotaged the FBI and Birmingham Police's investigation. They rounded up Klansmen under surveillance by the FBI and put them in the custody of Klan lawyers without notifying the FBI or the Birmingham Police beforehand. Perhaps more disturbingly, Hanes, a former FBI agent, played a key role in what unfolded on the evening of September 29. A Birmingham police informant described how it happened, but the essence of this report would not surface for fifteen years.

The informant reported a secret meeting at the St. Francis Hotel in downtown Birmingham and listed ten people in attendance, five of whom were low-level Birmingham "Klansmen." The other five included "Colonel Al Lingo," "Major William R. Jones" of the investigative division of the Alabama State Troopers, "Wade Wallace, a distant relative of Governor Wallace," "former mayor Art Hanes," and "Robert Shelton, Imperial Wizard, KKK." Hours later, these men orchestrated the rounding up of five Birmingham Klansmen and the eventual arrest of Robert "Dynamite" Chambliss, Charles Cagle, and John Hall. As the informant's report stated, "Same persons listed in above group, including Robert Shelton and Art Hanes, were also present at the Alabama Highway Patrol office later in the evening" where the Klansmen were placed under arrest. Immediately thereafter, the governor's office in Montgomery released a statement announcing that Lingo's state troopers had conducted an independent investigation and "are holding two persons in connection with the Birmingham bombings." Sources in Washington told the *New York Times* that Wallace's state police agency "acted without notifying the other investigating force. That procedure was viewed here and in Washington as unusual." Rather than rationalize it, a jubilant Wallace met with the press and gloated: "We sure beat that Kennedy crowd to the punch!"

A Klan attorney immediately appeared to serve as the Klansmen's council. His name was Matthew Hobson Murphy Jr., a direct descendant of the city's founders, a blue blood who proudly attended the same Klavern, Eastview 13, as his clients. Baby-faced and handsome, Murphy was a true believer, an undefeated third-generation Confederate. Like Hanes, he loved Birmingham and believed he was fighting a Second Civil War. The two attorneys had even more in common. During law school in Tuscaloosa, Hanes and Murphy were roommates and remained close friends.

Murphy allowed his clients to be questioned by the state police for two days, a process that also included polygraphs. On October 2, the state police released all three suspects on $300 bonds, opting instead to prosecute them for illegal possession of dynamite, a misdemeanor. A "few hours" after Chambliss's habeas corpus hearing, "Colonel Lingo announced that the state troopers had found 135½ sticks of dynamite hidden in a wooded area north of the city." Lingo claimed that Chambliss led him to this kudzu patch, and on October 9 and 10, all three Klansmen were convicted of illegal possession of dynamite and sentenced to one hundred eight days of hard labor. The Alabama state police read a statement attributed to Chambliss, a known bombmaker, claiming that he "bought the dynamite to blow out stumps and a basement for a building to be constructed for the Ku Klux Klan." Murphy, known in the Klan as Klonsel, made sure that all three were released on bond pending appeal.

President Kennedy was appalled. He ratcheted up pressure to solve the bombing, but Hoover balked. FBI agents had identified key suspects, particularly Chambliss, but Hoover knew better than to trust state prosecutors. To turn over the evidence now would only lead to an acquittal by an all-white jury. The right play was to wait it out, possibly for years, while protecting key informants inside the Klan. Hoover didn't just want to solve the crime, he wanted to dismantle the Klan itself. On October 28, he provided Attorney General Bobby Kennedy with an update of the investigation: "We then discussed the Birmingham bombing situation and I advised the Attorney General of the obstruction which the Alabama State Highway patrol had placed in our way of what was then an early solution of the case, but that we were working intensely upon it and hoped ultimately to be able to bring about the apprehension of the persons responsible for the bombing of the church in which the four little girls were killed."

⟫⟫ ⟫⟫ ⟫⟫ ⟪⟪ ⟪⟪ ⟪⟪

Birmingham was so full of violent racists that other suspects quickly emerged in the media. Number one on that list was an Atlanta attorney named J. B. Stoner, figurehead of the NSRP, who appeared in Birmingham just hours before Sunday's church bombing. An obvious suspect in the FBI's investigation, Stoner had arrived from Atlanta to honor a federal grand jury subpoena related to the NSRP's rock-throwing incident at Graymont Elementary in early September. FBI reports described him as a thirty-nine-year-old lawyer standing five-feet six-inches tall, one hundred and sixty pounds, with brown hair and blue-gray eyes. A childhood bout with polio marked him with a permanent limp, and like an Irish curse, Stoner trod the earth on a game leg. It made him easy to spot, even in the Klan robes he'd been wearing since adolescence. Though he had no criminal record, his FBI file could fill several cabinets. Each report included a warning: "Stoner has stated in the past he would shoot FBI agents who sur-veilled him," sometimes followed by Hoover's handwritten notation, "pursue vigorously."

The NSRP was a patchwork of longtime extremists led by Stoner and chiropractor Edward R. Fields, a disciple of Birmingham fas-cist Emory Burke, author of *Chain-Ganged by the Jewish Gestapo*. After World War II, Fields and Stoner attended law school together in Atlanta, formed an anti-Semitic political group, and stood beside Burke as he went to jail for inciting violence. Throughout the 1950s, Stoner and Fields took their message across the South, into Missouri, Iowa, and Kentucky, advocating the re-enslavement of blacks and the destruction of Jews. In 1958, they reunited in Birmingham, carving the NSRP out of remnants of the "United White Party, Christian Anti-Jewish Party, the Real Political Situation, the Columbians, and the 'outlaw' Klans."

Stoner wrote articles for the NSRP's monthly publication, *Thun-derbolt*. In those pages, he described the genocidal work of Adolf Hit-ler as "too moderate," while coining the nickname "Martin Lucifer Coon" for the distinguished preacher from Atlanta. As the party grew in size, Stoner traveled the country in an Oldsmobile convertible on the NSRP's dime, helping Fields to organize mobs of Klansmen and states-righters, incite violence whenever possible, and defend guilty white terrorists pro bono. Stoner was also a bombmaker. He enjoyed reminding journalists like the *New York Times*'s Gene Roberts just how much he knew about dynamite.

On the first day of Birmingham's school integration, Stoner and Fields organized an eight-car caravan. They drove to each school in a red sedan emblazoned with Confederate flags checking on NSRP pickets, who jeered as the first black student entered Jones Valley High. They held signs that read RACE MIXING IS ANTI-CHRISTIAN and MAKE JONES VALLEY A PRIVATE SCHOOL. When police broke up the protest, one of Stoner's lieutenants hit a detective with a brick. In the days preceding the church bombing, the NSRP held its seventh annual convention in the Emerald Room of the Redmont Hotel—the same room where Wallace had earlier sat them in a place of honor—and members from sixteen states listened to Stoner's keynote address: "The FBI is portrayed as being against Communism by the press and the T.V., but it is actually helping promote Communism. It knows that the Jews are behind Communism but will do nothing about the situation. All of our atomic secrets have been stolen and Jew spies are allowed to escape with these secrets."

In previous years, Stoner had taken an active part in blowing up synagogues in Atlanta and black churches in Alabama, but by 1963, he'd become a full-time instigator, not to mention a key distraction for law enforcement. His presence naturally drew attention away from other Klansmen willing to engage in terrorism. It allowed white vigilantes throughout the state, like Asa Carter and Bobby Shelton, to point a finger at someone rather than say nothing when the FBI came knocking. Stoner played that role well. He held rallies in Birmingham after the church bombing that drew ridiculous headlines, such as FBI BOMBED CHURCH, SAYS RALLY SPEAKER. He called Hoover a "black devil from Hell" and slurred FBI agents as "dirty, slimy traitors" and "shock troops of integration." On one occasion the NSRP passed out fliers that read, "White Rally: Bobby Kennedy Floods Birmingham with FBI. Agents to Scare White People and Make Way for Martin Luther King's Take Over."

The FBI responded by sending two agents to the NSRP headquarters, address 1865 Bessemer Road, at 10:15 AM on the morning of October 31. They wanted information regarding a "blue Nash automobile which was referenced during the course of our investigation." Upon arrival, the two agents were met with vile threats and hysterical tirades. Stoner's followers even called the Birmingham Police and reported that two Communists had trespassed on their property. As Birmingham's finest arrived, the states-righters taunted the FBI, only to get arrested for filing a fictitious trespassing charge. Strangely enough, Stoner did not represent the NSRP in court. Instead, he hired Imperial Klonsel Matt Murphy, the legal advisor for the Klan and bombmaker Chambliss.

Murphy pursued the case with zeal and became a hero to the NSRP. In February 1964, he was featured on the front page of the *Thunderbolt* as a "God fearing" man with "a well known and hard won reputation of dedication to the cause of White America." A copy of the criminal indictment laid out beside Murphy's picture announced the charges in capital letters: OBSTRUCTION OF JUSTICE. Both Stoner and Fields were listed as defendants. "The FBI has indicted eight men who led the White people in massive protest demonstrations against the forcing of Negroes into White schools," the article read.

It wasn't just a one-time gig for Murphy; he stayed on as counsel for the NSRP in the upcoming federal trial, not to mention a civil suit for libel.

⋙ ⋙ ⋙ ⋘ ⋘ ⋘

Those who knew about Stoner, like any journalist covering the race beat, believed he must have killed those four little girls. Surely no one else could be so evil as the outspoken Georgia fascist with a game leg. The first writer to take the bait was George McMillan, a William Bradford Huie wannabe and a native Southerner. In the June 1964 issue of the *Saturday Evening Post*, McMillan wrote about a lead suspect named "Mister X." The man carries a "distinguishing physical characteristic" and remains under "constant surveillance." He is the "ringleader," an "out-of-state man," involved in "more bombings than any one individual in the South," McMillan wrote. "Police and FBI either know or have good reason to believe that this Mister X planned the 16th Street church bombing at a meeting in Birmingham two weeks before it happened; that he was at the house of the men who planted it two nights before the bombing, and that his car was parked two blocks away from the 16th Street church on the Sunday morning the bomb went off."

The FBI dismissed McMillan's speculation, but only internally. "Such articles, including the *Saturday Evening Post*, were off base in naming J. B. Stoner and the National States Rights Party group as our principal suspects." The same story attracted the attentions of Murphy, who was handling the dynamite charge appeal for Chambliss, the real Mister X. In open court, Murphy cited "an article in the current issue of *Saturday Evening Post* concerning the Birmingham bombings, terming it 'judgment without trial.'" It surprised no one, especially Hoover, when Chambliss walked out of Birmingham Recorders Court in June 1964 a free man. His conviction for admittedly possessing over one hundred sticks of dynamite was thrown out.

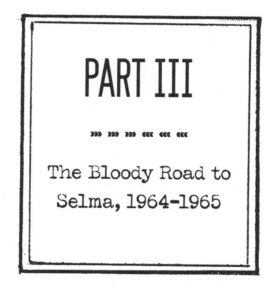

PART III

>>> >>> >>> ««« ««« «««

The Bloody Road to
Selma, 1964-1965

PART III

13

A $25,000 Lie
Philadelphia, Mississippi,
June-December 1964

The bloodshed that shamed Alabama quickly pivoted to Mississippi, the state with the least number of registered black voters. To remedy that evil, volunteers, both white and black, Jew and gentile, converged in 1964 for Freedom Summer. It was like walking into an ambush. Churches and voting registration outposts were bombed. Dozens of "outside agitators" were beaten, hundreds more arrested, and at least six killed. On June 21, a sheriff's deputy pulled over three civil rights workers passing through Philadelphia, Mississippi. They were coming back from investigating a church burning in Longdale on a sultry afternoon, and the deputy for Neshoba County refused to give them a ticket. Instead, the three men—college student Andrew Goodman, social worker Michael Schwerner, and a twenty-one-year-old Mississippi resident James Chaney—were arrested and clapped in jail. They were held incommunicado until midnight, long enough for the deputy to organize a posse of Klansmen at the county line. Later that night, the civil rights workers disappeared.

Walter Cronkite reported the story to the nation, noting that two days before their disappearance Congress had passed the Civil Rights Act of 1964, banning segregation in all public facilities and expanding voting rights for minorities. President Johnson viewed the incident as the Klan's rebuttal, and he ordered Hoover to take over the investigation. Soon agents from across the country took up posts across the state.

Huie received a call the day of the disappearance. He was at home, working on a novel, so he hadn't watched television or read the papers. In retaliation for his criticisms of Governor Wallace, the Klan had burned crosses on his Hartselle lawn. "Now I had to sleep with one eye open and one hand on my automatic shotgun," Huie later wrote. During the past six months, he'd done little but attack Wallace, denouncing him in the March issue of *Look* and lecturing across the country against Wallace's experimental run in the 1964 presidential primary, which Hanes was supporting as a Wallace elector tasked with rebutting the governor's critics on national television.

The caller was Huie's editor for the *New York Herald Tribune*, telling him to pack his bags. Huie tried to resist, telling the editor that he would not go to Mississippi for this one. He'd promised his family that he would not get involved. The editor didn't buy it. Did Huie really see no end to the violence? Or could his reporting help end it? Maybe Huie could show America what a white terrorist looks like? Huie quickly rolled over. The next morning at sunrise he left for Neshoba County in a white Oldsmobile. That summer, in the sweltering heat, he filed several front-page dispatches for the best-written newspaper in America.

Huie dug into the story and the editors couldn't get enough, allowing him to continue as a stringer for the *Tribune* even after accepting a $5,000 retainer from the *Saturday Evening Post*, the Philadelphia magazine with Norman Rockwell covers and millions of subscribers. What kept the story alive was the fact that the FBI could not find the bodies. To make this a big score, Huie needed to beat Hoover to the punch, then exclusively reveal the killers. Doing so would get him a lucrative advance on a Pulitzer-quality book, and for the first time, he might convince Hollywood to make a movie about racial violence. The story was that big.

Little did Huie know that Hoover was reading his stories and growing more suspicious with each new dispatch. "What do we know about Huie who writes so violently and indulges in wild speculation?"

Hoover queried on more than one report. A background investigation soon landed on his desk: "[Bureau files] contain considerable information regarding Huie, who has obtained his reputation by writing about very controversial subjects in which he has been critical of many prominent and respected individuals and organizations." Hoover read the report and wrote his judgment on the original. "He is a menace in his writings."

One Sunday afternoon near the end of July, Huie strolled into the FBI's new Jackson, Mississippi, headquarters, which was on the top floor of a bank building. More than one hundred fifty FBI agents had joined the manhunt, as well as four hundred sailors and former CIA director Allen Dulles. Weeks earlier, when they located the missing car, Hoover paid a visit to cut the ribbon on his newest field office. Agents soon located two bodies in a nearby river, but neither matched the description of the civil rights workers. It made people wonder how many killings in Mississippi went unpunished.

A Jackson FBI agent named Joseph Sullivan did not recognize Huie when he walked inside. Naming several of his best sellers and exhibiting recent clippings from the *Tribune*, Huie explained that he lived an independent life as a successful journalist. Then he pitched a shady proposition. Huie wanted to post a $25,000 reward for the bodies of the civil rights workers. The money would come from his publisher, and it would be paid to the man who gives up the bodies.

Agent Sullivan listened stoically, interjecting to ask one question: What do you expect to receive in kind? Nothing, Huie replied. He just believed that a reporter, rather than a cop, might have an advantage in obtaining this information using money. Huie also felt that finding the bodies was good for the United States and the state of Mississippi. Sullivan seemed skeptical and told Huie that the FBI would not cooperate.

Going it alone, Huie's approached a "shyster" Klan lawyer named Clayton Lewis and offered him, or anyone else in the Klan, a $25,000 reward for all three bodies. According to a subsequent FBI report, "Lewis did not discourage this offer; however, bodies were shortly thereafter located by the FBI."

The bodies were found on the evening of August 4 buried inside a dam near the Neshoba County fairgrounds. One of Hoover's lieutenants immediately informed President Johnson that someone had "come forward" and led the FBI to the bodies, but it was unclear whether Huie's money played a role. The nation learned the news from Cronkite, but only after the White House and President Johnson, who was consumed with the Gulf of Tonkin fabrication in Vietnam, ordered Hoover to embargo the bureau's press release for ten minutes. He wanted to call the families of the civil rights workers and inform them personally.

>>> >>> >>> <<< <<< <<<

Though possessing no proof, Huie felt sure that money played a key role in finding the bodies, even though the governor of Mississippi, Paul Johnson, described the discovery this way: "Mr. Johnson said he understood that FBI agents had searched the area once before and had noticed the new dam. Later, when they saw that the dam had collected no water despite heavy showers, they returned for a further investigation." Huie didn't buy that logical explanation, opting instead to fictionalize his suspicions as fact in a dangerous and lasting exposé called "The Untold Story of the Mississippi Murders." It ran in the *Saturday Evening Post* on September 5, 1964, with this invented lead: "At dusk, two cars met on a narrow lonely red-clay road. They stopped side by side. One driver passed a shoebox to the other. Then they sped away. In that box was $25,000 in $20 bills, belonging to the people of the United States. It was paid for the three bodies which had been hidden forty-four days in an earthen dam."

Huie then "revealed" that a paid FBI informant gave up the bodies. The informant drew a map that led agents to a tract of land called Old Jolly Farm, six miles from town. The FBI took over the site, hired a bulldozer, and started digging. The teeth of the machine chewed nearly twenty feet down into the newly packed dam. Lying face-first in the dirt were three decomposing bodies, still dressed. Huie speculated that the informant might have held out for $30,000, but he couldn't be sure. "I think I know his real name, but there are laws against writing what one merely thinks," Huie explained. "My strongest hunch is that the informer, lyncher or not, is the one who confided in his wife that he knew where the bodies were, and that he could get $25,000 for the information. Long ago I ran across a similar case, and I remember that stringy-haired, long-necked woman telling me how she couldn't get all that money out of her hair."

Weeks later, in what may have been his way of apologizing, Huie published a glowing profile of the FBI's new Jackson field office in the *New Republic*. It was clearly designed to counter criticism of the FBI coming from civil rights leaders. The FBI and Justice were under fire for not prosecuting racially motivated killings. Huie's story read like propaganda straight off the director's special correspondents' list. "The Rev. Martin Luther King Jr. has contributed to this criticism by saying that if the FBI can reassemble a dynamited plane and convict the dynamiters," Huie wrote, "why can't it similarly punish dynamiters and murderers in Mississippi? Punishment can only come if the majority of eighteen citizens of Mississippi forming a grand jury, decide to indict; and thereafter only if twelve citizens of Mississippi, forming a petit jury, and partially chosen by the defendants, *unanimously* decides to punish!"

While preparing the article, Huie called the Jackson field office to relate that he'd received a $40,000 advance for a book called *Three Lives for Mississippi*. His deadline was Christmas, and he expressed hope that the FBI would review the manuscript beforehand to make sure he was "guessing correctly." With the length of a book, Huie believed he could "take more license" and use his "imagination." Agent Sullivan brought up Huie's inventions in the *Post*, the rogue unattributed claim that the FBI paid $25,000 for the bodies. Huie shrugged and stammered before admitting that he had no "proof" the FBI paid anyone, but he "strongly suspicioned" it. Had the FBI waited any longer, Huie continued, he might have beat Hoover to the punch. Agent Sullivan asked how Huie planned to write a book when the article itself was a fabrication. Unoffended, Huie said he was paying a reporter for the *Birmingham News* named George Metz, whose wife was born in Neshoba County, to try to flesh out the details.

Metz was under instructions to write abusive articles against the FBI in hopes of gaining the trust of the Klan. "By taking potshots at the FBI," Sullivan reported, "Metz allegedly gains the confidence of the local officers and others who may supply the necessary information Huie needs for his forthcoming book." Huie also planned to pay the murderers to confess, just like in the Till case. It seemed abundantly clear to the FBI that he would not "let the truth interfere with a good fiction portrayal."

On the following Sunday, November 1, Huie's press rounds began. NBC's *Monitor*, a Sunday magazine for radio, broadcasted the interview into several million homes. The announcer wanted to know how someone could possibly write a book about a murder that had not yet gone to trial. "You've certainly spotted the fact," Huie replied. "I just told you that the people of the United States, through the FBI, have already paid these murderers $25,000. I probably will pay them another $10,000 for information during the next month. So not only will we not have brought these people to trial, but we will have paid them $35,000. So this must be one of the massive ironies of our time."

Birmingham FBI agents tracked Huie down after the *Monitor* interview for an explanation. They wanted to know why was he offering a $10,000 reward and making such a damn fool of himself. Huie called it a "technique being used as part of a maneuver which he expects will completely solve this case by creating an atmosphere in Neshoba County." He then provided a list of suspects and repeated his promise to clear the manuscript with the FBI before publication. True to his word, Huie called the Jackson field office during the first week of January 1965. The manuscript was not finished. Huie had missed his Christmas deadline because he needed more information. He wanted to know if the FBI would provide reports of the conversations that took place in the Neshoba County jail before the civil rights workers were killed. It would help "round out" the "characterization" of the book, Huie explained.

There were other concerns as well. "He stated the worse thing that could happen to the movie rights (he inferred he had sold them to MGM) would be that some of the defendants would be convicted of murder which would make them eligible for portrayal rights," Agent Sullivan's report read. "He states, however, he frankly doubts this will ever happen." Huie's cavalier brand of journalism did not sit well in Washington. Agent Sullivan immediately told the writer to be careful. He was going down a "self-serving," dangerous road: "At this point, Huie was very firmly and frankly informed that should he incorporate in any writings of his information that could be construed as evidence or admissions of the principals that we would take those steps necessary to insure that that information was treated as official evidence even if it meant subpoenaing him into court."

14

Cattle Prods and Plaited Whips
Selma, Alabama,
January-February 1965

The violent and historic change of 1964 ended with more conflict on the horizon. At the University of Oslo that December, Dr. King, at thirty-five, became the youngest laureate in Nobel Prize history. "I believe that wounded justice," King spoke in Oslo, "lying prostrate on the blood-flowing streets of our nations, can be lifted from this dust of shame to reign supreme among the children of men." King vowed to continue his struggle despite the threats on his life, and the new year found him true to his word, marching for the right to vote in Selma, Alabama. "Oppressed people cannot remain oppressed forever," he reminded the world in Oslo. "The yearning for freedom eventually manifests itself. The Bible tells the thrilling story of how Moses stood in Pharaoh's court centuries ago and cried, 'Let my people go.'"

There was historical significance in King's move on Selma. Nearly one hundred years earlier, during the first week of April 1865, South Alabama still had not fallen. As Union forces attacked the city in three columns, the South's invincible general, Nathan Bedford Forrest, arrived covered in blood. His patchwork forces were outnumbered and outgunned, but they formed a line around Selma's fortifications and stood their ground, taking and delivering heavy casualties, as the Union Army advanced. The fighting deteriorated into hand-to-hand combat until soldiers loyal to Forrest surrendered the city. The general was nowhere to be found, having fled with his guerrillas down Burnsville Road. Two years later, Forrest became the first imperial wizard of the Ku Klux Klan.

Selma remained under siege a hundred years later. King believed the city of thirty thousand had "become a symbol of bitter-end resistance to the civil rights movement in the Deep South." It continued to subscribe to a religion of states' rights and segregation. It continued to maintain "white" and "colored" signs in public facilities. But most importantly, it refused to let African Americans register to vote. Changing Selma called for taking to the streets and demanding a stake in America's democracy, King believed.

A series of marches to the county courthouse began on January 18. That afternoon, King arrived at the city's safest accommodation, the Hotel Albert, planning to become its first black patron. The hotel covered an entire block, with gothic arcading inspired by Doge's Palace in Venice. Slaves built it in 1854, and it stood tall, a survivor of the Civil War, a relic of an unforgotten era. As King stood at the registration desk, ensconced by his entourage, a jackal from Birmingham's NSRP, a wiry, tall fellow with a pointed nose, wormed through the crowd, calling out, "I want to talk to you," before slamming King's head into the hotel counter, punching him in the temple, and kicking him in the groin. A white woman, a bystander, cheered. "Get him, get him!" she yelled. Later that night, J. B. Stoner held a rally on the outskirts of Selma to applaud the attacker.

City authorities, committed as they were to segregation, refused to play the foil. It took until February 1 for King to go to jail. Confined and desperate, King purchased a plea for help in the *New York Times* that ran in all caps. "THIS IS SELMA, ALABAMA. THERE ARE MORE NEGROES IN JAIL WITH ME THAN THERE ARE ON THE VOTING ROLLS." As he'd done in Birmingham, King scribbled a plan to sustain media attention, some of which had already proven significant. But as in Birmingham, King knew that it would take more scenes of police brutality, in the face of nonviolent protests, to stoke the nation's consciousness. Thankfully, the people of Dallas County had elected the perfect target: Sheriff Jim Clark. "Consider a night march to the city jail protesting my arrest (an arrest that must be considered unjust)," King wrote. "Have another night march to court house to let Clark show true colors."

A Bull Connor wannabe, Clark stood six-foot-two, two hundred twenty pounds, and wore a pin on his shirt that read NEVER. Colonel Lingo of the state troopers considered him a friend and resource. In May 1963, during the night of rioting that followed King's attempted assassination in Birmingham, Clark's posse, a group of racist volunteers who rode horses and acted more like vigilantes, busted heads with billy clubs and attacked innocent bystanders with abandon. Now that Selma was the target, Clark and his posse traded clubs for cattle prods. They took pleasure using them to run blacks out of restaurants and movie theaters. Even church gatherings were broken up with tear gas and declared "riots." Luckily for King, it was Clark's turf, not the city's, to secure the courthouse from would-be black voters.

The sheriff could be baited, the marchers had already witnessed, because he feared change. He was so scared of African Americans that he moved his family into the county jail. The mother of his five children took up a residence on the third floor, just down the hall from Dallas County's undesirables. The Clarks' trepidation was biblical. The sheriff referred to Browns Chapel, the rallying point for the marchers, as a "house of thieves," and he considered it his Christian duty to attack them "with plaited whips" to "get the money changers out of the temple," as Jesus had done in Jerusalem. His wife adored him because he was fighting "to preserve our way of life" and "not let the niggers take over the whole state of Alabama."

Sheriff Clark dressed like a combat soldier. Some days he donned a colonel's hat to complement his green fatigues, on others he sported a white helmet emblazoned with the Confederate flag. When King came to town, Clark started out firm but disciplined, refusing to take the bait. But day after grueling day of civil disobedience was more strain than he could bear. His first mistake, back on January

18, was arresting two hundred peaceful protesters in a very brusque manner, grabbing women by their necks and leading them off to jail like unruly cattle. Those scenes inspired headlines like CLARK MAN-HANDLES MRS. BOYNTON. Then a federal judge ruled part of Alabama's literacy tests unconstitutional. Dallas County was ordered to start registering at least a hundred voters per day, but Clark's obstinacy endured and arrests spiked.

The first major episode of brutality to capture significant national attention came at the sheriff's expense. On January 25, a two-hundred-twenty-six-pound African American woman named Mrs. Annie Lee Cooper had seen enough. She had been waiting for hours to register to vote, and in her periphery she watched Clark beat a young civil rights worker into submission. "Don't hit me again!" the man yelled, as Clark continued the thrashing. That's when Mrs. Cooper suddenly stepped out of line and landed what *Newsweek* called "a non-nonviolent overhand" on Clark's left eye. An Associated Press photographer captured the rest of this ugly scene with a still image. The now hatless sheriff, his left eye swelling, his pate bald and sweaty, appears to ram his extended billy club into Mrs. Cooper's midsection while two deputies hold her down. It was raw, the symbolic rape of a would-be voter by a racist sheriff.

Then Alabama killed another Negro. On the evening of February 18, in the neighboring hamlet of Marion, a crowd of five hundred worshippers left a church service at dusk to sing hymns at the Perry County jail, where a young civil rights worker was held incommunicado. Sheriff Clark was called off his reservation to help quell the "riot." He appeared on scene next to Wallace's state troopers, champing for a fight. As the crowd reached the police barricade, the streetlights suddenly went dark and all hell broke loose. It became a melee of swinging fists, billy clubs, and tear gas. When the smoke cleared, a "six-dollar-a-day woodcutter" named Jimmie Lee Jackson, who lived at home with his mother, lay in a nearby hospital with a bullet in his stomach. As Jackson fought for his life, Colonel Lingo entered his hospital room to serve an arrest warrant. But Jackson never made it to jail. He died eight days after being shot by an Alabama state trooper.

King led the eulogy from a church in Selma. More than a thousand people witnessed the sermon. The weather that week had been
a tyranny of rain, but King promised light, promised that the dark
streets of oppression would lead to the passage of a new voting law.
He vowed that Jackson would not die in vain. "There is an amazing
democracy about death," King preached. "Farewell Jimmie! You died
that all of us could vote, and we are going to vote." But the chant
that drove the marchers forward, drove them into a fury of civil disobedience, was the one coined by a preacher named James Bevel,
mastermind of the Birmingham and Selma projects, a spiritual man
so committed to the movement he'd fought off a one-hundred-two-
degree fever and a bout of pneumonia to continue the struggle. The
night of Jackson's funeral, Bevel interrogated the Old Testament to
relieve his anger. A phrase that touched him was quickly amended
into a declaration: "We must go to Montgomery and see the king!"

15

Bloody Sunday
Selma, March 7, 1965

The route from Selma to Montgomery is fifty-one miles, eastbound on Highway 80. It crosses the Alabama River by a steel bridge with a lone arch. The bridge is named after Confederate general Edmund Pettus, who was captured three times during the Civil War but kept fighting. One hundred years later, the bridge proved to be a right of passage for a column of five hundred twenty-five marchers hoping to hand deliver a petition to Governor Wallace. They left Brown Chapel unarmed, advancing over the bridge past more than two hundred journalists confined to a parking garage off Highway 80. Governor Wallace's orders were to stop the marchers at the county border, and there to enforce the law stood Alabama's state troopers, forming a battle line with Sheriff Clark and his mounted posse at the end of the bridge.

As the train of marchers steadily approached, the journalists got into position. There was an eerie silence, interrupted by a bullhorn that stopped the long procession of marchers at the police cordon. Major John Cloud, head of the troopers, called out, "This is an unlawful assembly. The march you propose is not conducive to public safety. . . . You've got two minutes to turn around and go back to your church." The clicking shutters of telephoto lenses then captured what President Johnson would call "an American tragedy." Sixty seconds into the order, Cloud shouted: "Troopers advance!" The marchers were bull-rushed, and Clark's mounted posse charged. A gallery of white toughs cheered, as the trampling of horses and the screaming of innocents became a bloodletting.

The unfolding horror was broadcast into millions of middle-class homes. Americans watched as women were whipped like slaves and men, like Freedom Rider John Lewis, were beaten unconscious. Through clouds of tear gas, marchers dispersed into the grass as if fleeing a fire. They were pushed all the way back to the church, their forfeited possessions strewn along the route of their retreat. The next morning, this national shame slammed against the doorstep of nearly every American home. Journalists dubbed it "Bloody Sunday."

King was not among the victims. He did not approve of the first march, but from Atlanta, he called for a second march two days later. Clergymen of every cloth were urged to join him in Selma, and overnight four hundred religious leaders—Jews and gentiles—flooded into the Alabama Black Belt. They came from all over the country, landing in Birmingham and riding to Selma in nervous caravans, like pilgrims to a disputed site of worship. Everything happened so fast that by 5:00 AM on "D Day," President Johnson was begging King to stand down. Violence was the inevitable end to such a rash endeavor. The president pleaded, How many people would be killed trying to walk those fifty-one miles without a police escort?

King refused to cancel the march until a federal judge issued an injunction. King obeyed the order on one condition: a column of marchers would be allowed back onto the bridge to dramatize the previous week's injustice. So the second failed march to Montgomery ended with King leading a column of fifteen hundred onto the bridge to pray.

》》 》》 》》 《《 《《 《《

Proud white Southerners watched in disbelief as the following hours unfolded. On the Monday night of March 15, President Johnson called a joint session of Congress to address the situation. No one expected more than an appeal for patience, a middle-of-the-road plea for law and order. Certainly, no one expected the president to go all in for a new voting rights bill. But in a moving exhibition of political courage, Johnson threw his Southern allies under the bus and ended his own chances of reelection. He called for a total end to the institution of segregation.

> This was the first nation in the history of the world to be founded with a purpose. The great phrases of that purpose still sound in every American heart, North and South: "All men are created equal"—"government by consent of the governed"—"give me liberty or give me death." . . . Those words are a promise to every citizen that he shall share in the dignity of man. This dignity cannot be found in a man's possessions; it cannot be found in his power, or in his position. It really rests on his right to be treated as a man equal in opportunity to all others. It says that he shall share in freedom, he shall choose his leaders, educate his children, and provide for his family according to his ability and his merits as a human being.

Federal judge Frank M. Johnson, residing in Montgomery, shared those sentiments. He lifted his injunction on Wednesday, and marchers celebrated in the rain. Now the fifty-one-mile march was on for good. It would require cooks, drivers, and babysitters, so thousands of "outside agitators" went flooding into Alabama to share the burden. They arrived in a chaotic hurry, for King had set an ambitious and symbolic date: Sunday, March 25.

Governor Wallace responded with defiance. To mock the president, he called a special session of his own legislature and gave a twenty-minute speech that was broadcast statewide. Wallace described the marchers as "mobs, trained in the street warfare tactics of Communists." All the elements of Asa Carter's rhetorical flourish shined through his remarks. "I say to you tonight that the street warfare and demonstrations that plagued Czechoslovakia, that ripped Cuba apart, that destroyed Diem in Vietnam, that raped China, that has torn civilization and established institutions in this world into bloody shreds, now courses through the streets of America, rips asunder the town of Selma and laps at the doorsteps of every American, black and white," Wallace swore.

Art Hanes wanted to confront the marchers head-on. He began organizing a white countermarch from Montgomery to Selma, an old-fashioned showdown along Highway 80 that would inevitably lead to bloodshed. The idea, popular among the NSRP, was short-lived, the *New York Times* reported, because "former Mayor Art Hanes said he would 'stay away from the scenes of tension' in deference to Governor Wallace's appeal to citizens to 'support law and order.'" In doing so, Hanes gave the governor, his friend and ally, a tangible card to play if accused of inciting violence, a card he lacked in the church bombing aftermath. In a campaign book, Wallace later claimed that he "had been responsible for the cancellation of a proposed white march, led by former mayor Art Hanes, from Montgomery to Selma."

Not every member of the white resistance heeded Wallace's plea. On March 21, a motorcade of two hundred forty Klansmen paraded around the white marble buildings of Montgomery in eighty-three cars, starting from a parking lot on Madison Avenue, turning onto Bainbridge, then Dexter, before passing through court square and fanning off. The city permit approving the rally forbade them from wearing masks, but for fifty-five minutes, from 2:40 to 3:35 PM, a sea of Confederate flags looped around those tense Montgomery streets, casting shadows on the stark white marble of Alabama's Capitol. Imperial Wizard Shelton signed the permit application and led the parade. Klonsel Murphy, who had defended Chambliss and the NSRP, drove his 1964 Chrysler convertible while other Birmingham Klansmen carried signs that read "Be a Man Join the Klan." In tow was J. B. Stoner, riding in his Oldsmobile convertible with a giant Confederate flag tied to the antenna. It was not the first nor the last time the Klan and the NSRP would publicly stand together, in non-violence as well as violence, to prevent racial change.

>>> >>> >>> <<< <<< <<<

It took five days and four nights for the marchers to reach Montgomery, snaking through Lowndes County along the Alabama River and emerging out of the wilderness. Three thousand national guardsmen and federal marshals patrolled the route as the media covered it like a sporting event. CBS brought in thirty-five hundred pounds of gear on two DC-3s, then rented two helicopters, one to provide aerial shots of the march and the other to monitor the crowd buildup in Montgomery. NBC, wrote *Newsweek*, "used a rebuilt Cadillac fitted with a video tape recorder, and installed a film processor in the linen room of Montgomery's Diplomat Motel. As a precaution against hostile whites, the network taped over the 'NBC' on its Cadillac." As the tired marchers converged around the Capitol, Governor Wallace became a hostage in his own castle. He could only peek out, training his binoculars on the change that was now so real. "That's quite a crowd," he said.

Addressing the marchers twenty-five thousand strong, an exhausted King stood on a flatbed trailer, working the crowd into a call-and-response reverie, dusting his broom, as the bluesmen say, on the carcass of segregation. "He is trampling out the vintage where the grapes of wrath are stowed," King told the crowd, because "no lie can live forever." Once removed from Jefferson Davis's own mouth emerged this line, the final nail in Jim Crow's legal coffin. "Truth crushed to the earth will rise again!"

16

Baby Brother
Selma, March 25, 1965

A white Impala appeared in Selma as the sun set on the march. The four men inside, all from Birmingham, had driven south that morning for the Klan rally in Montgomery. Tonight, they were in Selma looking for trouble. After a few beers at a bar called the Silver Moon Cafe, they rode through town scouting potential victims. Military police and marchers were everywhere, making any violent attack more risky, but just before heading back to Birmingham, they spotted the perfect victims in an Oldsmobile with Michigan plates. The driver was a middle-aged white woman, and riding shotgun was a much younger African American man. "Lookie here, Baby Brother," Klansman Collie Leroy Wilkins said. "Will you look at that. They're going to park someplace together."

The Impala followed the Oldsmobile across the Pettus Bridge. For twenty miles the two cars retraced the route of the march into the outreaches of Lowndes County. It soon became a chase, as each vehicle accelerated to more than eighty miles per hour, slowing down as they passed jeeps full of national guardsmen, then racing past the Jet Drive-In and Craig Air Force Base, out near a desolate spot known as Big Swamp. The woman from Michigan, Viola Liuzzo, was calming her panic by singing "We Shall Overcome." But when the

Impala pulled even, shots rang out, and Liuzzo's car veered sharply off the road.

Around 2:00 AM, one of the Klansmen in the Impala, Gary Thomas Rowe, called his case agent, Neil Shanahan, at the Birmingham FBI and reported the shooting. Rowe was Hoover's prize informant inside the Klan, and he agreed to meet Shanahan at a parking lot, where he got into an unmarked vehicle and returned to the crime scene to find a dragnet of state troopers surrounding the blood-spattered Oldsmobile. Liuzzo had run off the road and slammed into a fence. The African American man in the passenger seat, nineteen-year-old Leroy Moton, was nowhere to be found. Liuzzo, a mother of five, was lying across the seat covered in blood. She was dead.

Rowe then led Shanahan to a wooded ravine where the Klansmen discarded their shell casings. He said two of the men had worked for the steel mills in Fairfield, just outside Birmingham. On Monday, they planned to destroy the murder weapon, a .38-caliber revolver, by shoving it into a blast furnace. By midmorning, FBI agents were applying for search warrants and staking out the three suspects. The accused triggerman, Collie Leroy Wilkins, was arrested with shell casings on the windowsill of the Impala, and the twenty-one-year-old killer, when handcuffed, was so frightened he defecated in his pants.

At 1:00 PM, the White House called a press conference. Flanked by J. Edgar Hoover and Attorney General Nicholas Katzenbach, President Johnson stunned the world by announcing arrests in a sensational crime that was less than fifteen hours old. It was sold as a moment of justice, and the president went out of his way to praise Hoover's FBI. Then he went even further, speaking candidly about his lifelong hatred of the Klan, lashing out at terrorism, and calling the clandestine order a "hooded society of bigots." Journalists noted that while preparing to speak, the president penciled a key phrase into his remarks. "Mrs. Liuzzo went to Alabama to serve the struggle for justice," the president said. "She was murdered by the enemies of justice who for decades have used the rope and the gun, the *tar and the feathers* to terrorize their neighbors."

When asked for a response, Imperial Wizard Robert Shelton called the president "a damn liar." As for Liuzzo, Shelton believed she got what she deserved. "If this woman was at home with the children where she belonged, she would not have been in jeopardy," he said on the radio. "I notice they are using pictures of the children crying. I wonder if the children were crying when she left them three weeks ago or if they just started crying today." Shelton later arrived at the US Post Office Building in downtown Birmingham to witness the four Klansmen's arraignment. US commissioner Louise Charlton, seventy-six, sat at a walnut desk, hooked to an oxygen tank, with a flower in her hair. The first three Klansmen, Collie Leroy Wilkins, William Eaton, and Eugene Thomas, arrived together in federal custody. Charlton deposed the federal agents with a single question: "Are these men in connection with the tragedy in Lowndes County?" When told "Yes," Charlton explained the charges and filled in her forms with a pencil, then typed up her notes using the two-finger method. She set a much higher bail than anyone expected: $50,000 per man.

Shelton and Murphy could not find Rowe. They waited four long hours outside Charlton's office for Rowe to appear under arrest. They called, sent emissaries, and talked with reporters, who demanded to know how four low-wage workers would come up with $200,000 in bail. Murphy, who was up to his ears defending J. B. Stoner and the NSRP, told the *New York Times* that "some other of our friends" will raise the money immediately, and the bail bonds later showed that Murphy vouched for half of the bail in his own name. The rest came from his predecessor, Klonsel emeritus James Easdale.

Rowe finally arrived that afternoon through the back door. Handcuffed and escorted by FBI agents, the informant played his role well. He cursed the government and threatened reporters who put cameras in his face. But Murphy and Shelton were not convinced by the act. They stared at Rowe like a mangy dog, as Charlton quickly took down his information and set the same bail. Shelton ordered Rowe to appear at Murphy's office inside the Frank Nelson Building after getting released. The Klonsel had long suspected that Rowe was a snitch. This time they aimed to prove it.

Assembled in Murphy's office was the entire Klan executive council—Imperial Wizard Shelton, Alabama grand dragon Robert Creel, and the head of the Klan Bureau of Investigation, Ralph Roton. It was a test. If Rowe didn't have the guts to show, then he was surely the rat. They waited until after 9:00 PM when Rowe entered the building and stepped calmly up to the second floor. "Where the fuck you been, Baby Brother?" Murphy asked.

Rowe shrugged. In an exhausted voice, he said the FBI picked him up at his apartment that morning and drove him all over the state, into Leeds, Anniston, and Vestavia, trying to convince him to turn state's evidence. He had no choice but to hear them out, Rowe explained. Before he could finish, Shelton interrupted, yelling that Rowe was a no-good Judas, a traitor to the Klan, and a damned liar, but Murphy waved him off.

"What bribe did they offer you?" Murphy asked.

"Oh, a few acres of apple land in Wisconsin," Rowe replied.

Murphy's eyes lit up. He found a pen and paper and began drafting an affidavit. Make it five hundred fifty acres plus $186,000 in cash, he demanded. And put your oath to it—by signing this document. Rowe headed for the door. "I'm not signing anything," he said. "I'm exhausted and going home." He just walked out, later telling Shanahan that neither Murphy nor Shelton had the guts to stop him. After midnight, he called the FBI from a pay phone to report that he was still alive. Someone did follow him, Rowe said, but he confronted the tail and got free.

Without Rowe the investigation was a toss-up. Any one of the four men in that Impala could have pulled the trigger. When the time came, Rowe would have no choice but to testify, but staying in character now could provide the FBI with crucial evidence. Shanahan was adamant: he must stay in the Klan until the grand jury met. After that, Rowe would go into hiding, testify at the trial, and receive immunity from prosecution. Blowing his cover now endangered the possibility of getting a conviction, and it would put Rowe's life in imminent peril. After all, Rowe was in the car, holding the same type of gun as the murder weapon; Rowe failed to stop the shooting, so without his cooperation, Shanahan explained, the FBI would not protect him.

Rowe acted frustrated, confused, and exhausted. What should I do tomorrow? he asked. How do I pretend this never happened? The FBI told him "to get lost," then reenter his life as if nothing had changed. Any fear the informant would turn yella disappeared soon after, when agents spotted Rowe devouring breakfast with his fellow defendants off Highway 31, "south of the large green water tower with the sign Prattville written thereon."

17

The Klonsel's Stage
Hayneville, Alabama, April–May 1965

The year of the snake, 1965, brought Huie many spoils. The Klan kill-ings in Dallas and Lowndes Counties could not have come at a more lucrative time. In April, the *New York Herald Tribune* commenced running his new book, *Three Lives for Mississippi*, in a sixteen-part serial. Forty-five newspapers syndicated the articles, and it earned Huie an untold stash of money. To fuel sales of the book, Huie's pub-lisher took out a full-page ad that was charming, in a morbid sort of way. A cropped picture of Huie's no-nonsense gaze was positioned above a quote the publisher described as the author's "ominous pro-phetic statement." It read: "A missing civil rights worker in Missis-sippi today is a dead civil rights worker." There was even a caveat emptor: "Be warned: 'Three Lives for Mississippi' is not a political or sociological study. Not a collection of articles or a diary. It is the sear-ing authentic story of an historic encounter. And will stand as one of the greatest and more moving documents of our time."

Another humble promotion compared it to *Uncle Tom's Cabin* but with "irrefutable documentation." The installments continued into April, as the Liuzzo murder remained in the papers. A rumor was circulating that one of the Klansmen involved in the Liuzzo murder might have been on Hoover's payroll. The *New York Times* confirmed it on April 22: "The case includes the involvement of an informant for the Federal Bureau of Investigation, Gary Thomas Rowe, 34, of Birmingham, who was a helpless witness to the shooting. Mr. Rowe is reported to have been a paid informant for the bureau on Ku Klux Klan activities for the last six years."

To Huie it sounded like a cash drawer popping open. Without a second thought, the *Herald Tribune* dispatched him to Hayneville, site of the upcoming murder trial. Huie found the white community seething with outrage, though not concerning the murder of an innocent woman, but by Rowe's betrayal of the Klan. President Johnson might believe that the war to end segregation was in its final throes, Huie wrote, but the Klan envisions a protracted, guerrilla-like conflict. "The Klan," Huie wrote, "through its Imperial Klonsel Matt Murphy Jr. will charge that the president, by not stopping the march from Selma to Montgomery, 'released on Alabama a horde of homosexuals, whores, mobsters, beatniks, atheists, Jews and Communists,' and is therefore 'more guilty of this murder than the man who held the gun.'" Huie described Murphy, fifty-one, as a "shaggy, shambling bear of a man who believes that this 'victory' the Klan wins here will bring thousands of Americans into the Klan, will make certain that Alabama Governors remain supporters of the Klan, and will put a Klansman in the White House by 1972."

Huie then accused Governor Wallace of secretly supporting the Klan. The governor's picture hangs in every Alabama Klavern, Huie wrote, and he helps the Klan financially by putting "money in Klan coffers by compelling road builders and engineering firms to pay Klan Wizard Robert Shelton for 'public relations counsel.'" That money helps the Klan find legal representation for its soldiers. As Klonsel Murphy freely admitted to Huie, there is a "numbered bank account in a Birmingham bank" to accept all donations for the three Klansmen's defense. "Martin Luther King has a private secret account in a Swiss bank," Murphy claimed. "He is now a millionaire and is getting richer every day. Every Klansman knows this, and we are going to give white men a chance to fight King by making secret contributions to us."

The *Herald Tribune* could not afford Huie for the entire week of the trial. Instead, editors sent down a full-time columnist, a thirty-four-year-old commoner and a true Yankee, a writer who earned his keep profiling everyday, blue-collar Americans like the gravedigger who prepared President John F. Kennedy's tomb. His name was Jimmy Breslin, an irreverent and blunt shoe-leather reporter with a literary flair that could not be tamed. Breslin also covered the Selma March and jolted his readers by capturing the unguarded actions of white bystanders, whose accents he nearly perfected. Not all the voices in his copy were unsympathetic, but he pulled no punches documenting the epidemic of bitter racism in Alabama.

Breslin's first dispatch from Hayneville painted an opposing scene. It was a narrative of gas stations, quiet streets, live oaks, and flowering pastures. The romance of spring pitted against the backdrop of stale oppression. As the trial approached, Breslin found Murphy on the eighth floor of a Montgomery hotel, dressing for court and small-talking with his clients. The accused triggerman, Wilkins, was smoking a cigar while his co-conspirator, Eaton, thumbed through the Bible. Breslin asked about the previous day's voir dire. "I've had that jury list in my pocket for twenty days now," Murphy bragged. "We know everybody who was on that panel."

Down at the Lowndes County courthouse, Breslin spotted Sheriff Clark in sunglasses, standing in the yard talking to Imperial Wizard Shelton, with his "close-cropped hair, a pinched face with a prominent nose, and ears which rise to red-tipped points at the top." Breslin was approaching Shelton for an interview when a "fat-bellied kid with sunken blue eyes and a crew cut" scurried past. It was Wilkins, hurrying into the courthouse, where an all-white, all-male jury selected in haste would try him.

Inside the courtroom, on the second floor, it was more like a pep rally than a trial by jury. States-righters worked the crowd with abandon, handing out issues of the *Thunderbolt* while Sheriff Clark pinned a NEVER button to the lapel of Murphy's coat. Klansmen sat at every pass, as eighty-five people took their seats for the trial to begin. They sat on church-like benches exhaling cigarette smoke that exited out of big-frame windows. From the outset, it became clear that the defense team would prey on the jury's fears, insecurities, and prejudices. Murphy would frame Liuzzo, the victim, as an unchaste "nigger-lover" who got what she deserved. One of the first witnesses he called was Leroy Moton, the young man in Liuzzo's car on the night of the murder. Moton fled the crime scene virtually unscathed. Terrified and shocked, he hitchhiked back to Selma rather than wait on the police.

Murphy called Moton the true killer, whose motive was the money in Liuzzo's pocketbook. The witness was so frightened he could barely defend himself. State judge T. Werth Thagard let the disgraceful examination go on with few objections, so Murphy made it more macabre by gesturing wildly with his three-fingered right hand, which had been mangled in an industrial accident.

"What did you do to Mrs. Liuzzo while you were there in the car?"

"I didn't do anything to Mrs. Liuzzo while I was in the car," Moton answered, in a weak trembling voice.

"Did you reach over and touch her?"

"No, I didn't."

"You didn't lay your hands on her?"

"No, sir."

"What kind of gun did you have with you?"

"I don't carry a gun."

"What kind of gun was in the glove compartment?"

"There wasn't no gun in the glove compartment."

"Now who fired the bullet holes in the windshield? Did you do it?"

"I did not fire no shots through the windshield," Moton swore, "and I did not go through her pocketbook and get no money and I didn't have a gun and I didn't do anything. You are trying to pin something on me, that's what you're trying to do."

"Oh, I am?"

Murphy seemed to enjoy himself that morning. He relished the terror in Moton's eyes and tried desperately to invent a sex angle, deposing the state's toxicologist, who answered all Murphy's questions, even the most appalling.

"You say Mrs. Liuzzo had on a dress, a slip, and a bra," Murphy asked, "and that was it . . . no underpants?"

"No underpants," the toxicologist answered.

Murphy demanded to know whether Liuzzo's vaginal cavity showed any signs of intercourse. He already knew the answer but brought it up for an effect. The answer was no. The report showed no sign of bruising and no semen residue. Murphy then asked whether "some contraceptive device could have been used?" Again the answer was no.

"Did you find any puncture marks in her arms?"

"No I did not."

"No puncture marks in her arm at all where a hypodermic needle might have been used?"

"I did not detect any."

"Did you look for it?"

"Yes."

When the court recessed at noon, those who weren't disgusted bought lunches across the street and ate them on the lawn of the courthouse. Reporters purchased "souvenir-sized" bottles of whiskey to drown their disillusionment. Very soon, the Klan would package Murphy's lies and racism into a thin, little magazine called *Night Riders*, the cover of which showed Liuzzo's bloodied corpse sprawled out across the seat of her car.

》》 》》 》》 《《 《《 《《

At 3:30 PM, Gary Thomas Rowe walked into the courtroom through a green door. He was dressed like a G-man, wearing a suit, tie, and aviator sunglasses. Not a word was spoken as he paced across the creaking wooden floors and took his oath on the Bible. The attorney general of Alabama, Richmond Flowers, commenced a long deposition in which Rowe recounted the entire day of March 25, 1965. The informant spoke in a calm, confident voice over the episodic revving of car engines and braking Trailways buses. He began at the beginning and walked the jury through the high drama of cold-blooded murder. It all built up to the shooting.

Wilkins rolled down the window. He was sitting just a little ahead of the front window of the other car. His arm went out the window right out to the elbow length. The woman driving the other car, Mrs. Liuzzo, turned her head a little and she was looking straight at him. Wilkins fired two shots through her front window. And Thomas yelled, "All right, men, shoot the hell out of 'em." Wilkins turned to me and said, "Put your gun out the window." I had a .38, Wilkins had a .38. Wilkins and Eaton emptied their guns. I made believe I was firing mine. Their auto went straight off the road.

The newsmen who listened to Rowe's testimony went away convinced. The informant showed no emotion. He spoke in a matter-of-fact, plainspoken, Southern drawl. It was obvious to Breslin that some of the jurors were "shattered" by the informant's cool performance. FBI agents later propped up his testimony by showing evidence that the bullet recovered from Liuzzo's brain matched two additional slugs found inside her car. All of those bullets were fired by a gun that Rowe attributed to Wilkins. Murphy and Shelton could only sit there and fume with rage. All along, Baby Brother had been their Judas.

As the first day of testimony ended, one point seemed clear: the defense would have trouble breaking the unflappable Rowe. But as Breslin put it, Murphy is the "kind of man the people in Lowndes County understand," a man "who claims that Jews own the Federal Reserve Bank and are causing wars and that Alger Hiss runs the country through Felix Frankfurter." Murphy "believes that Negroes were created as part of the animal world," and a man that crazy was capable of anything, especially on cross-examination.

〉〉〉 〉〉〉 〉〉〉 〈〈〈 〈〈〈 〈〈〈

It was a muggy, packed house the next day. Murphy sat at the defense table with a Bible and two pistols, laurelled in segregationist paraphernalia. Rather than argue that Rowe actually did the shooting, Murphy would paint the Klan as an agent of Christ, and Rowe's betrayal as sacrilege. After Judge Thagard called his court to order, Murphy ripped a sheet of paper out of a legal pad. "Did you hold up your right hand and swear before God," Murphy yelled at Rowe, before reciting the entire Klan oath from memory: " 'I most sacredly vow and most positively swear that I will never yield to bribery, flattery, threats, passion, punishment, persecution, persuasion, nor any other enticements whatever coming from or offered by any person or persons, male or female, for the purpose of obtaining from me a secret or secret information. I will die rather than divulge the same, so help me God.' Did you swear to such an oath?"

"I could have possibly, yes," Rowe answered.

Rowe's flat, affirmative response left Murphy at a loss. His cross-examination quickly turned into something of a paranoid sermon. He talked incessantly about President Johnson trying to break the back of the Klan, about Fidel Castro and Communism, about the NAACP, about Supreme Court justice Felix Frankfurter and the Federal Reserve. As the day dragged on, Murphy sweated himself pale and screamed until he was hoarse, losing his way with each new word. The most effective aspect of his cross-examination concerned Rowe's compensation from the FBI. Shanahan, Rowe's case agent, testified that the informant had received $112 per week since April 1. Murphy scoffed at the figure and brought up the meeting with Rowe at his office in the Frank Nelson Building, the night Murphy personally posted Rowe's $50,000 bail.

"Isn't it true that the FBI offered you 500 acres in Minnesota and enough money to live the rest of your natural life if you'd help break the back of the United Klans of America?"

"I would like to answer that," Rowe perked up. "No, sir, Mr. Murphy, you instructed me to put that information out."

The Klonsel slammed his hat to the ground and cursed under his breath. He stomped around the room and banged on the table.

"You . . . you . . . " he screamed, pointing at Rowe with the marked hand.

His outburst was so disquieting that the judge granted a five-minute recess for Murphy to calm himself. When the Klonsel returned, he apologized profusely to everyone in the room except the witness. A long day was about to get even longer.

»»» »»» »»» ««« ««« «««

Clocking in at sixty-seven minutes, Murphy's closing statement was an epic travesty of courtroom civility and judicial ethics. He started by defending racism through a tortured reading of the Old Testament. "Niggers are against every law God ever wrote," he told the jury. "Noah's son was Ham and he committed sin and was banished and his sons were Hamites and God banned them and they went to Africa and the only thing they ever built was grass huts. . . . And do unto the white people what God said you shall not do because there'll be thorns in your eyes, thorns in your flesh; if you intermarry with a servile race, then you shall be destroyed."

Murphy ranted until he ran out of energy, until his flabby physique was covered in sweat. The jurors looked confused when they left for deliberations, and a few hours later, word came back that Wilkins would not be acquitted after all. Ten of twelve white jurors actually wanted to convict him for Liuzzo's murder, but it wasn't enough. The two hard-liners held out, which meant there would have to be a retrial. The jury was hopelessly deadlocked.

PART IV

»»» »»» »»» ««« ««« «««

Krossings in Klan
Kountry, 1965–1966

18

I Was a Ku Klux
Hayneville, Alabama,
May–September 1965

Huie came away from Hayneville as jaded as ever about justice in the Deep South. But it also warmed his heart to know that ten brave Alabamians could still stand up to a bully like Murphy. With Congress now committed to investigating the Klan through public hearings, Huie never doubted who would become the protagonist of his next book: Gary Thomas Rowe. The informant's infiltration of the Klan was the stuff of spy fiction. To weave a compelling narrative, Huie needed complete access to the biggest fish in the FBI's tank. So on May 5, he "expressed a desire to contact Rowe" through the informant's handlers at the Birmingham FBI. "Huie stated he has always been 'pro-FBI,' and that he would assure us that anything he wrote pertaining to Rowe would be favorable to the FBI," the report read. When it reached Hoover's desk several days later, the director scribbled a one-sentence reply: "I don't trust Huie."

Rowe was told that if he accepted Huie's offer, "the Bureau could no longer assume responsibility for his safety or the safety and welfare of his family." But Hoover did agree that Rowe should be informed of Huie's proposition. In case the informant later went rogue, he could not claim the FBI withheld this lucrative offer. Undeterred, Huie pitched the idea to senior editor Richard Kennedy of Dell Publishing, owner of *Look* magazine. At a meeting in Manhattan, Huie's literary agent Ned Brown proposed two $75,000 advances, one for the book and one for the movie. It would be a three-way split among Rowe, Huie, and a New York writer named Michael Dorman, a Huie admirer and fellow journalist whom Huie had known since Dorman covered the 1963 Project C demonstrations in Birmingham.

No one bothered to get Rowe's permission before proceeding, but the FBI became aware of the contract when Dorman walked into a field office in New York looking for a sympathetic face. Again it backfired. Hoover was told that Huie's coauthor left understanding "that the FBI would have absolutely nothing to do with any of this, could not and would not help." But Huie ignored these warnings and kept at it. He sent a letter to Kennedy, proposing a signing session in Manhattan for July 29 or July 30. "The working title should be I WAS A KU KLUX FOR THE FBI by Thomas Gary Rowe, With William Bradford Huie and Michael Dorman. Essentially, it should be a first-person 'spy' story, written so that the reader can associate with Rowe from first to last," Huie wrote. "This is the race conflict in Alabama as Rowe lived it . . . the drifter-bartender in his first contacts with the FBI agents . . . his decision to join the Klan as a spy . . . why, how, etc. The reader must travel every road with Rowe, join the Klan with him, meet Klansmen, and be present at every secret meeting with an FBI agent."

Huie imagined that the story would cover Mrs. Liuzzo's murder, as well as "the Klan connections with Alabama Governors Patterson and Wallace . . . material on Klan figures like Matt Murphy and Bob Shelton." It would also require some serious embellishing, like *Three Lives for Mississippi*. "We must write this story like a novelist would write it, not like a reporter," Huie explained. "We must get inside Rowe and create a three-dimensional character who feels and thinks as well as acts." The deadline would be built around the second trial, slated for October. "The Delacorte-Huie contract should specify that we begin work on August 1, 1965, and deliver the completed manuscript on December 31, 1965 . . . with a possible 30-day extension if the trial is delayed until after October 1."

Despite Hoover's intransigence, Huie could hardly contain his excitement. *Three Lives for Mississippi* was selling fast, and each new day made him richer. He was on another big story, he was flush with cash, and he had a backdoor plan. "It should be understood by all parties that there is an element of calculated risk here," Huie wrote to Kennedy and Dorman. "Rowe might die or be killed. Or we might not 'get Rowe.' If we wait until we 'get Rowe' to begin work, we'd be at least six months delivering the book. By starting on the preliminary work now, and betting on 'getting Rowe' by October 15th, we can bet that we can deliver the book by the end of the year."

》》》 》》》 》》》 《《《 《《《 《《《

Months earlier, on March 26, 1965, the story broke that Paul Johnston, a prominent Birmingham lawyer, would defend Rowe in a $6,000 civil suit for unpaid legal expenses. Birmingham's "Man of the Year" in 1958, Johnston was a graduate of both Harvard and Yale, a former member of Supreme Court justice Robert H. Jackson's staff during the 1945 Nuremberg trials, and an outspoken liberal on the subject of race. Johnston took Rowe's case after an entreaty from US attorney general Katzenbach and famed defense attorney Bernard Segal, who explained that Klonsel Matt Murphy sought to reclaim expenses for bailing Rowe out of jail the day after Liuzzo's murder. Johnston accepted the unpopular assignment, and within days, he was kicked out of the law office that his father helped establish, by partners that included his own brother.

Johnston was Huie's backdoor hope of "getting Rowe." Both men walked in a milieu of educated and tolerant Alabamians, people who took a stand for integration, faced down ostracism, and stomached violent threats. When approached by Huie that spring, Johnston agreed to pass his offer along, but only after resolving the lawsuit. It dragged on until August 18, when Johnston asked the FBI for permission to speak with Rowe, who was in hiding somewhere out West. The lawsuit against Rowe would be heard the first week of September, and Johnston wanted to prepare a defense. During the same conversation, he made it clear that he would also make Rowe aware of a publishing contract of "$25,000 for the privilege of writing a story on Rowe's activities as a Klan informant." Johnston was claiming no part in the matter, and he promised to "advise Rowe not to sign this contract until the trials in this matter are disposed of." Rowe agreed to call Johnston at 2:00 PM on August 20.

In the interim, Huie showed up unannounced at the Birmingham FBI's office to further lobby the proposition. He admitted "gambling" on getting Rowe but called Johnston "a close personal friend" and an honest broker. Huie said he understood the FBI could not help him before the retrial in Lowndes County. However, he wanted the bureau to know that he and Dorman were in town "developing background." They were staying at the Downtowner Motel, Huie said, the same hotel where Rowe was hidden during Wilkins's first trial. The agent who wrote the report said Huie "asked for no information, and, of course, none was furnished."

That same week in August, through a "bit of managing," Huie scored an interview with Rowe's father in the boardroom of the Reynolds Metals Company. Johnston, "a friend and fellow club member of the general manager," arranged the meeting. The elder Rowe, an illiterate millwright and a thirty-three-year employee, was "brought up from the plant" to meet Huie. At some length, he provided good background to help make Rowe a sympathetic figure. Huie even asked his editor to amend the publishing contract so that Rowe's parents would also benefit financially. Soon after, Huie realized that his brash moves in Birmingham "attracted Ku Klux attention." The plant supervisor at Reynolds Metals was a known Klansman, and Huie was sure that word was out, because two days later, the Grand Dragon of the state of Alabama, Robert Creel, held a rally in Huie's sanctum of Hartselle. Before leaving town, Creel asked the chief of police to pass Huie a message: the Klan knows you're dealing with Rowe.

》》》 》》》 》》》 《《《 《《《 《《《

On the day Johnston was to deliver Huie's pitch to Rowe, a tragedy crippled the Alabama Klan. During the wee hours of August 20, Klonsel Murphy left the Patio Bar in Birmingham to investigate a shooting. Nightriders on US Highway 11 had followed a young white woman for several miles before firing upon her with a shotgun. She was struck in the eye and rushed by ambulance to the University of Alabama hospital in the college town of Tuscaloosa. Believing the shooters to be black, or just saying so to cover for the Klan, Murphy left his seat at the bar to investigate. Entering the town of Cottondale, six miles outside of Tuscaloosa, Murphy passed out behind the wheel, crossed the centerline, and struck an asphalt tanker. The collision knocked two back wheels off the tanker's axle and spun it into a figure eight. Murphy's car ended up on the side of the road, mangled and disfigured. The Klonsel was killed on impact.

Murphy died optimistic. Earlier that day, he gave what might have been his last interview to Huie. The deadly Watts Riots, which had been burning for days in Los Angeles, took some heat off the Klan. Thirty-four lives had been lost, turning parts of the country against the faltering civil rights movement. "A few hours before his death," Huie wrote, "Matt Murphy said to me: 'Do you remember I told you four months ago that the Klan would elect the President in 1972? I was wrong by four years. We will elect George Wallace in 1968. This black insurrection in California has revealed to every American that Niggerism is Communism and Communism is Niggerism. . . . This is a Godsend to America and to make the most of it, I'm working day and night.'"

The Klan went into mourning after Murphy's demise. Statewide rallies eulogized him as a hero to the South, a true Confederate. Speakers urged young racists to stand up and continue his rebellion. Grand Dragon Creel put it this way: "God has a special place for Murphy, and I'm sure he has one for Martin Luther King. . . . Murphy was an inspiration to everyone in Alabama, but he is no longer with us to fight your battles, so it's time you realized that you are the federal government and begin your own fight."

The funeral attracted more than three hundred segregationists, Klansmen, and states-righters from across the nation, including the three accused of killing Liuzzo. The men came in suits, the women in gowns, to a funeral chapel in Birmingham. The pastor held a simple, ten-minute ceremony that included a reading from Scripture and ended with the reading of "Crossing the Bar," a poem by Lord Alfred Tennyson.

The pallbearers and the family then left in a convoy for Greenville, Alabama, a one-hundred-twenty-mile trek to Murphy's hometown. Art Hanes, one of the men holding Murphy's casket, held back tears as his friend was laid to rest. Emotional and defiant, Hanes later told reporters that he was not ashamed to admit the depth of their friendship: "I am proud to say Murphy was my friend. We even roomed together for a while at Woods Hall [men's dormitory at the University of Alabama]. I have known him a long time and in my opinion he was not only a brilliant lawyer but a good man, as well as a man who did not have a wicked or evil bone in his body, and would never willingly have done anything to anybody. During his very successful career here as a lawyer, at least seventy-five to eighty percent of his time had been in vigorous defense of negroes who were accused of various crimes."

>>> >>> >>> <<< <<< <<<

The same day that Murphy died, August 20, a part-time sheriff's deputy in Hayneville walked into a grocery store and shot dead an Episcopal minister named Jon Daniels. A twenty-six-year-old clergyman from New Hampshire, Daniels had heeded King's call to register black voters in Alabama, knowing too well that it might cost him his life. Huie reported the story for the *Tribune*. "The citizen-deputy who fired the buckshot is a graying fifty-two-year-old highway engineer," the story read. "His son is a state trooper working for Al Lingo. His heroes are Jim Clark, George Wallace and Matt Murphy." A similar tragedy occurred back on March 11, two weeks before Liuzzo's murder, when a gang of Klansmen beat a Unitarian minister named James Reeb to death. Reeb's killer was also in custody, and the district attorney had convened a grand jury.

Huie was worried that the Reeb trial could make the docket before Wilkins's. Such a scenario, being upstaged by a trial with national implications so similar in nature, would take even more wind out of the Rowe story now that the flamboyant Murphy was out of the picture. Much of the testimony would repeat what happened in May, and no one could guarantee that whomever the Klan hired to replace Murphy would provide the same fireworks and diatribes that a mass-market book required. For that reason, Johnston's eventual pitch to Rowe—delayed by Murphy's death—was delivered by Birmingham FBI agent Everett Engram on August 27 with caveats: "Huie has advised that the opportuness [sic] of your story has been influenced, probably adversely, by three recent happenings, (1) the Los Angeles riots, (2) the recent murder in Hayneville of the Episcopal clergyman, Jonathan Daniels, and (3) Murphy's death. However, he still is very much interested in your story and today presented a contract drawn by his New York lawyers."

The contract contained nine stipulations and included two signature lines, one for the informant and one for Huie. The stipulations demanded that Rowe make himself available for "not less than four weeks" and that he must "impart to Huie his true and complete life story." However, the author would not be responsible for "any inaccuracy, distortion, fictionalization, inference, innuendo, inconsistency or any other variation, error or omission." Rowe also had to agree "to inform Huie, to the best of his knowledge, as to those persons from whom Huie has the most fear, so that Huie may protect his life and property accordingly." In return, the author promised to pay Rowe up to $50,000 in $10,000 increments.

Johnston also spoke to Rowe by telephone on Friday, September 10. Rowe thought about Huie's offer over the weekend but turned it down flat on Monday, September 13. He did not want his picture in a book, and he did not want anyone telling his story. Nor did he want to lose FBI protection. "I have read Mr. Huie's proposed contract to me," Rowe wrote to Johnston, "and it is unacceptable for many reasons. As you may know my life has been threatened by the Klan and the Klan has discussed several methods of carrying their threats out. . . . Also I resent Mr. Huie's talking to my parents and implying to them that he was going to write my story before he had contacted me."

The king of checkbook journalism gave it one more shot. In a letter addressed to Johnston but meant for Rowe, Huie said it disturbed him to read accounts of Rowe and other informers as "finks." He said the pending acquittal of Wilkins meant that they should "try to retrieve by journalistic effort what has been lost in the Lowndes County courts." He proposed that Rowe meet him in Montgomery on October 18, right after testifying. If the meeting should go well, then Huie would fly Rowe to New York, where they could sign off on the deal just before Huie left for his European book tour to promote *Three Lives for Mississippi*. "We see in the Rowe story, a possible vehicle with which we can damage the Klan and all such terrorist organizations." Huie also had a backup plan: "If I do not write the Rowe book, I will write a general book, perhaps titled *The Ordeal of Alabama*, about the machinations of Wallace, Lingo, Jim Clark, and the Klan, with a good deal of emphasis on Lowndes County and what it represents."

But even that would be tricky. Huie worried that *Look* would not support him against future libel claims. "Money-wise, the present contract leaves me in a horribly exposed position," Huie wrote to Dorman. "I can proceed with the story. I can collect and spend $75,000. And then I can be beaten by the lawyers." More ominous fears also made him consider abandoning the project altogether. "Alabama is a more dangerous place today than it has ever been," Huie explained. "My trip last week to Lowndes County convinced me of this. When and if there is publicity about me and Rowe, I must have my homes guarded every night; and I probably will have to have a bodyguard in both Jefferson and Lowndes Counties."

19

The Parable of Two Goats
Hayneville, October–December 1965

Just as the Rowe story seemed to falter, a new character emerged on August 28, the day after Johnston pitched Huie's proposition to Rowe. Rejuvenated by the news, Huie wrote his editor immediately: "From the enclosed cutting you will note that Art Hanes has replaced Murphy and that the trial is NOT to be delayed. If [Hanes] is not a Ku Klux, he acts like one. He is a half-assed lawyer, but even he is smart enough not to ask for a continuance. What with the federal registrars in Lowndes County, along with the new murder, acquittal of the Liuzzo murderers is all but certain."

Ku Klux or not, Hanes was up-front about his motivations. He told reporters that he felt "incensed over the way President Johnson attacked the Klansmen on national television." Men accused of crimes should be assumed innocent, not judged by the president in a blitz of pretrial publicity. The three Klansmen had come to him, Hanes explained, and they deserved a vigorous defense, regardless of their guilt or innocence. Journalists brought up Hanes's friendship with Murphy and his outspoken views on race, not to mention the racist speeches he'd given to various Klan fronts. Hanes waved them off. "To my knowledge," he said. "I have never been within fifty miles of such a meeting."

Hoover did not buy it for a minute. When a subordinate suggested that Hanes be "deleted from the Special Correspondents' List," Hoover signed off with one word: "Right." Unlike his predecessor, Hanes vowed to try the case on the facts, to stay away from the heated rhetoric. But though he may have carried himself in a more civilized way, Hanes's legal tactics mirrored those of the Klonsel. During voir dire, Hanes put eleven members of the White Citizens' Council on the jury. When the trial began on October 17, Hanes, like Murphy, invented a sex angle. He also disrespected the only black witness by dropping the courtesy title "Mr.," a point noted by Huie in one of his dispatches.

"Leroy, was it part of your duties . . . to make love to Mrs. Liuzzo?" Hanes asked.

The prosecutor objected, the judge sustained, but Hanes refused to stop.

"Leroy, did you at any time park in an automobile with Mrs. Liuzzo in front of Brown's Chapel?"

"No, I didn't."

"Did she touch you?"

"No, sir."

"At no time you never touched her?"

"No, I didn't."

"Or she never touched you?"

"She never touched me or I never touched her."

Rowe really did not want to testify again. His nerves were shot, but after numerous FBI pep talks, he went back on the stand, feigned confidence, and retold the story of Liuzzo's murder in a flat, calm voice. Rowe painted Wilkins as the triggerman and linked him to three shell casings from a .38-caliber pistol, the murder weapon. On cross-examination, Hanes devastated Rowe's credibility by exhibiting a photo from the 1961 Mother's Day Riot at the Birmingham depot, an event that saved Hanes's campaign for mayor. Tommy Langston's picture, the only one to survive the savage beating of Freedom Riders, clearly showed Rowe and a group of Klansmen beating an innocent black bystander. Hanes asked if Rowe was the man with his back turned to the camera. Rowe committed perjury in saying no, but the judge took no action against him, even after Hanes told the jury that Rowe was cut in the neck during the riot and that a fellow Klansman saved his life. Hanes then carefully attacked Rowe's actions on the night of March 25.

"Did you tell Wilkins not to shoot?" Hanes asked.

"No, sir."

"Did you make any attempt to jostle Wilkins to distort his aim?"

"No, sir."

"Well, you work for the FBI, don't you?"

"Yes, sir."

Hanes never accused Rowe of firing the fatal shot, despite the fact that the FBI did not take fingerprints from the murder weapon. Perhaps he knew that was unnecessary. Three weeks earlier, in the same courtroom, the killer of clergyman Daniels was easily acquitted despite smoking gun evidence. So Hanes played it safe. He took Murphy's path using a more acceptable tone while continuing to portray Rowe as a traitor to the South. Hanes dubbed his closing statement, "The Parable of Two Goats." Wilkins was the scapegoat for the FBI and Rowe was the "Judas" goat. "You are God-fearing men. You read the Bible," Hanes told the jury, adding, "Maybe the murderer is from the Watts area of Los Angeles!"

Huie hung his head when the jury returned a not-guilty verdict in one hour and forty-seven minutes. They'd hurried through deliberations in order to make the 7:00 PM Friday night football kickoff. "Hayneville is too small to have a drive-in movie or a bowling alley," Huie wrote in the *Tribune*. "Fewer than two hundred white persons live within a mile of the courthouse. So football and sex are the only available amusements, and everybody agrees that Hayneville is crazy about football." The local high school football team had put together a thirty-two game winning streak, and "the fathers of [the team's] two stars, Lewis McCurdy Sr. and O.P. Woodruff, were both in the jury weighing the fate of Collie LeRoy Wilkins."

Hanes stood proud as the verdict was read, thanking members of the jury as they scurried home to collect their pompoms and cowbells. "Not only was the verdict of not guilty justifiable," Hanes told the press. "I think the evidence demanded this verdict."

Huie left town disgusted. His failed attempt to make a deal with Rowe was quickly salvaged into a fictionalized assault on Wallace, Lingo, and the Klan. The novel was called *The Klansman*; Hollywood pounced on the dramatic rights.

》》》 》》》 》》》 《《《 《《《 《《《

Since the *Brown* decision, only a handful of Southern juries had ever convicted a white man for a racially motivated murder. Legal forums like the courtroom, designed precisely to exact justice, had been perverted into a safe harbor for racism and murder. But finally, a silent minority decided to stand up. It happened first in Anniston, Alabama, site of the 1961 firebombing of a Freedom Riders bus. Four years later, in December 1965, an NSRP member named Hubert Strange, twenty-five, stood trial for killing Willie Brewster, a blue-collar African American.

The crime occurred in July, two hours after Stoner and his lieutenants held a public rally in Anniston. That night, one of the NSRP speakers yelled, "If it takes killing to get the niggers out of the white man's streets and to protect our constitutional rights, I say yes—kill them." Minutes after those words were spoken, Brewster was leaving his job at the foundry for the last time. On the ride home, a bullet fired by Strange struck him in the back of the neck, and as he lay dying, Brewster felt compelled to deny any involvement in the civil rights movement.

The trial was held in a Calhoun County courthouse. Stoner represented Strange and made little attempt to lay out a defense. That offended the jury. It deliberated for more than ten hours, each man casting twenty ballots, before the final holdout relented. The man who delivered the verdict was a typewriter salesman, the rest worked in factories or on farms, in the National Guard or as firemen. The jury returned a guilty verdict on December 2, 1965, exactly one hundred years after Alabama ratified the Thirteenth Amendment and ended slavery for good. Stoner was so shocked that he actually wept.

"I would rather have some good black niggers than the white niggers on the jury," he cried.

>>> >>> >>> <<< <<< <<<

Judge Frank Johnson, forty-seven, must have been moved by the Strange verdict. Appointed by President Eisenhower to the Northern District of Alabama, Johnson's legacy extended back to the Montgomery Bus Boycott. In that pivotal case, *Browder v. Gayle*, Johnson ordered Alabama's capital city to integrate public buses once and for all. For more than a decade thereafter, he relentlessly employed the equal protection clause of the Fourteenth Amendment, striking down segregation ordinances and voter suppression laws with abandon. He also enjoined and later approved the Selma–Montgomery march. As much as anyone, Johnson understood the reach of white terror in Alabama and the fear it bred among good men. After all, Klansmen had bombed his mother's home and burned crosses on his yard. Like Huie, Johnson slept with a shotgun under his bed.

The day after Strange's conviction, Judge Johnson oversaw a historic federal conviction in the Liuzzo murder. Hanes's clients—Wilkins, Eaton, and Thomas—were prosecuted in Johnson's court for violating Liuzzo's civil rights, a federal charge separate from the state charges of murder. John Doar, assistant attorney general of the United States, tried the case, and Hanes, whom some reporters described as flat-footed in federal court, represented all three Klansmen. Judge Johnson would not allow him to prey on racial prejudices, disrespect black witnesses, or play the "nigger lover" card. In less than ninety minutes, Hanes deposed ten witnesses, including Rowe, and closed with a passage from the Bible. "Then one of the twelve, Judas Iscariot, went to the chief priests and said, 'What will you give me if I deliver him to you?'"

The jury deliberated for eleven hours before declaring itself "hopelessly deadlocked." Judge Johnson wasn't buying it. He wanted a verdict, so he gave what in law is called the Allen charge: "You haven't commenced to deliberate long enough to be hopelessly deadlocked." The jury fought it out the following morning, and after lunch, a guard passed Johnson a note: they'd reached a verdict. For the second time in two days, twelve all-white, all-male Alabamians returned a guilty verdict against the Klan. Dr. King was stunned. Two convictions in two days seemed impossible in Alabama. For the first time, the hammer of democracy had cracked the seemingly impregnable duplicity of Southern justice. Those two historic verdicts were, as King put it, "rays of light and hope which penetrate the darkness which hovers over a long line of unpunished killings."

Hanes did not cry like Stoner. He knew how to play a bad hand, calling the jurors "highly intelligent people" who had done "a good job." He even complimented the FBI's professionalism on the stand. But his civility did not extend to Judge Johnson, a fellow alumnus of the University of Alabama School of Law and a longtime nemesis of Governor Wallace. Hanes told reporters Johnson's "dynamite charge" to the jury effectively "railroaded" his clients. A few weeks later, Hanes would continue his new role as Klonsel by filing a libel claim against *Life* magazine on behalf of the Mississippi lynch mob responsible for the *Three Lives for Mississippi* killings.

20

The Klokan
Los Angeles, January 1966

At 12:45 PM on January 10, Philip Manuel, an investigator for the House Un-American Activities Committee (HUAC), arrived at the Mayflower Hotel in downtown Los Angeles with a subpoena. The clerk at the registration desk passed him a note jotted down at 10:37 AM from the Klansman that Manuel had flown from Washington to serve. The note claimed that the man's flight was delayed. Worried and anxious, Manuel thought it might be an excuse not to show, but for the next six hours he waited patiently in a room on the third floor.

The phone finally rang at 6:45 PM. It was FBI informant Gary Thomas Rowe. The Department of Justice had refused to give Congress access to him until the Liuzzo trials were over, and the FBI had assured Rowe that his cooperation with HUAC did not require testifying. "Do you have a subpoena?" Rowe asked. When Manuel said yes, Rowe called it off. "He wanted to make it clear that if a subpoena was to be served, that he felt that this was a doublecross," Manuel's notes read. So Manuel offered Rowe a deal: if he would come to the hotel and answer questions about the inner workings of the Klan, the subpoena would disappear. Rowe would not have to testify publicly before the HUAC.

Around 7:15 PM, Rowe walked into the Mayflower and made his way to the third floor. Manuel found him to be "very nervous, emotionally upset, and suspicious." Rowe believed that Klansmen might try to kill him at any moment. He carried a .38-caliber pistol and looked ragged with fatigue. He had less than $300 in the bank, even though his new job, working for a former FBI agent in an "investigative capacity," paid $400 per week. Walking into the room, Rowe gave no pleasantries. His return flight left at 11:15 PM, so Manuel had less than four hours.

The thought of going back on the stand for the second trial in Hayneville still terrified Rowe. It had taken a campaign of backslapping and beer drinking just to make him do it the first time. Now, Rowe claimed the FBI was throwing him to the wolves because he refused "to bow to certain pressures to write articles and a book" and because he "really did not want to testify in the second trial." He never mentioned anyone by name, so Manuel never knew whether Rowe felt pressured to cooperate with Huie or with someone on Hoover's special correspondents' list.

When Rowe finally calmed down, he diagrammed the inner workings of the Klan and its violent connection to the NSRP. In doing so, he dissected the most organized terrorist apparatus in America. He dropped the names of suspects in the Sixteenth Street Baptist Church bombing and speculated as to where the Klan received its dynamite. The conversation took Rowe back to the early sixties. Born in Savannah, Georgia, he moved to Birmingham with his father as a high school dropout. He dreamed of becoming a cop but lied about his education on the application.

In 1960, he was working as a bartender when the FBI recruited him at his parents' home to infiltrate the Eastview 13 Klavern, the scene where he first met Imperial Wizard Bobby Shelton. Rowe said he could immediately tell that something was wrong. Shelton took the stage and suddenly called out Rowe's name. Then he told everyone else to leave. Rowe just stood there stunned, as the doors of the Klavern were bolted shut. Shelton then accused Rowe of spying for the FBI and ordered him killed.

Manuel listened to the rest of what may have been a highly exaggerated story. Rather than beg for his life, Rowe said he took Shelton hostage and yelled, "This bastard is going with me." He ordered the Klavern doors unlocked and started downstairs with Shelton held hostage. He could have just run away, but instead he shoved Shelton into a wall, knocking him out cold. Rowe then strutted back upstairs, challenging everyone else to a fight. Those events amused Shelton, and after that he protected Rowe from Klonsel Murphy, whom Rowe described as "his greatest enemy in the Klan." As Manuel noted, "In early 1965, there was a plot to kill [Rowe] on the farm of the late Matt Murphy. . . . Rowe claimed that someone in the Klan tipped him off as to the plot and Rowe avoided contact with Murphy."

What Manuel seemed to want most from Rowe was evidence of a violent connection among Shelton, Murphy, and Stoner. Rowe's response confirmed Manuel's suspicion. "J. B. Stoner and his associates were very close to Robert Shelton and during his life Matthew Murphy was very close to J. B. Stoner," Manuel's notes read. Murphy and Stoner were planning to become law partners at the time of Murphy's death, and Rowe believed that Stoner and Murphy were "the guilty parties in the Birmingham church bombings," despite having no "direct knowledge" of the planning. Rowe wanted it on the record: Klonsel Murphy was "a constant cause of violence in the entire South."

Other HUAC sources, as well as Rowe, suggested that ties between the Klan and the NSRP could best be understood by considering a bombing that shamed Jacksonville, Florida, for the better part of 1964. That February, Klansman William Rosecrans Jr. threw twenty sticks of dynamite under the home of a six-year-old boy named Donald Godfrey. The child and his mother were targeted because they'd won a federal order to integrate Lackawanna Elementary School. Both survived the explosion, and within weeks Rosecrans confessed to the crime. He pled guilty to a federal civil rights violation and took a polygraph. It proved his guilt but also cleared him of any wrongdoing in the Birmingham church bombing, as well as other crimes committed across the South. In July 1964, the US government brought civil rights charges against Rosecrans's co-conspirators using the same federal law that would bring down the Liuzzo killers in Judge Johnson's court. Like Rowe in Hayneville, Rosecrans shocked the Klan by testifying against his comrades on July 3, 1964, in Jacksonville, but not surprisingly, the first attempt at justice ended in a mistrial.

In November 1964, the retrial began. Rosecrans's co-conspirators were defended by Murphy and Stoner, the two most important Klan attorneys in the country and the spiritual leaders, respectively, of the Klan and the NSRP. Rosecrans refused to testify, opting instead for seven years in prison. He was too scared, and without his testimony it took eight days for the government to establish its evidence. The effort was futile. Having picked an all-white jury, Stoner and Murphy got the Klan off with the usual rhetoric, attacking what Stoner called "some of the most disreputable witnesses ever put on a witness stand." As with Rowe, they branded Rosecrans as Judas, the Klan as defenders of Christendom. When all the defendants were acquitted, Murphy and Stoner stepped out of court elated. "I'm very happy the Federal Bureau of Integration has gone down to defeat again," Stoner told reporters.

Rowe may have been partially responsible for Rosecrans's backing out, Manuel learned, because of legitimate threats that were put on his life by a special intelligence unit that's sworn to secrecy. "The Klokan Committee," as Rowe described this outfit, "plots and commits acts of violence. It also obeys orders in carrying out predetermined acts of violence. These acts are never discussed outside of this select group, and they are never discussed in the Klavern meetings." It all goes through Shelton, Rowe claimed. Shelton ordered Rowe, and the rest of the Klokan, to Jacksonville on November 21–22. They flew commercial and stayed at the Capri Motel, whose invoices would soon be subpoenaed by Congress. It was quite a scene. Shelton was there. Murphy was there. Alabama grand dragon Robert Creel was present. So were Wilkins, Thomas, and Eaton—the three men later tried in Liuzzo's murder.

Rowe and other HUAC witnesses recalled the scene in Room 318, Murphy's room. Under the bed was a small "pasteboard" box containing two bundles of dynamite, six or seven sticks apiece. There were also blasting caps with green, yellow, and white wires, not to mention a small arsenal of guns and ammunition. A rumor had circulated that a splinter Klavern might try to assassinate Shelton that night in Jacksonville, so everyone was assigned surveillance duties and given weapons. Just before the Klan rally began, Stoner and his lieutenants dropped by to confer with Shelton and Murphy. Rowe was certain of what happened next: the principals went into a private room and put their heads together. "Rowe stated that J. B. Stoner and several other of his men conferred with Shelton, Murphy, and Creel, and the decision was made to assassinate Rosecrans." When Stoner left, Shelton turned to Rowe and Wilkins to officially contract the hit on Rosecrans. "We didn't bring you all the way down here just to go to a rally," Shelton said.

Hundreds of Klansmen showed up that night at Jack's Truck Stop on Cedar Bay Road. They'd come from as far away as Texas to eat a fried chicken dinner and hear angry speeches. Armed to the teeth, Rowe and the Klokan policed the crowd, packing automatic weapons, a "foreign made burp gun," a carbine, and two hand grenades. The grenades were in a box beneath the speaker's platform. Not surprisingly, the hit on Shelton never materialized. But nor did the Klokan go after Rosecrans. Either Rowe did not explain why or Manuel omitted it from his notes. The dangerous situation just sort of fizzled out, Rowe implied.

However, when the final report was released, HUAC explained the situation this way:

> The [United Klans of America's] Imperial Klonsel Matt Murphy was serving as one of the counsel for some of the defendants, although the UKA had no organizational tie with the United Florida Ku Klux Klan. At this same motel meeting, furthermore, the UKA agreed to "take care of Rosecrans" if the opportunity presented itself. Certain klansmen from Alabama were assigned to the task of eliminating Rosecrans. Rosecrans, however, remained in Federal custody. Legal action initiated by the klans to free him from jail was unsuccessful. It appears that

klandom planned to free Rosecrans from prison in order to kill him as an object lesson to others.

As 11:00 PM closed in, Rowe walked out of the Mayfair Hotel like a spy into the night, ostensibly back to the airport. In just a matter of days, the information he shared that evening would air publicly in Congress's most notorious court.

21

Klan Kourt
Washington, February 1966

Acting on President Johnson's suggestion, Congress announced its investigation of Klan terrorism on March 30, 1965, just five days after the Liuzzo murder and the afternoon of a deadly car bombing outside the US embassy in Saigon. Investigations were broken down by state, and the hearings began on October 24, 1965, with a presentation of flowcharts, maps, and diagrams, all of which revealed the reach of the Klan throughout the country, as well as its papal-like protocols and pagan-like customs, not to mention its childlike vocabulary that added *Klan* or the letter *K* to almost every possible word. Headline writers had a field day slugging stories like KLAN KOURT, or more obscurely, KLUDD SILENT ON BUCKSHOT IN KLAN PANTS, a reference to the Klan chaplain's alleged possession of ammunition.

On the first day of public hearings, Imperial Wizard Shelton appeared before a panel of suits in an intimidating caucus room. He was unapologetic, sarcastic, and ironic; having expended so much blood and treasure fighting what Hanes called the Second Civil War, Shelton saw no contradiction invoking the Fifth Amendment to the US Constitution. He did it so often that no one could keep up. Nor would he cooperate with orders to turn over Klan files. He flatly refused. The hearings continued throughout the second and third

Liuzzo trials, giving outsiders a complete education on how to escape justice in the Deep South. But it wasn't until after the meeting with Rowe that Congress honed in on the Alabama Klan, home base of the invisible empire and America's most dangerous Klaverns. During the first and second week of February 1966, a parade of Shelton's top lieutenants appeared before Congress and pled the Fifth.

Despite a complete lack of cooperation from witnesses, the hearings disclosed the clandestine nature of Shelton's operation. America learned that the Klan legally conducted business, almost exclusively, through an incorporation called Alabama Rescue Service. Shelton used the fictitious name to acquire a citizens band radio license from the Federal Communications Commission (FCC) to monitor police calls. All told, the Klan maintained over a dozen fronts just in the state of Alabama, many of which listed a Tuscaloosa or Birmingham address, under such aliases as the Young Men's Social Club and the Benevolent Brotherhood. That didn't include the insurance company, the entities to publish propaganda, nor the shell companies set up to loot the state of tax dollars. Investigators also revealed that Matt Murphy, when still alive and serving as Klonsel, created a "White Man's Defense Fund" for the Liuzzo killers through the Birmingham Trust National Bank. It was the same account Murphy bragged about to Huie on the day before his death. At least two additional accounts existed in Birmingham for the sole purpose of hiring lawyers to defend killers.

Unlike Klansmen from other states, the boys from Alabama refused the pro bono services of J. B. Stoner, who represented the lion's share of several dozen Klan witnesses. Shelton had someone else in mind for the job. Weeks before his public appearance, he told investigators "he might hire as his lawyer the ex-FBI agent who has been retained by other accused persons and who was formerly the mayor of Birmingham." But Hanes was apparently too tied up with the lynch mob libel claim, or too reluctant, to take the case, so Shelton settled for a lawyer from North Carolina named Lester V. Chalmers Jr.

Chalmers was good at telling his clients to plead the Fifth Amendment. None of the Alabama Klansmen subpoenaed before Congress could be described as cooperative, and only a few answered even a single question. But the most talkative of that small lot proved to be the most important. His name was Ralph Roton, chief investigator for the Klan Bureau of Investigation, or KBI. Roton was a cocky veteran and electrician who still sported a crew cut. For two days he sat before a microphone in the caucus room, answering in defiance, often dropping the line "I could not say beyond a reasonable doubt with all certainty," but answering nonetheless. He testified without counsel.

"Did you, on behalf of the United Klans of America, make any investigation as to the circumstances relating to the death of Viola Liuzzo?" asked chief investigator Donald Appell.

"I did, under the direction of attorney Matt Murphy . . . I made some photographs . . . I talked to State investigators, talked to the FBI, was at the trial, and all information was turned over to the attorney."

Appell then produced a check for "attorney's fees." He wanted to know which lawyer Roton was working for and why the Klan paid attorney's fees in the Liuzzo trial. Roton hesitated, then answered the question without revealing any names. "It could be for the attorney that was hired in the Wilkins case," he testified. Congress later confirmed that the money, $500, went to Hanes. Several checks made out in his name were put into the official record, but investigators failed to address his broader role in the Klan despite Hoover's longstanding suspicions, not the least of which was Rowe's assertion that Hanes was a "card carrying Klansman." Out of respect for attorney-client privilege, Hanes never received a subpoena to testify, not even in executive session.

》》》 》》》 》》》 《《《 《《《 《《《

Under congressional protocol, Roton could no longer plead the Fifth after he started testifying. This inconvenience led to a breakthrough when Roton revealed that he personally investigated Martin Luther King Jr.—on state orders. In August of 1963, as Birmingham schools prepared to integrate, Roton, the head of the KBI, was the man hired by the state of Alabama to infiltrate civil rights organizations and investigate Dr. King's March on Washington. Roton quit his job "to come to the Washington march to take pictures, make tape recordings, and identify as many known Communists as I could for a committee such as this for the state of Alabama, known as the Commission to Preserve Peace." On the morning of the Birmingham church bombing, Roton appeared on the scene with his "press pass." He took pictures of grieving innocents who were crowding around the carnage. A congressman suddenly interrupted the story.

"You have any knowledge that the Ku Klux Klan might have been engaged in that?"

"Do you want my opinion, sir?"

"Yes. That is what we are up here for?"

"I don't think they did, in my judgment, because I was down there."

"Whom do you think did it?"

"I don't know sir."

"Do you think the Communists did it?"

"There is a possibility. I can read you some statements that I have available."

"What ground do you have for saying that?"

"Well, I can read you some statements that have been documented and turned over to the commission and the FBI when they asked me what information I had about the bombing of the 16th Street Baptist Church, if you would like to hear them, sir."

"Surely. Go right ahead."

"James Bevel, field secretary for the Southern Christian Leadership Council, made a statement at the Unitarian church in the latter part of 1963, stating, 'The bombings in Birmingham will stop when we get what we want.'"

With both defiance and calm, Roton continued the Klan's propaganda war but assured the committee that only five or six people in the Klan knew of his secret role in the KBI. Roton didn't feel the committee should assume that the state hired him because of his affiliation with the Klan. But the "coincidence" naturally led to an obvious question.

"Alright, now, sir, who recommended you to the legislative committee for employment?"

Roton suddenly became very uncomfortable. He answered the question, the *Washington Post* reported, "only after long minutes of indecision and a five minute recession that he requested 'to make a phone call.'" Whom he called was not publicly revealed, but when he returned, Congress demanded an answer.

"Gentlemen, if I go in and keep this in context, I certainly would appreciate it . . . I talked with Governor Wallace—he had no idea that I was ever associated with the United Klans of America—and I told him that I did investigative work; for whom, I did not say, and that I understood there would be a position open with this committee and I would appreciate anything he could do to help me. Now, whether Governor Wallace did or not, I do not know. I only worked for the committee, as you know, a short time."

Congressman Joe Pool, D-Texas, refused to "keep this in context."

"Did Governor Wallace talk to you about your investigative work?" Pool asked.

"Yes sir; we talked that one time."

"After you went to work for the committee you talked to Governor Wallace?"

"Yes sir."

"What did you talk about?"

"To the best of my knowledge, I don't think I saw the governor for four, five, or six months."

"Did you tell him about the results of your investigation?"

"Yes sir."

"Did he have any suggestions?"

"I don't remember sir."

"Did Robert Shelton ever talk to Governor Wallace about you working for this committee?"

"Not to my knowledge, sir."

A short recess ensued while a member of the Alabama Legislative Commission for the Preservation of the Peace wrote a hurried letter that was subsequently entered into the record. It confirmed Roton's employment with the state but swore ignorance of his Klan ties. Congressman Pool was not satisfied.

"The question that occurs to me is this: Was the State of Alabama paying you for investigating for the United Klans?"

"No sir, definitely not."

"That is really what the question is. You claim the State of Alabama, but you are a member of the United Klans and you are an undercover agent for them. You had two masters, so to speak. Which one were you working for? I know who paid you, but whom were you working for?"

Roton refused to cave. He expected the nation to believe that the most powerful, ambitious governor in the nation did not know that he was recommending a Klansman for the state's only full-time job investigating Dr. King's movement. Skeptical news reports circulated the following morning dressed in disturbing headlines: KLAN AIDE SAYS ALABAMA GAVE HIM A STATE JOB; ASKED WALLACE FOR JOB SAW NO CONFLICT.

》》》 》》》 》》》 《《《 《《《 《《《

The hearings ended two weeks later with the anticlimactic testimony of J. B. Stoner. Nothing new emerged because Stoner ignored the committee's authority. His only truthful response was his rationale for silence. "I refuse to answer on the ground that to do so may incriminate me," Stoner said, "and I also refuse by invoking all of my rights under the 1st, 4th, 5th, especially the 6th Amendment, also the 8th, 9th, 10th, 14th amendments to the Constitution of the United States, and further respectfully refuse to answer because to do so would waive my right to invoke constitutional rights and privileges in response to further questions."

The committee resorted to putting his stories from the *Thunderbolt* into the record, one of which referred to the committee chairman as "an ape." Other gems included the time Stoner told a Birmingham mob how to make a bomb, as well as his anthropology lesson in Bogalusa, Louisiana. "The nigger is not a human being. He is somewhere between a white man and an ape," Stoner claimed. "We don't believe in tolerance. We don't believe in getting along with our enemy, and the nigger is our enemy!" HUAC quit its yearlong inquiry with a blunt summation. "The record is not a pretty one. It is a record of floggings, beatings, killings, of talk of and plans to assassinate public figures and others for no other reason than the color of their skin or the fact that they disapprove of the ideas, policies, and activities of the Klan." Imperial Wizard Shelton and six others (but not Stoner), faced contempt charges. In six months, Shelton would be tried and convicted in a Washington, DC, courtroom. And after a few years of appeals, he would finally serve a nine-month sentence beginning in March 1969. The lag time on bond allowed him and all the other Klansmen to rally around Governor Wallace, widely rumored to be a third-party candidate in the 1968 election.

22

The Escape
Missouri State Penitentiary,
Jefferson City, March 1966

Two weeks after the HUAC hearings ended, on March 11, James Earl Ray tried to escape the gothic walls of the Missouri State Penitentiary. He had served half of a ten-year sentence for armed robbery, but the dream of running free in the world, of making a statement of some kind, drew on his mind as faithfully as he tugged his right ear. "I began collecting tools," Ray would later write, "hacksaw blades and a long pole with a hook at the end used to open hard-to-reach casement windows—and watching for my chance."

Why he decided to risk it all that winter remains a mystery. When questioned years later about his cryptic motivations, Ray protected them like sacred trophies. "I do read the papers quite a bit" was about all he would say. So there's no way to know, for sure, whether he read about the segregationist rebellion in Wallace's Alabama, about unpunished murder and state-funded harassment. Did Ray know about the assault of King in Selma, about the brutality on the Pettus Bridge, about the killing of Viola Liuzzo, about the show trials in Hayneville, about the death of Matt Murphy, or about the hiring of Hanes and subsequent acquittals? Had Ray heard of Huie or read in *Look* about the scope of Wallace's ties to the Klan? No one can say for sure.

After putting a dummy in his bunk, Ray busted out by crawling up a tunnel, past a guard office, to another building where he hoped to get onto the roof. As he mounted a gutter in the rain, it suddenly gave way. He slipped and fell fifteen feet, landing hard and causing a commotion. Stranded by his own ineptitude, Ray hid out in a small building that housed a generator. He stayed hidden there for twenty-seven hours until an alert guard seized him without incident.

Ray spent the better part of that lost year avoiding punishment for the failed escape. In September 1966, as Hanes persuaded a jury of eight black men and four whites to acquit Eugene Thomas in Liuzzo's murder, Ray was transferred to a state hospital for a psychiatric evaluation. Doctors learned that he possessed an average IQ of 105, that he suffered no hallucinations or delusions, no mental disease nor serious depression. But he did appear to be antisocial, and the doctors concluded that he was a sociopath, though not a "psychotic" one. Another doctor examined him that December and drew similar conclusions. Ray suffered from anxiety and obsessive impulses. In other words, he'd become restless. His escape "was the result of undue anxiety and tension with the need to actually do something."

In early 1967, Ray returned to Jeff City, to the caged existence he'd known for the past twenty years, a life of solitude, meaningless chores, and voracious newspaper reading. Two big stories out of New Orleans remained in the papers until his ultimate escape in the spring of 1967. The first appeared in the *New York Times* on February 18 under the headline WALLACE ASSAILS 2 PARTIES' CHIEFS. Addressing the annual leadership conference of the White Citizens' Council of America, Wallace took the stage in a smoky room, surrounded by banners that read "Stand Up for America." There in New Orleans, Wallace took a vow. "At the end of his speech," the *Times* reported, "he said that if Republican and Democratic leaders 'don't swing around and fly right, we're going to see them all the way from Maine to California.'" Wallace's words were taken by some as a confirmation of his presidential ambitions. Members of the audience "laughed, clapped, and stamped their feet" at his irreverent and plainspoken diatribes.

Missouri, the state Ray called home, immediately began the arduous challenge of putting Wallace's American Independent Party on the November 1968 ballot by collecting thousands of signatures from ordinary citizens. It started at a Baptist church in downtown St. Louis, where Sheriff Clark, acting as an official representative of the Wallace campaign, delivered the governor's blessing to Missouri's hard core. Soon American Independent Party literature began to appear in a corner tavern that Ray's brother Jack opened in the most racist part of the city, the Third District, just a few hundred feet from Missouri's Wallace headquarters.

The second big story appeared in a small New Orleans paper called the *States-Item*. It also ran on February 18, the same day Wallace rallied the White Citizens' Council. The article reported that New Orleans district attorney Jim Garrison had spent $8,000 since November researching "the possibility of a well-organized plot in which New Orleans and New Orleans citizens were somehow directly involved." Garrison was convening a grand jury and deposing witnesses. "New Orleans authorities were searching for a Cuban who lived in Miami," the article read.

Garrison thought he'd solved President John F. Kennedy's assassination. He was trying to show that Lee Harvey Oswald's sympathy for Communist causes was a front, that while living in New Orleans and championing "Fair Play for Cuba" on Camp Street, Oswald was secretly plotting the assassination of Fidel Castro. "Black is white, white is black," Garrison told the *New York Times*. "I don't want to be cryptic, but that's the way it is." Garrison claimed knowledge of a secret plot hatched by an anti-Castro fanatic and possible Bay of Pigs pilot named David Ferrie, who once supervised Oswald as a commander of the Civil Air Patrol. As the FBI already knew, Garrison would falsely claim that Ferrie's library card was found in Oswald's wallet and that Ferrie transported Oswald to Dallas to kill President Kennedy.

On February 22, Ferrie killed himself just minutes after telling a *Washington Post* reporter that Garrison's investigation was a "witch hunt." But his suicide note was vague, and the death of Garrison's "lead suspect" sent the dogs of conspiracy barking even louder. Garrison seized the moment, announcing in a tight corridor of reporters and rolling cameras that "we have solved the assassination of President Kennedy beyond any shadow of a doubt." His investigators wanted to question a Cuban man who was never identified by the FBI, a "Latin" who was seen handing out pro-Castro fliers with Oswald in an old television station newsreel. The only way "people involved can get away is by killing themselves," Garrison boasted.

》》》 》》》 》》》 《《《 《《《 《《《

Ray finally escaped on April 23, 1967, just four days short of his long-awaited appeal to the Missouri Supreme Court. In his last hours as a ward of the Show-Me State, he purchased a transistor radio and a sack of candy bars. As Wallace officially announced his candidacy for president on *Meet the Press* that Sunday morning, Ray hid inside a huge breadbox in the bakery that was immediately placed on a truck bound for the prison farm. Somewhere along the route, Ray broke free and made his way to St. Louis, then to Chicago, where he hid out for several weeks working as a dishwasher at the Indian Trail Restaurant in Winnetka, Illinois. In June, Ray moved to Montreal for two months in a failed attempt to acquire a Canadian passport, before doubling back through Illinois and then on to Alabama.

On August 26, Ray arrived at the Birmingham depot ready to reinvent himself. He purchased a .38-caliber pistol and rented a safe deposit box from Birmingham Trust National Bank, where the Klan maintained its "White Man's Defense Fund" account. He took dancing lessons, studied photography, and read the paper. In the classifieds, he found a 1966 white Mustang, a hot rod with red interior, styled with "Heart of Dixie" license plates. He bought it for $1,995, and on October 6, he set out for California by way of Mexico. How he paid his expenses—possibly explained by the July 13, 1967, robbery of the Bank of Alton—has never been definitely established. Clearly, his wages as a short-term dishwasher during the summer of 1967 hardly explain this rambling, international lifestyle.

PART V

》》》 》》》 》》》 《《《 《《《 《《《

Stand Up for
America, 1967–1968

23

Meet Me in California
Los Angeles, 1967

As Ray moved from Birmingham to Mexico to Los Angeles, Wallace hit the campaign trail. One of his first stops was Ray's hometown of St. Louis, where on November 12 more than two thousand blue-collar workers reached out to him on a "dial-a-question" radio show. Later in the day he honored an invitation to speak to the city's Rotary Club, and it tickled him to learn that so many upper-class whites shared his outrage and frustrations. He seemed to view it as a seminal moment, an omen that his support outside of the South was stronger than he expected. "They really liked me," Wallace gloated on the way out of town.

The big test would come in December. The campaign needed to collect 66,059 signatures to make the California presidential ballot. It would require a major financial commitment, one that would never pay off in electoral votes. Some questioned why Wallace would even try, because polls showed that he had a better chance of winning the black vote than he did of winning the Golden State. Wallace's advisers recognized the dilemma. If he didn't make the ballot in all fifty states, few donors would take him seriously. On the other hand, if he did make it in California, the publicity would push him over the edge in other states. The money would pour in, and the media would pounce on the story.

The problem was logistics: Wallace needed an army of volunteers that he didn't have time to recruit. So he found a back door. Having exhausted his one-term limit as governor, Wallace ran his cancer-stricken wife, Lurleen, as a stand-in. She won the election handily, allowing Wallace to simply order state employees and loyal volunteers to California. It must have cost hundreds of thousands of dollars in plane fares, hotel bills, and telephone calls, but Lurleen let taxpayers foot the bill. By late November, eager Alabamians were flooding into L.A. on something of a mass junket. It was a flagrant misuse of public funds but a hell of a good time. Preaching "Law and Order," Wallace made his stand in Los Angeles, where two years earlier the deadly Watts Riots scorched portions of the troubled city.

At least one volunteer arrived on his own dime. After a month of sun-saturated debauchery in Mexico, Ray and his "Pride of Dixie" Mustang rolled up at the "Wallace for President" precinct in Hollywood on November 14. Ray had served time in Los Angeles back in the 1950s, so he brought along a certain nostalgia. He planned to stay on Skid Row for several months and settled into a forlorn hotel. He spent his days learning to dance, seeing a psychologist, drinking at bars, and studying how to become a locksmith. In testimony before Congress a decade later, Ray downplayed his interest in Wallace, which more than anything, seemed to explain his presence in California: "When I first came there, I was looking for a—some type of cover—some type of front for me to stay in Los Angeles for however long I stayed there, particularly if it was four or five months. And I think I called this Wallace Headquarters once and asked them something about how long they were going to be there or something."

A cover or not, Ray arrived in L.A. with politics on the brain. To get a phone in his first hotel room, he claimed to be a canvasser for the Wallace campaign, and phone records show he dialed the local precinct on three separate occasions. By December 15, Ray had moved over to the St. Francis Hotel, which housed his favorite bar, the Sultan Room. A female bartender named Marie Martin asked

Ray for a ride to New Orleans because she needed to pick up the children of her cousin, Rita Stein. To her surprise, Ray said yes, on one condition: Marie, her cousin Rita, and her brother Charles Stein—an acquaintance of New Orleans DA Garrison—must all sign the ballot petition for Wallace. Ray was serious. On December 15, he drove them all to the Hollywood precinct, and while they signed the petition to put Wallace on California's ballot, Ray stood around comfortably, as if he "worked there." When they finished signing the petition, Ray and Charles Stein headed out for New Orleans on Ray's dime.

They returned to Los Angeles on December 21, just as Wallace's push in California started getting tight. The deadline was January 2, 1968. By Christmas, the official tally stood around fifty thousand signatures, seventeen thousand short of the benchmark. But it was not an accurate figure. The bureaucrats simply could not keep up because by New Year's Eve, Wallace had actually crossed the threshold, ultimately securing one hundred thousand signatures, the lion's share from Los Angeles County. On December 28, possibly intoxicated by Wallace's unapologetic support for Rhodesia's white farmers, Ray wrote the American South African Council to learn about immigrating to Rhodesia. He'd helped Wallace conquer California, and now he wanted to help the ancestors of British and Dutch colonists stave off a native insurgency.

Ray usually kept his views on race to himself, with a few glaring exceptions. After King's assassination, journalist Louis Lomax scoured L.A. for more information about Ray's life in the city. He discovered that someone scribbled "down with Mexicans, niggers and Martin Luther Coon" on the wall outside "a phone booth used by Ray in the lobby" of the St. Francis Hotel. The FBI later confirmed the graffiti, but there was no way to prove who wrote it. However, another FBI report later confirmed that Ray scribbled the same slur, "Martin Luther Coon," on the back of a portable television set that he sold to Rita Stein before leaving California. As the election heated up, Ray's views on race continued to show.

⟫⟫ ⟫⟫ ⟫⟫ ⟪⟪ ⟪⟪ ⟪⟪

Whether conscious of it or not, Ray had joined a movement that included some of the most notorious racists in the world. On January 2, 1968, the day of Wallace's official California triumph, an Associated Press reporter found Imperial Wizard Bobby Shelton in Georgia, jubilant and defiant as ever. His federal prison sentence would be delayed another year, and it pleased him mightily to have the chance to work for Wallace in his quest for the White House. Shelton had flown to Atlanta on a Klan-owned twin-engine plane with six seats, a symbol of what the AP would soon report: the number of dues-paying Klansmen in the United States was now higher than at any other time since World War II. The Anti-Defamation League put the figure at fifty-five thousand members, and a congressional report confirmed the surge. Those draconian HUAC hearings of 1965–1966 had, in many ways, backfired. "The secret organization is expanding in the North and the Midwest," the AP reported.

Shelton stepped out of the plane and into a waiting automobile, headed to a courthouse in rural Georgia to address one of his aligned Klaverns. The reporter tagged along, scribbling down every word and baiting Shelton with Wallace questions. The imperial wizard predicted a "military coup" if segregationists received no concessions as a result of the election. That's where Wallace came in. "I think he's our only salvation now," Shelton said. The reporter asked whether he spoke in an official capacity, as a member of the Wallace campaign. "He and I understand each other," Shelton replied.

When they arrived at the old courthouse in Winder, a small group of Klansmen stood waiting. Shelton gave a short speech before exhibiting a John Birch Society film called *Anarchy U.S.A.*, a crude documentary starring mobs of angry black rioters. The premise was simple: if blacks could be inspired to riot en masse, it would help Wallace and grow the Klan. If more cities burned and more people died, Wallace and the Klan might make the world white again. Shelton even cited empirical data from the New Jersey riots that left twenty-six people dead the previous summer. "A week after the riot in Newark, we chartered six units alone," Shelton told Klansmen in Winder.

24

A Sick White Brother
Memphis, April 4, 1968

The evidence suggests that Ray spent three months in L.A. mentally preparing himself for a life in hiding. He tried hypnotism and read self-help books. He underwent plastic surgery, altering the tip of his nose, so "when the FBI put me on the Top Ten and circulated my old pictures, and stressed my nasal tip and low-hanging ear, then nobody would recognize me." In hopes of finding work abroad, he "graduated" from a six-week bartending school on March 2. He also continued to study locksmithing.

The war in Vietnam escalated that winter as the Viet Cong broke the Tet Truce, but Ray continued to obsess on another conflict. That February he wrote to "Friends of Rhodesia," asking for a subscription to "Rhodesian Commentary" and thanking the director of the organization for clarifying "most of my questions regarding immigration. Such as Passport." Ray apparently dreamed of boarding a steamer bound for White Africa while foreign headlines, in foreign tongues, roared with the news of his masterful crime.

Before leaving California, Ray almost threw it away trying to spread the Wallace religion to barflies. In February 1968 at the Rabbit's Foot Club, another watering hole where Ray enjoyed fifty-cent screwdrivers, a bartender named Bo Del Monte observed Ray in a

"heated discussion" with a "Caucasian female" over Alabama's reputation of racism. Del Monte "acknowledged that Ray often spoke support for Governor Wallace" and on this occasion lost his cool, telling
the liberal young woman, "I'll drop you off in Watts and we'll see
how you like it there." Del Monte remembered the incident because
Ray claimed to be from Alabama. It did not strike him as a coincidence that shortly afterward "a Negro patron of the Rabbit's Foot
Club, and his date, were struck on the head by a rock or brick while
in a nearby parking lot."

Another bartender at the Rabbit's Foot recalled a "political discussion" with Ray concerning "Robert F. Kennedy and George Wallace."
The bartender said Ray "became rather incensed and vehemently supported Wallace." He too remembered the Watts incident, but with
more theatrics. He said Ray lost his cool and "another customer who
knew the girl separated them." In what became a pattern, Ray vigorously denied that Wallace or racism had anything to do with the
incident. Rather, he simply remembered getting jumped by two men
in the parking lot for no reason. "Everybody was stirred up out there
at that time over politics or something," Ray later testified, "and somebody said something about my driver's license, the tags on my car, and
something about blacks in Alabama and I didn't say much because I
didn't want to get in no kind of brawl in a tavern and get arrested."

Ray's motivation to leave California suddenly matured on the
very weekend that Martin Luther King Jr. appeared in L.A. to
recruit for the Poor People's Campaign. This massive civil rights
occupation of the nation's capital was planned for summer, and critics of Dr. King, like Governor Wallace, were framing the initiative
as a Communist plot. King's visit appeared on the front pages of the
city's newspapers, almost forcing Ray, who read them religiously, to
hear about King's address to the California Democratic Council,
where he vowed to oppose President Johnson's re-election. King
said he would put his powerful, if waning, influence behind either
Eugene McCarthy or Bobby Kennedy. But some on the hard right
did not take King at his word. A paranoid minority of segregationists thought he was secretly planning a last-minute run. "A change

is absolutely necessary," King told the audiences he addressed in California. "We must end the war in Vietnam. President Johnson is too emotionally involved and face-saving is more important to him than peace."

The following morning, Sunday March 17, King clarified his statements during a sermon at the Second Baptist Church on Griffith Avenue. "I've made it very clear that I have no intention of running on any ticket," the *Los Angeles Herald-Examiner* reported. "I don't have any political aspirations." As King addressed the congregation on Griffith Avenue, Ray prepared to leave L.A. for good. Sometime that day he provided the St. Francis Hotel with a new forwarding address: "General Delivery, Main Post Office, Atlanta, Georgia." It seems evident, though hardly proven, that Ray's sudden exit from California had plenty to do with King's visit.

Over the next several days, Ray drove across the country and through the Deep South. He stopped in New Orleans sometime before March 22 to drop off clothes for the Stein family, before ultimately spending the night of March 22 in Selma. King planned to recruit in neighboring Eutaw the following day, so Ray registered at the Flamingo Hotel, whose neon sign illuminated the infamous Edmund Pettus Bridge, where state troopers beat civil rights marchers three years earlier. While in town, Ray likely read the previous day's *Selma Times-Journal*, which included this passage: "King and his followers moved into Alabama late Wednesday after a two-day swing through Mississippi. He planned to drive to Lisman, Linden, Camden today, then fly to Atlanta."

On March 24, Ray trailed King back to Georgia. In Atlanta, he rented Room 2 at a boarding house on 113th–114th Street and studied a map of the city, making circles near landmarks where he might find King exposed. But armed only with a small revolver that he purchased in Birmingham, he likely found it impossible to get close enough for a shot. He needed something more powerful if he was going to shoot from a distance.

》》 》》 》》 《《 《《 《《

As Ray scouted out King's domain in Atlanta, the civil rights leader traveled to Memphis on March 28 to lead the city's sanitation workers in a march against poverty. As the procession made its way down Beale Avenue, black militants hurled bricks and bottles through shop windows, creating a riot that police, wielding nightsticks and tear gas, struggled to put down for several hours. Never before had King participated in a violent march, much less fled the scene in a waiting car. His critics, including both Wallace and Hoover, quickly took advantage. On March 29, 1968, Memphis FBI agents handed off this fake news report to "cooperative" media outlets.

> Martin Luther King, during the sanitation workers' strike in Memphis, Tennessee, has urged Negroes to boycott downtown white merchants to achieve Negro demands. On 3/29/68 King led a march for the sanitation workers. Like Judas leading lambs to slaughter King led the marchers to violence, and when the violence broke out, King disappeared.
>
> The fine Hotel Lorraine in Memphis is owned and patronized exclusively by Negroes but King didn't go there for his hasty exit. Instead King decided the plush Holiday Inn Motel, white owned, operated and almost exclusively patronized, was the place to 'cool it.' There will be no boycott of white merchants for King, only for his followers.

The riot in Memphis put King's itinerary on the radio and in the papers. That same day, March 29, Ray drove to Birmingham to purchase a Remington .243-caliber rifle from Aeromarine Supply, located across the street from the city's integrated airport. On March 30, Ray returned the rifle because of a defect that prevented it from loading; he swapped it out for the Remington Model 760 Gamemaster and returned to Atlanta. Knowing that King would return to Memphis on April 3, Ray dropped off his laundry at Piedmont Laundry on April 1 and hit the road. Two days later, as King checked into the Lorraine Motel, Ray took Room 34 at the New Rebel Motor Hotel in the Whitehaven section of Memphis. That evening he sipped cans of Schlitz while King delivered his final sermon at the city's Mason Temple: "And then I got into Memphis, and some began to say the threats, or talk about the threats that were out. What would happen to me from some of our sick white brothers?" King asked. "Well, I don't know what will happen now. We've got some difficult days ahead. But it really doesn't matter with me now, because I've been to the mountaintop. And I don't mind."

A court injunction kept King in town until April 4. That morning, his lawyers had appeared in court to convince local authorities that a second march would not lead to violence or looting. Across town, Ray read a fateful passage in the Memphis *Commercial Appeal*. The article reported that King had taken a room at the Lorraine Motel, an exposed and vulnerable lodging at the corner of Mulberry St. and Huling Ave. that many black celebrities, like Louis Armstrong, frequented on trips to River City. Throughout the day, radio and television broadcasts also made note of King's hotel, some even announcing his room number.

All Ray had to do was get in position. Just after 3:00 PM, he parked on South Main Street and saw a sign that read APARTMENTS ROOMS. Proprietor Bessie Brewer showed him several rundown accommodations, but he picked Room 5-B, which had a clear view of the Lorraine. Sometime that afternoon, Ray carried the rifle inside, most likely by wrapping its box in a green bedspread. He left the room to purchase a pair of Bushnell binoculars for $41.55 and spent the next hour glassing Room 306. He did not have to wait long. King walked outside at 5:50 PM and Ray identified him with the binoculars, then went into a community bathroom holding the rifle. While standing in the tub, Ray balanced the rifle on the windowsill. At 6:01 PM King stepped back outside and Ray opened fire. The bullet splayed King's neck open and shattered his spinal cord. He fell to the ground, secreting a pool of blood, as his associates scrambled to comprehend the mortal wound.

Ray fled immediately, jamming everything he owned, including a copy of that morning's paper, into the green bundle. He charged down a side staircase, opened the door outside Canipe Amusement Company, and inexplicably dropped the entire bundle—which included the murder weapon and a radio from the Missouri State

Penitentiary—onto the sidewalk. Fleeing the city in the Mustang, Ray made it out of town before an all-points bulletin could be issued. As Ray raced back to Atlanta, President Johnson prepared to address the nation. "The dream of Dr. Martin Luther King, Jr., has not died with him," Johnson said on April 5. "Men who are white—men who are black—must and will now join together as never in the past to let all the forces of divisiveness know that America shall not be ruled by the bullet, but only by the ballot of free and just men."

Ray made it back to Atlanta before dawn. He parked the Mustang at Capitol Homes apartments and spent the night in the Five Points rooming house, eventually leaving behind a John Birch Society letter about South Africa and a copy of *Los Angeles Weekly*. Just after noon, he boarded a bus headed for Detroit. Around 8:00 AM on April 6, he crossed into Windsor, Canada, in a taxi, then boarded a train for Toronto. He spent the next thirty days hiding out and scheming to acquire the forged Canadian passport. In the name of Ramon George Sneyd, he made it to England on May 6 despite having recently made the FBI's "Ten Most Wanted Fugitives" list. When captured at Heathrow Airport on June 8, Ray was carrying two copies of the forged passport, a Rhodesian guidebook, and a "South African Airways timetable on which the next flight to Salisbury, Rhodesia, was marked in pencil, and the phone number of the South African Embassy in Lisbon was written in ink."

25

Stoner's Visit
Memphis, June–September 1968

As the Klan predicted, black riots broke out immediately after King's death and burned for days. Memphis suffered a week of terror as helicopters circled overhead through plumes of smoke, while national guardsmen enforced a twenty-four-hour curfew by carrying submachine guns and shooting out street lamps to protect themselves from roaming black snipers. In Washington, DC, hundreds of fires were set over the next three days along Fourteenth Street, forcing the cancellation of the city's Cherry Blossom Festival. Firefighters and national guardsmen combed the charred streets, day and night, until the violence finally ceased. A dozen people were killed in the riots.

Segregationists wasted no time trying to sully King's legacy. The White Citizens' Council called media coverage of King's murder "an orgy of public breast-beating." It slandered the deceased as an alchemist of propaganda and an "instigator of violence." Wallace, the eighth most admired man in a 1967 Gallup poll, was more strategic in his public statements, marking the assassination as "regrettable" and "typical of the breakdown in law and order." Though many people blamed racism for King's death, Wallace could only see red. "I want to get to the bottom of why people are being assassinated in this country," he said on television. "And we've had some assassinations recently. In my judgment somewhere the Communist movement is involved in this country in the assassinations."

As the FBI hunted for Ray across the globe, Wallace took a break from the campaign to mourn the loss of his wife, Lurleen, who died of ovarian cancer on May 7, just weeks after Wallace claimed "she has won the fight." Ten days after Ray's capture, on June 18, Gallup reported that Wallace could very possibly sweep the entire South and throw the election into the House of Representatives, a play that pundits called the Virginia Plan. In the Deep South alone, Wallace seemed likely to win 47 percent of the popular vote. On June 28, Wallace returned to the stump in Eutaw, Alabama, for a twenty-five-dollar-a-plate campaign dinner. Busty belles serving sweet tea and drunken country singers belting out patriotism charmed the event. Sympathy for Wallace's grief combined with anger over the riots had given the candidate a modest bounce in the polls.

ABC News was in Eutaw and cameras were rolling when a strange guest, Imperial Wizard Shelton, suddenly forded the crowd to greet Wallace like an old friend. For those who witnessed this encounter, like correspondent Sam Donaldson, the scene was disquieting. An aspiring presidential candidate embraced the admitted leader of America's largest terrorist group—right in front of the camera. But before Donaldson could get the film to New York, Wallace's men "seized and destroyed" three hundred feet of newsreel while the candidate personally chewed out the journalist for doing his job. "The whole conclusion in your mind and that of your network was to contrive the picture," Wallace cursed, "like some of you have contrived marches to get TV coverage."

A few weeks later, Wallace addressed eight thousand people in Ray's hometown of St. Louis. It took seventy policemen, state troopers, and Secret Service to protect him from black protesters who broke into the auditorium. They were taunting Wallace with the Nazi phrase "Sieg Heil!" before Wallace supporters starting throwing punches. "Let the police handle it! Let the police handle it," Wallace pleaded to the mob. Cops took control quickly and led away the protesters who were steadfastly singing "We Shall Overcome."

》》》 》》》 》》》 《《《 《《《 《《《

The surreal summer of 1968 found J. B. Stoner trudging onward in an oblivious fever, advancing his hate into the Midwest and selling Wallace for President as the last hope of the white race. When not defending racist killers, Stoner drove across the country continuing his libel of Jewish people and haranguing "niggers" at Klan rallies. Like a counterinsurgent in a lost war, he infiltrated blue-collar slums and organized pockets of resistance as far away as St. Louis, which had recently started its own branch of the NSRP.

Back on April 4, as King stepped onto the balcony of the Lorraine Motel, Stoner spoke to a small group of Mississippi supporters "inside a barber shop across the street from the Meridian Federal court-house." Informants reported that Stoner was overcome with glee and hate, telling the little mob that King was a fraud, a violent man, and a vile creature who, like all "niggers," loathed the Anglo-Saxon race. "He has been a good nigger now since six or seven o'clock!" Stoner declared. "The Black Power niggers will now say that nonviolence has failed and that violence is the only answer!"

On June 14, six days after Ray's capture, Stoner's NSRP mailed a letter to Wandsworth Prison offering to defend Ray pro bono, just as it had done for all the Klansmen dragged before Congress. The states-righters, Ray soon learned, were taking donations for his defense through the Patriotic Legal Fund, a clone of the account Klonsel Matt Murphy commissioned to defend Liuzzo's killers. Ray received Stoner's offer the same day that Hanes boarded that July 4 red-eye with Huie's proposition in hand. He must have been tempted to dismiss Hanes on sight and take his chances with the NSRP. After all, he had apparently never met Hanes, and he had not signed any-thing except the letter requesting representation. As far as Ray was concerned, Hanes was traveling to London on his own dime. Even if he insisted on being compensated, Stoner would surely cover the reimbursement.

Instead, Ray declined Stoner's offer on July 4. He'd read enough to know that Hanes, not Stoner, possessed the courtroom discipline to lead a jury to acquittal. Going with the NSRP would expose his

racial motive in a much more obvious way. In a handwritten letter on ruled Wandsworth stationery, Ray told Stoner that he would
await Hanes's counsel before taking on more attorneys. To cushion
the blow, he hinted at their shared political sympathies and asked
that Stoner help him down the road in civil court by filing claims for
libel. "As for my personal views on the case," Ray wrote, "I am more
concerned with the personal charges made against me by the leftist
press than the murder charge."

The legal attaché in London secretly acquired this missive and
passed it to the FBI. Nothing more emerged for a month, until a story
appeared on the wire in late July suggesting that Hanes and Stoner
might be cooperating in Ray's defense. The source of the allegation
was Stoner's longtime partner in hate, Dr. Edward R. Fields, who was
speaking from the NSRP's new command center in Savannah, Georgia. "Art Hanes is a personal friend of mine and would be a good attorney to defend Ray," Fields told the AP, leading Hanes to vigorously
deny any alliance with the NSRP and dial Savannah immediately to
respond in an unfriendly manner. An NSRP informant reported that
Hanes "acted mad and pointed out that he did not even recall meeting them and he was not their friend." The states-righters were crestfallen. Hanes masked his racism with French cuffs and tailored suits,
cocktails and conversation, while Stoner and Fields lived it openly,
in Klan robes and bow ties, waving Confederate flags and burning
crosses. But they were all committed segregationists with clear ties
to the Klan, and they all defended Klansmen to advance political
objectives. Stoner claimed to have met Hanes on only one occasion,
the informant later reported, but he assumed their mutual friendship with Murphy and their shared affinity for Wallace counted for
something. When later asked why he loathed Stoner so much, Hanes
bit his tongue: "I don't mind saying that I would not allow that man
Stoner to be associated with any case that I was involved in."

Ray stayed in touch with Stoner through mail, and on September 18 he requested that Stoner come to Memphis. Without a dime
to his name, Ray offered to pay full price for a consultation. Stoner
was eager, forwarding his reply by airmail with "Special Delivery"

written across the bottom of the envelope. "Please forgive me for failing to answer your letter sooner, but I was in Kentucky where I am
representing eight innocent men who are falsely charged with murder," Stoner replied. "I will leave Savannah next Wednesday and will
head straight to Memphis to see you as soon as I stop off in Atlanta
for one day. . . . It is nice of you to offer to pay me, but that will not
be necessary."

Hanes knew as early as August 14 that Ray and Stoner had plans
to file libel actions against the press. But by late September, as Hanes
began to prepare his client for trial, Ray started acting out by demanding to testify and threatening to hire Stoner if Hanes wouldn't agree.
Sheriff Morris intercepted Ray's mail and forwarded it to the FBI
with the observation that Ray "was losing interest in Arthur Hanes,
his present attorney, and might conceivably let Stoner defend him
in the forthcoming trial." It confirmed what the sheriff was hearing
from Ray's guards, fellow Wallace supporters who played gin rummy
with the assassin several times a week. Ray's own words even seemed
to confirm the rumor. "I don't think Hanes can do everything that
needs to be done," he wrote to his brother Jerry, who was also in
contact with Stoner.

To make matters worse, Judge Battle suddenly called on Hanes
"to show cause" why he should not be held in contempt of court after
telling an Associated Press reporter in Birmingham that Ray might
not be physically competent to stand trial in November because of
"cruel and inhuman treatment," the constant light in his cell and
the constant electronic surveillance, not to mention the two guards
"breathing down his neck twenty-four hours a day." That veiled threat
to delay the trial clearly violated Battle's gag order. Served with a
summons, Hanes immediately appeared before a two-day inquest led
by Judge Battle and the lawyer's committee. Upon taking the stand,
Hanes denied making prejudicial statements to the media but inexplicably admitted that "serious differences have arisen between me
and my client on the best way to handle this defense." Shocked by the
news, Battle called those differences "a very grave matter" while still
holding Hanes in contempt of court, the penalty for which included

jail time. In a show of restraint, Battle "withheld" sentencing to prevent an appeal. As one editorial put it, Battle left the "Sword of Damocles" hanging over Hanes's head until after Ray's trial.

》》》 》》》 》》》 《《《 《《《 《《《

Ray's guards documented Stoner's arrival in Memphis on September 28. "At 2:30 PM Mr. J. B. Stoner, attorney, entered A Block and conferred with Ray until 4:00 PM. Mr. Stoner brought a note out of A Block with him which Ray had given him. This note was addressed to Mr. Stoner and requested that he file a libel suit against *Life* magazine in behalf of James Earl Ray." The press did not learn of Stoner's visit until October 3 when the *New York Times* reported this headline on page twenty-three: A KLAN ORGANIZER MADE VISIT TO RAY. As the story's placement suggests, media coverage failed to emphasize Stoner's partnership with Klonsel Murphy, Hanes's friend and predecessor, from 1963 to 1964, much less the NSRP's support for Hanes's mayoral campaign in 1961–1962. Perhaps more disturbing, Ray's guards soon discovered a cryptic note in the trash alluding to a conspiracy, as well as a payoff. "I got a murder charge instead of 10,000 for listening to promises," Ray wrote. "No more fool pants."

26

A Blond Latin
Look, October 1968

William Bradford Huie viewed Stoner's entrance into the case as a threat to the publishing deal. Until he sold the movie rights and delivered a book manuscript, the money would continue to come out of his pocket. He'd already paid Hanes nearly $25,000. By not including Ray in the initial proceeds—all of Ray's 30 percent stake was assigned to Hanes for legal expenses—Huie and Hanes opened the door for Ray to sabotage the entire agreement by firing Hanes for Stoner, whom everyone understood would never be able to come to terms with Huie.

To try to save the deal, Huie paid a visit to Battle's chambers to denounce Stoner's meddling. It must have been an awkward conference in light of Huie's flagrant disrespect for Battle's publicity order. "I urged the judge not to allow Stoner to visit Ray contending that Stoner was not an attorney for Ray and therefore had no right to visit Ray," Huie later wrote. "Of course, when I urge, I soon become bitter, and then goddam bitter. But despite my bitter urging, Judge Battle gave Stoner unlimited visiting privileges with Ray. And Stoner did nothing from the beginning except to agitate Ray against Hanes, against me."

But Ray did finally back down. Rather than switch trial attorneys, he put the NSRP on a futile libel crusade and acknowledged that Stoner's presence would poison the effort to sell the jury a conspiracy. "I guess Mr. Hanes is right in not wanting Stoner associated with the defense," Ray wrote to Huie, who was not allowed to visit Ray's cell. "I agree that we should leave politics out of it at this time. But Stoner wants to file the libel suits right now, while Hanes wants to put the libel suits off until after the trial. So while I'm not going to push Stoner in on Mr. Hanes in the main case, I'm going to retain Stoner to file the libel suits. Also Stoner says he can raise hundreds of thousands of dollars for me if I need it."

》》 》》 》》 《《 《《 《《

Huie never had a better scoop. By mid-October, he had trekked across much of North America confirming evidence of an explosive conspiracy. Armed with Ray's hand-drawn diagrams and following the money, he logged thousands of sky miles and lodged in the finest of hotels: the Rivermont in Memphis, the Drake in Chicago, the Berkeley in Montreal, and the Bel-Air in Los Angeles. It was a sharp contrast to the seedy boarding houses, bordellos, and municipal underbellies where Ray spent his lost year on the run. Huie soon learned that nearly everything Ray described in his writing checked out, yet many unanswered questions and outright omissions about the conspiracy remained, riddles that would take time to solve. These complexities, Huie seemed to believe, would make it harder to compete with other "Trials of the Century" because Memphis was not the only game in town. Both New Orleans and Los Angeles were gearing up for prosecutions in both Kennedy assassinations. Sirhan Sirhan, the killer of Bobby Kennedy, had even forged a publishing deal of his own.

Huie decided to shoot first and verify later. On October 16, as the first two *Look* articles headed to the printer, comedian Johnny Carson peppered Huie for the scoop on the *Tonight Show*. Did Ray's motivations mirror those of Lee Harvey Oswald or Sirhan Sirhan? Carson asked. Why did he do it? Huie couldn't help himself. He assured several million Americans that Ray was not an ideologue or a racist. He explained that King's murder differed from the Kennedy assassinations in one distinct way: Ray was a part of "a conspiracy that had been in progress for quite some time. There was a lot of money paid for that killing."

The *Look* series ran over a three-week period beginning October 29. The first installment was called "The Story of James Earl Ray and the Plot to Assassinate Martin Luther King." Its black-and-white cover hit Memphis newsstands two weeks before the scheduled trial and just a week before the election. The writer was introduced in a foreword that Dr. King wrote for *Three Lives for Mississippi*: "Mr. Huie recognizes that the unholy alliance of violence and 'Southern justice' indicts not only murderers but the larger society that shelters them." The article laid the groundwork of conspiracy, but only after an exclusive look at Ray's escape from prison, his first job in Chicago, and his one-night stand at a polished resort just outside of Ottawa. Huie located Ray's love interest and convinced her to pose for pictures. In an anonymous silhouette, she wore a seductive nightgown and held a burning cigarette.

" 'Tell me about the sex,' I said. 'Did you go to Ray's room at Gray Rocks?'

" 'I did,' she answered. 'And I stayed till morning.'

" 'Well. What about him? I had concluded that he is some sort of neuter. His prison record indicates he isn't homosexual. Yet when he got out on April 23, 1967, and reached Chicago, he avoided women. So what about him.'

" 'Nothing unusual,' she said. 'My experience has been limited. But with me, I thought he acted perfectly normal.' "

Having gotten the reader's attention, Huie sketched out the plot. In late July 1967, he wrote, Ray wandered into the Neptune Tavern in Montreal and fortuitously met a "blond Latin about 35" named "Raoul," who called himself a "sea man" with ties to New Orleans. The description conjured up a fair-skinned Cuban immigrant. This mysterious Latin, Huie wrote, met with Ray more than five times in Canada. Together they forged a criminal scheme that would allow Ray to get what he needed: money and a fake passport.

Look editors handed off tear sheets of this article to the FBI, and skeptical agents across the country scrambled to confirm the sensational story before publication. Headquarters put it this way: "The entire article is leading the reader to believe that a conspiracy took place as early as August 1967, and continued up to the day King was assassinated; however, no specific detail is provided to bear this out." A search of the greater New Orleans area revealed no evidence of Raoul, so Hoover asked the Royal Canadian Mounted Police to conduct its own investigation, to find this Canadian seaman with a New Orleans connection. Skepticism soon turned to fear when Hoover learned that "newspaper reporters from the US" were seen at the Neptune Tavern showing bartenders pictures of Ray and a man they believed to be Raoul. Hoover wanted to confirm that it was Huie, not a more credible journalist, so he contacted the legal attaché in Ottawa and requested that the Canadian police show pictures of Huie to the bar owner.

Getting a search warrant for Huie's files would also help, as would bringing the journalist before a grand jury. But after weeks of debate, the Justice Department sent legal guidance that left Hoover hamstrung: "This responds to an inquiry from your Bureau. We have no present plans to obtain a search warrant or issue a subpoena in order to obtain the notes and letters in the possession of William Bradford Huie, allegedly received by him from James Earl Ray through Attorney Arthur Hanes." Miraculously, Huie also escaped a contempt of court citation despite the fact that Judge Battle's lawyer's committee ruled on November 4 that he'd "probably violated the judge's order restricting pretrial publicity."

>>> >>> >>> <<< <<< <<<

The second *Look* article was called "I Got Involved Gradually, and I Didn't Know Anyone Was Going to Be Murdered." It began with a stipulation of facts more certain than a grand jury indictment, complete with numbers.

1. That the plot to murder Martin Luther King Jr., existed as early as August 15, 1967, eight months prior to the murder on April 4, 1968

2. That Ray was drawn unknowingly into this plot in Montreal on August 18, 1967, and thereafter moved as directed by the plotters

3. That as late as March 23, 1968, less than two weeks before the murder with which he is charged, Ray did not know that the plot included murder or that it was aimed in any way at Dr. King

Huie picked up with Ray's move to Birmingham in August 1967. Raoul and Ray arrived by train and spent the night at the Grenada Hotel, next to the Birmingham depot. For unknown reasons, Raoul left the next morning, instructing Ray to move into a boarding house on Highland Avenue and then open a safe deposit box at Birmingham Trust National Bank. Surprisingly, Huie failed to mention that Birmingham Trust was the same bank that oversaw Klonsel Murphy's "White Man's Defense Fund" and other national Klan accounts. Huie claimed that the selling of narcotics, not Klan financial support, explained Ray's splurging on a white 1966 Mustang with low mileage. Huie confirmed that Ray paid $2,000 cash to a respectable citizen, and under the alias Eric S. Galt, he acquired an Alabama driver's license and "Heart of Dixie" license plates.

Ray stayed in Birmingham for forty-two days. A quiet life of dancing lessons, doctor's visits, photography practice, and barhopping ensued. But that fall, on October 6, Raoul suddenly ordered Ray to the United States–Mexico border to traffic more "contraband." The job was quick and lucrative, earning Ray $2,000 for a single day's work. When it was complete, he acquired a tourist visa and spent the next few weeks tanning in the dueling paradises of Acapulco—where he'd been once before in 1959 just months before his arrest in St. Louis—and Puerto Vallarta—a haven for expats made famous by newlyweds Elizabeth Taylor and Richard Burton. Huie had not yet traveled to Mexico or New Orleans to confirm Ray's story, so he just quoted Ray's handwriting. "I spent most of my time on the beach," Ray explained. "I was in one brothel in town about four times, plus twice during the day on business."

The debauchery came to an end that November when Ray drove north as Governor Wallace began his critical push to get on the California presidential ballot. Ray crossed the border in Tijuana, then drove north to Orange County. In the months that he would spend in L.A., Ray would undergo plastic surgery, try hypnosis, drink at bars, and wait for more instructions. When Dr. King arrived in Los Angeles that March, Ray followed him back to Atlanta, then on to Memphis for the final job.

Huie closed the six-thousand-word piece by illuminating what he called "features of the plot." He believed that unnamed conspirators who wanted King murdered by a white man for dramatic effect during the 1968 presidential election ordered Ray to Memphis. They wanted to stoke racial tensions, and they hoped Ray could pull it off in Montgomery, Birmingham, or Selma, because those places marked milestones—the Montgomery Bus Boycott, the Project C demonstrations, the Selma–Montgomery march—in King's career. Unfortunately, Ray had to settle for Memphis, where he found the perfect vantage for a nearly perfect crime. "Dr. King was the secondary, not the primary target. The primary target was the United States of America," Huie wrote. He was so certain that he picked a title and booked a flight to New York to finalize the publishing contracts for *They Slew the Dreamer.*

27

Election Night
Tuesday, November 5, 1968

Not surprisingly, the grand finale of a historic presidential election—marred by political assassinations and violent protests—overshadowed Huie's *Look* articles. The country was barreling toward a constitutional crisis because it remained quite plausible that Wallace might toss the election into the House of Representatives by denying Nixon or Humphrey two hundred seventy electoral votes. Should he pull it off, Wallace could legally auction away his electoral votes to the highest bidder rather than leave it up to Congress. By ordering his electors to vote for the candidate who made the most concessions to the South, Wallace could say he picked the president.

Wallace's campaign office in Montgomery could hardly handle all the money pouring in through the mail. It amounted to upwards of $150,000 per day, mostly in five-dollar increments. On October 24, an overflow crowd of more than sixteen thousand gave Wallace a standing ovation at Madison Square Garden as protesters battled with police along West Thirty-Fourth Street. Polls in late October showed that seventy-five million people would vote in the election, and in the final weeks of the campaign, Wallace seemed poised to pick up nearly 50 of 538 electoral votes, plus 20 percent of the popular vote. Now that Humphrey had begun to make a late surge, it became increasingly likely that Nixon, the favorite, would need to win California to avoid the Wallace scenario.

Rumors circulated that Nixon's aides had already courted Wallace electors with the hope of avoiding this situation. They wanted Wallace's electors to become "faithless," to betray the voters they represented, by giving away electoral votes to Nixon in states that Wallace might win. As a litmus test, the *Washington Post* interviewed dozens of the 177 Wallace electors across the country and found them in no mood to play Judas. "They are, on the whole, obscure. Their one common bond is loyalty to George Wallace and that for which he stands," the article read. "Most have ratified their fealty to the Alabama candidate in an unusual signed and notarized oath that commits them to Wallace—'or whomsoever he may direct'—in the Electoral College balloting."

Faithless electors were nothing new in Wallace Country. When President Kennedy won the election of 1960, Democratic electors from Alabama and Mississippi—incensed over Kennedy's stance on civil rights—tried to sabotage democracy by voting for Senator Robert Byrd of West Virginia—a former Klansman who wasn't even on the ballot. Had enough electors followed suit, the election of 1960 would have been thrown into the House, and Nixon might have won. It almost happened again in 1964, when Wallace ran in the Democratic presidential primary and handpicked segregationists like Hanes to serve as loyal electors. After strong showings in three primaries, Wallace dropped out of the race, but his campaign asked the electors to cross over and vote for the Republican nominee, Barry Goldwater, should President Johnson win in their state. Wallace appointed these electors, but they had also taken the Democratic Party's oath not to vote Republican.

Despite giving his word to the party, Hanes told reporters that he would obey Wallace's orders and vote for Goldwater "if the governor decided this was the best course for the South and Alabama." But it never got to that point. Goldwater, not Johnson, took Alabama with segregationist support. It was the first time since Reconstruction that a Republican won a state in the cradle of the Confederacy, and no one was more responsible for that shift than Wallace.

WANTED BY THE FBI

CIVIL RIGHTS – CONSPIRACY
INTERSTATE FLIGHT – ROBBERY
JAMES EARL RAY

FBI No. 405,942 G

Photographs taken 1960

Photograph taken 1968
(eyes drawn by artist)

Aliases: Eric Starvo Galt, W. C. Herron, Harvey Lowmyer, James McBride, James O'Conner, James Walton, James Walyon, John Willard, "Jim,"

DESCRIPTION

Age:	40, born March 10, 1928, at Quincy or Alton, Illinois (not supported by birth records)		
Height:	5' 10"	**Eyes:**	Blue
Weight:	163 to 174 pounds	**Complexion:**	Medium
Build:	Medium	**Race:**	White
Hair:	Brown, possibly cut short	**Nationality:**	American

Occupations: Baker, color matcher, laborer

Scars and Marks: Small scar on center of forehead and small scar on palm of right hand

Remarks: Noticeably protruding left ear; reportedly is a lone wolf; allegedly attended dance instruction school; has reportedly completed course in bartending.

Fingerprint Classification: 16 M 9 U OOO 12

M 4 W IOI

CRIMINAL RECORD

Ray has been convicted of burglary, robbery, forging U. S. Postal Money Orders, armed robbery, and operating motor vehicle without owner's consent.

CAUTION

RAY IS SOUGHT IN CONNECTION WITH A MURDER WHEREIN THE VICTIM WAS SHOT. CONSIDER ARMED AND EXTREMELY DANGEROUS.

A Federal warrant was issued on April 17, 1968, at Birmingham, Alabama, charging Ray as Eric Starvo Galt with conspiring to interfere with a Constitutional Right of a citizen (Title 18, U. S. Code, Section 241). A Federal warrant was also issued on July 20, 1967, at Jefferson City, Missouri, charging Ray with Interstate Flight to Avoid Confinement for the crime of Robbery (Title 18, U. S. Code, Section 1073).

IF YOU HAVE ANY INFORMATION CONCERNING THIS PERSON, PLEASE NOTIFY ME OR CONTACT YOUR LOCAL FBI OFFICE. TELEPHONE NUMBERS AND ADDRESSES OF ALL FBI OFFICES LISTED ON BACK.

EXHIBIT II
TO THE AFFIDAVIT OF
CHARLES QUITMAN STEPHENS

DIRECTOR
FEDERAL BUREAU OF INVESTIGATION
UNITED STATES DEPARTMENT OF JUSTICE
WASHINGTON, D. C. 20535
TELEPHONE, NATIONAL 8-7117

Wanted Flyer 442-A
April 19, 1968

▶▶▶ FBI Most Wanted poster for James Earl Ray.
Federal Bureau of Investigation, Department of Justice, April 1968

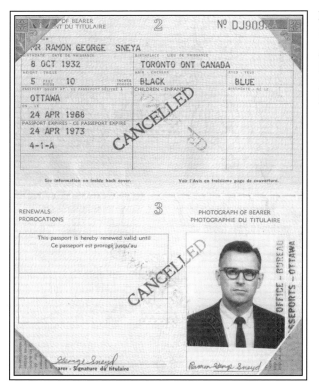

▶▶▶ Busted: the fake Canadian passport that got Ray arrested at Heathrow Airport, London, June 1968.

Shelby County Register of Deeds

▶▶▶ Pretrial publicity: lawyer Art Hanes interviewed by television media outside the Memphis courthouse, 1968.

Jim Hansen, photographer, LOOK Magazine Photograph Collection, Library of Congress, Prints & Photographs Division

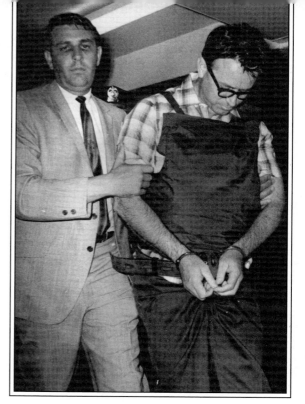

>>> Operation Landing: Ray and Shelby County Sheriff William Morris, July 1968.
Shelby County Register of Deeds, Memphis, Tennessee

>>> Judge Preston Battle's bench: courtroom where Ray pled guilty on March 10, 1969.
Shelby County Register of Deeds, Memphis, Tennessee

>>> Mayor Hanes (standing) announcing the closing of Birmingham's parks, December 11, 1961.
Birmingham Post-Herald *Civil Rights Photographs, Birmingham Public Library*

>>> King assassination attempt: bomb wreckage near Dr. King's Gaston Motel headquarters during the Birmingham campaign of the civil rights movement, May 14, 1963.
Library of Congress, Prints & Photographs Division, U.S. News & World Report *Magazine Collection, Marion S. Trikosko, photographer*

▶▶▶ Standing in the schoolhouse door: Governor George C. Wallace attempting to block integration at the University of Alabama, June 11, 1963.
Library of Congress, Prints & Photographs Division, U.S. News & World Report Magazine Collection, Warren K. Leffler, photographer

▶▶▶ No more Birminghams: September 22, 1963, March in Washington for the four little girls killed in the Sixteenth Street Baptist Church bombing.
Library of Congress, Prints & Photographs Division, U.S. News & World Report Magazine Collection, Thomas J. O'Halloran, photographer

>>> John H. Sutherland, founder of the St. Louis White Citizens' Council and elector for the Missouri American Independent Party; in 1978, Congress concluded that Sutherland had offered a $10,000 bounty for King's life at the time of Ray's April 1967 prison escape.
House Select Committee on Assassinations

>>> United Klans of America rally: Klonsel Matthew H. Murphy, Eugene Thomas, Collie Lee Wilkins, William Eaton, and UKA Imperial Wizard Robert M. Shelton on April 17, 1965, weeks after the murder of Viola Liuzzo.
Jerry Colburn, photographer, the Tuscaloosa News

⟩⟩⟩ National States Rights Party fuhrer J. B. Stoner, who became Ray's libel attorney in 1968. Stoner, a self-proclaimed bomb-maker, died a convicted white terrorist.
Memphis Press-Scimitar Morgue, Special Collections, University of Memphis Libraries

⟩⟩⟩ Candidate Wallace, having successfully made it onto the California ballot, officially announcing his third-party candidacy on national television, February 8, 1968.
Library of Congress, Prints & Photographs Division, U.S. News & World Report *Magazine Collection, Marion S. Trikosko, photographer*

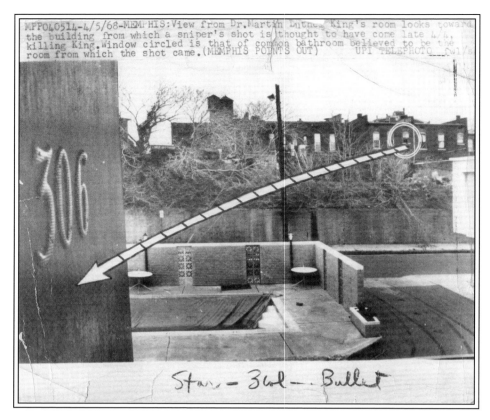

MFPO40514-4/5/68-MEMPHIS:View from Dr.Martin Luther King's room looks toward the building from which a sniper's shot is)thought to have come late 4/4, killing King.Window circled is that of common bathroom believed to be the room from which the shot came.(MEMPHIS POINTS OUT)   UPI TELEPHOTO

Stan - 3col - Bullet

▶▶▶ Trajectory of the bullet; note the bushes below.
Memphis Press-Scimitar Morgue, Special Collections, University of Memphis Libraries

▶▶▶ Riot, riot, riot: soldier in Washington, DC, street near buildings destroyed by the Martin Luther King Jr. assassination riots, April 1968.
Library of Congress, Prints & Photographs Division, U.S. News & World Report *Magazine Collection, Warren K. Leffler, photographer*

>>> Three tramps being taken into custody by Dallas police after the assassination of John F. Kennedy, November 22, 1963; later identified as Harold Doyle, Gus Abrams, and John Gedney.
Courtesy Fort Worth Star-Telegram *Collection, Special Collections, the University of Texas at Arlington Library, Arlington, Texas*

>>> Aeromarine Supply, near the Birmingham Airport, 1968.
Shelby County Register of Deeds, Memphis, Tennessee

▶▶▶ Floyd G. Kitchen, Missouri American Independent Party elector from St. Louis, was paid by John H. Sutherland and served on Wallace's national staff during the 1968 presidential campaign.

St. Louis Mercantile Library at the University of Missouri-St. Louis

▶▶▶ Brigadier General Reid Doster (middle) with Governor John Patterson and Lt. Col. Joe Shannon, Alabama Air National Guard participant in the 1961 Bay of Pigs invasion. Doster was fingered by Huie as a possible accomplice in the King assassination.

Joe Shannon Collection, Southern Museum of Flight Foundation

▶▶▶ Racist propaganda, previously titled "I Saw Selma Raped," and "Sex and Civil Rights" ghostwritten by Albert C. Persons, a Bay of Pigs participant. The second editions were sanitized with less outrageous titles, 1965.
House Un-American Activities Committee

▶▶▶ The prosecution: Executive Assistant Attorney General Robert Dwyer, District Attorney General Phil Canale, Assistant Attorney General James Beasley, 1968.
Special Collections, University of Memphis Libraries

▶▶▶ Ray's trial lawyers: Percy Foreman, Arthur J. Hanes, and Arthur Hanes Jr., with journalist William Bradford Huie.
Memphis Press-Scimitar Morgue, Special Collections, University of Memphis Libraries

▶▶▶ Memphis criminal lawyer Russell X. Thompson, approached by a mysterious blond Latin man in April 1968. Thompson told the FBI that Hanes might have passed the story along to Ray as inspiration for Raoul.
Memphis Press-Scimitar Morgue, Special Collections, University of Memphis Libraries

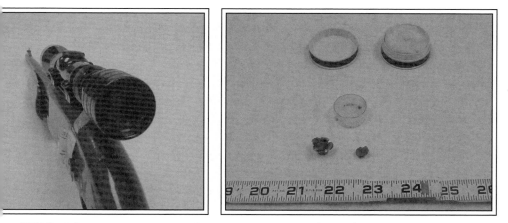

▶▶▶ An unnerved Dr. King, locked arm-in-arm with others, marches during the sanitation strike, March 1968.
Memphis Press-Scimitar Morgue, Special Collections, University of Memphis Libraries

▶▶▶ (left) Smoking gun: Ray's rifle and scope. (right) No ballistics: the death slug. *Shelby County Register of Deeds, Memphis, Tennessee*

▶▶▶ Blond Latin: May 6, 1968, frontpage of the *San Francisco Chronicle*; "Picture Parallel" article (center) by former FBI agent and Garrison coconspirator William Turner.
San Francisco Chronicle

▶▶▶ Gary Thomas Rowe (in sunglasses) on October 21, 1965, in Hayneville, Alabama, where he testified in the second Liuzzo murder trial and faced a grueling cross-examination by Klonsel Hanes.
Bettmann/Corbis

〉〉〉 〉〉〉 〉〉〉 〈〈〈 〈〈〈 〈〈〈

As millions of Americans began voting in the presidential election of 1968, Ray slept past noon. He awoke to an early supper of peas, corn, stew, and bread. When finished, he walked over to the sink and shaved. It must have occurred to him, as he lathered up, that in some strange way his own life might be riding on the outcome of tonight's vote. Despite overwhelming evidence to the contrary, Ray's brothers had convinced themselves that Wallace would win the election outright. They clung to the quixotic hope that Wallace would pardon Ray, much like he paroled Asa Carter's followers in Judge Aaron's castration. Several weeks earlier, Ray, too, seemed optimistic about Wallace's odds. In a sloppy, handwritten letter, he teased Huie that Wallace, when elected, would put him in jail for all the liberal diatribes he'd published in the last five years.

> I wouldn't worry to [sic] much about a contempt charge. Judge Battle has said himself that the order doesn't extend out side [sic] of his jurisdiction which is confined to Shelby County. However if you did get convicted of contempt I think the maximum penalty is only six months which would go by pretty fast, also if your ex. Governor [George C. Wallace] gets elected you would be uses [sic] to it.

It proved to be a horse race of an election between Humphrey and Nixon. Humphrey took most of the North and the West but nothing in the South. Wallace pulled in a respectable nine million votes across the country, winning Georgia, Alabama, Mississippi, Louisiana, and Arkansas. Like many Southerners in the Deep South, Ray wanted Wallace to get thirty more electoral votes to sabotage the election. "After supper Ray lay on his bunk and read the paper until 4:15 PM, at which time he asked for and received three aspirins and started watching TV," Ray's guards noted on election night. "From 4:15 PM until 4:00 AM Ray watched the election returns on TV or listened to them on the radio; talked freely with officers, making several comments as who he wanted to win, etc. At 4:00 AM Ray went to bed and was asleep at 4:30 AM. At 6:00 AM Ray was awake and at 6:15 AM, a breakfast of eggs, grits, toast, and coffee was served and Ray ate almost all of his breakfast. He watched TV until shift change."

When Ray woke that next morning, it must have felt like a hangover. The Virginia Plan was dead. Nixon won the election outright, taking more than three hundred electoral votes and beating Humphrey by a meager five hundred thousand popular votes. Wallace lost more Southern states than he won. He lost Florida, Texas, Kentucky, North Carolina, Virginia, and most importantly, Tennessee. If Ray was looking for an indication as to how "liberal" a potential jury might be, the news wasn't good. The tally in Shelby County looked even worse. Earlier in the week, the *Commercial Appeal* predicted that Memphis would be divided along racial lines, and it proved prescient, because Wallace, the far-right candidate, lost to Humphrey, the black-vote candidate, by more than five thousand ballots. Now that Wallace was powerless to help him, the prisoner was forced to mull the greatest decision of his life: was a trial in Memphis, a jury of his peers, and a defense built on the back of an international conspiracy really a gamble worth taking?

28

Pink Slip
Memphis, Tuesday,
November 12, 1968

Hanes and son landed in Memphis thirty-six hours before the trial. It was a Sunday night, and they arrived in the rain with their exhibits held close. Everything was in order, down to the gray tailored suit that Ray would wear. Come Tuesday morning, after the Monday holiday, they planned to put Ray's life in the hands of twelve jurors, two of whom would surely be black because of the state's voir dire strategy.

A front-page story in the Nashville *Tennessean* explained Hanes's motivation for taking the case. His wife, Eleanor, said, "Arthur is fighting for the old American principles," which are "doomed to go the way of the Dodo bird." Both denied speculation that he was a closet Klansman. "I have never been within fifty miles of a Klan meeting to my knowledge," Hanes claimed. "Why the Klan couldn't get together $25 tonight and couldn't get a hundred people together in Alabama without fifty-two of them being FBI agents. As far as planning is concerned, they couldn't plot the theft of a gallon of water from the creek. If the Klan had been involved it would have been solved in thirty minutes and Lyndon Johnson would have been on television telling you about it."

The FBI was not so sure. Back on August 19, a Memphis FBI agent received intelligence that Imperial Wizard Shelton came to

Memphis looking for Klansmen "amenable to donating money for Ray" because Hanes "allegedly told Shelton Ray had no money." In the same conversation, Shelton said that Hanes wanted him to return to Memphis "in the near future, time not specified, to look at a jury list that would be given to him by Hanes." Whether that happened is unknown, but based on previous Klan trials, it seems quite probable.

During the trial, Hanes would not argue Ray's innocence but instead wager that the white citizens of Memphis, angered by black riots, would acquit King's assassin out of reasonable doubt and racism. To counter a murder weapon with fingerprints, Hanes would try to put segregationists on the jury and attack the eyewitness, Charles Quitman Stephens, a forty-six-year-old alcoholic veteran of World War II. Stephens was a resident of the rooming house, and on the afternoon of the slaying, he claimed to have caught a fleeting glimpse of Ray as he hustled down a staircase holding the bundle. His testimony was suspect, Hanes would show, because a taxi driver claimed to have transported a drunken Stephens back home just hours before the assassination. Perhaps more damaging was the fact that Stephens had once been involved in a shooting and knew his way around the county jail.

After discrediting Stephens, Hanes would depose an eyewitness of his own. His name was Harold "Cornbread" Carter, a wino suffering from a recent stroke. Carter told Hanes's private investigator, Renfro Hays, that the real shooter fired from the bushes below the rooming house, not from above in the rooming house bathroom. Carter claimed that he was in the shrubbery drinking wine when this "bushman" suddenly appeared. A fresh footprint, as well as the initial reaction of King's chauffeur, Solomon Jones, supported Carter's testimony. As King lay dying on the balcony, Jones pointed police to the bushes, not the rooming house. His testimony was similar to that of Earl Caldwell, a reporter for the *New York Times* who was staying on the bottom floor of the Lorraine on April 4 and thought a bomb exploded. Caldwell saw policemen running from the bushes and initially thought they might have fired on King. How can both Caldwell and Carter be so mistaken? Hanes would ask the jury. Culpability would be determined by a parable of two drunks, Charles Stephens and Cornbread Carter.

Hanes also planned to introduce a bogus police broadcast to conjure up the Raoul conspiracy. On the night of the assassination, an amateur radio broadcaster—with a sick sense of humor—hacked his way onto police channels. In a fantastic bit of theater, he claimed that two white Mustangs, not one, were seen fleeing Memphis city limits. When FBI agents located the source of the fake transmission, they found a young boy with a professional-grade radio transmitter in his room. The kid denied doing it, but authorities left convinced he was too scared to tell the truth. To Hanes, however, the fake report pointed to conspiracy. He listened to the broadcast multiple times and took extensive notes. He thought the jury should consider the odds that such a thing could be a coincidence. Why, after all, was there no eyewitness besides Stephens? How did Ray get out of town so easily? The parable of two Mustangs leant itself to reasonable doubt.

Last, and most significant, Hanes wanted to attack the theory of the murder weapon. During discovery, he learned that the FBI's ballistics report proved inconclusive. The bullet that struck King was extracted from his corpse intact, but when the FBI tried to trace its markings, the slug broke into pieces. Even though the shell was still in the chamber of the rifle, the state could not absolutely prove the death slug was fired from the rifle in Ray's bundle. Having worked for the FBI, Hanes would question the ballistics as further proof of a conspiracy. "A six-year-old kid could have traced it," he later scoffed to reporters.

》》》 》》》 》》》 《《《 《《《 《《《

Those arguments were well rehearsed in Hanes's mind on November 9 as he taxied to his headquarters at the Holiday Inn Rivermont when the radio crackled with a report that Ray had asked Judge Battle for a new lawyer. Hanes and his son were shocked. They dropped off their wives at the hotel and stormed down to the jail in disbelief. Reporters were camped outside the building when Sheriff Morris handed Hanes a copy of Ray's note. "Due to some disagreements between me and you in regards our handlings of my case, I have decided to engage a Tennessee attorney and perhaps someone else," Ray wrote. "Therefore I would appreciate it if you would take no further action on my case in Memphis, Tenn. Also, I appreciate what you have already did for me."

Sheriff Morris told Hanes that Ray's brothers showed up that morning with Percy Foreman, the legendary defense attorney from Houston. Ray had penned the note, Hanes learned, in front of his guards, but only after Foreman demanded that he also sign an affidavit admitting that he changed attorneys on a voluntary basis. At sixty-six years young, Foreman epitomized flamboyance and showmanship. Saving killers from the electric chair was his specialty. In hundreds and hundreds of capital cases, Foreman had lost just one client to the death penalty.

Hanes was still processing the news when Foreman called the jail. "I expect you to cooperate, Mr. Hanes, and to let me have your files," Foreman demanded. Apoplectic and humiliated, Hanes let him have it. "Foreman, you'll get my files when I get the rest of my fee." He wanted $12,000 in addition to the $30,000 that he'd already been paid. To try to pressure Huie and Foreman to turn over the money, Hanes even threatened to sell his files to *Life* magazine. He also attacked Foreman personally, calling his motives "typical of a certain breed of Texans, such as LBJ and Ramsey Clark, who do things in an unusual way and pay scant attention to what is going on in the world."

Rumors were circulating that Huie might have influenced Ray to hire Foreman and delay the trial. The theory was that other journalists writing about the King assassination—like *New Yorker* writer Gerold Frank—might get access to the information that only Huie now possessed. It had already come out that Ray's brother Jerry flew to Huntsville, Alabama, just days before Hanes's firing. His ticket and hotel room were paid by Huie, who arrived at the airport without Hanes's knowledge carrying a bottle of liquor. But it turned out that Jerry Ray wanted Foreman to represent his brother as early as July 1969, just as Huie, Hanes, and Ray signed off on the publishing deal. Media reports and FBI documents show that Jerry's preference for Foreman was long-standing and unyielding. Even Ray's own writing proved that he hired Foreman without any input from Huie. The reason was understandable: Ray wanted to avoid the electric chair.

>>> >>> >>> <<< <<< <<<

Hanes's firing meant the trial would almost certainly be delayed. On the morning of Tuesday, November 12, reporters watched as Foreman cleared security and sat down at the defense table to address Hanes in confidence. Reporters could not make out the terse conversation, but one audible word did emerge: "fees." About that time, Ray appeared barricaded by police. They seated him behind the defense table as Judge Battle called for order. Immediately, Hanes rose to inform the court of the obvious: "Your honor, may it please the court, it is my understanding that the defendant in this case has written a letter to me requesting that I do nothing further in his behalf in this case and I have not seen the letter yet although I do have a copy."

The sheriff handed Hanes the original and Battle asked Ray to confirm it.

"Mr. Ray, I have here a copy of, what reports to be a copy of a letter dated November 10, 1968, from you directed to Mr. Hanes. I wish you to examine and see if you wrote that letter."

"Yes, Sir."

"Did you send that letter?"

"Yes, Sir."

"And, I believe in that letter you state that you wish to terminate the services of Mr. Hanes in this case?"

"Yes, Sir."

The state knew about Hanes's firing, but Tennessee attorney general Phil Canale and his team vowed to fight it. After all, they had subpoenaed three hundred and sixty witnesses across the world, including British attorney Michael Eugene and FBI forensics expert George Bonebrake. Scores of detailed exhibits were prepared, and eight policemen were taken off the beat to guard the eyewitness. More to the point, the citizens of Shelby County were footing the tremendous bill, which included thousands of dollars in electronic surveillance equipment and one-time security renovations. To delay now would double, if not triple, expenses.

In a long speech of protest, Assistant Attorney General Robert Dwyer denounced the entire defense table in a voice that resonated with anger. He told Battle that Ray was "trifling with the court" and should be ignored. "It is the state's position that the motion should be disallowed," Dwyer nearly yelled. "I don't know this gentleman [Foreman] from Texas. I have read something about him and heard some things along the way. . . . From what I've read, these gentlemen [Hanes and son] have been paid. . . . Let him [Ray] sit where he is and let's go to trial today!"

Foreman stood up to protest the "the diatribe spoken in my direction." He described his presence in Memphis as an inconvenient but profound professional duty. "Frankly, I'd be much better off physically and financially if the court adhered to the adjuration of the attorney general," Foreman said, "but if this man needs me and wants me, I feel an obligation to my oath as an attorney to make myself available."

Judge Battle clearly wanted to go to trial. All this commotion and bickering, the press coverage and the showmanship, was affecting his health and tarnishing Memphis's reputation. But to deny Ray a continuance now would poison the process of justice and provide grounds for an appeal. He understood that Ray possessed the right, under the Sixth Amendment, to receive a fair trial and to change counsel. After much debate, Battle accepted Ray's wishes and ordered a new trial set for March 3, 1969—one hundred and ten days away. He agreed to "conditionally" release Hanes and son from the case under certain stipulations.

> They shall remain counsel of record insofar as they both continue to be bound by the Court's orders on publicity.
>
> They shall co-operate with Mr. Foreman in making available to him everything disclosed by their investigation in this case and fully acquainting him of their actions in readying the case for trial.
>
> That Mr. Arthur J. Hanes, Sr., being now under a finding of Contempt of Court with sentence withheld by the Court shall

make an appearance bond of one thousand dollars before leaving this jurisdiction.

When the hearing ended, Hanes took out his checkbook and fled Memphis fuming, vowing not to return for sentencing. "They can keep the $1,000," he told a reporter. "But I guess I'll have to find a new ski resort. I don't suppose I can ever go to Gatlinburg again." Despite the insult of his firing, Hanes still insisted that Ray was just a patsy for Raoul and the black militants who arranged the assassination. America needed to hear the truth about this conspiracy, he believed. "A pall hangs over the country," Hanes claimed. "A cloud is hanging there over Memphis. It would be well if these were lifted. I had some bombshells to drop on them."

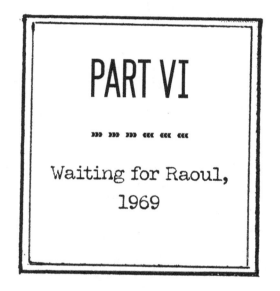

PART VI

>>> >>> >>> ««« ««« «««

Waiting for Raoul,
1969

29

Tramps
New Orleans, December 1968

Just as Foreman replaced Hanes in the publishing deal, Canada's national television network, CBC, revealed that Huie's ongoing conspiracy investigation might be headed in a very controversial direction. The interview gave listeners more texture to the sensational plot, and it opened up a Pandora's box of potential suspects. Huie downplayed Ray's significance in the conspiracy and put no emphasis on his documented affection for George Wallace. He now seemed to agree with Hanes that Ray was "not the kind of man who would kill deliberately in the hope of preventing racial change," but he believed that Raoul worked for an unknown group of white and black instigators working together. "I am convinced that the people behind the conspiracy wanted to use the death of Martin Luther King to cause more racial ruble [trouble] in the United States," Huie said. A few days later, on December 2 in Atlanta, he elaborated, calling the plot a "conspiracy between black and white persons who hoped to trigger widespread racial violence across the nation. They killed him not because they hated him—but to cause trouble."

Huie also compared Raoul to the mysterious Cuban being hunted by New Orleans DA Garrison, who was preparing to try businessman Clay Shaw on January 21 in New Orleans for conspiracy in the

Kennedy assassination. More than fifty telephone calls reached Huie from people who believed that Raoul was the same man seen with Lee Harvey Oswald on Camp Street before Kennedy's assassination. One caller was meeting him in New York with photographs. "It appears from what I now know that the assassination of Martin Luther King was largely Louisiana based," Huie said.

》》》 》》》 》》》 《《《 《《《 《《《

The pictures from New York were of three hoboes found in a coal car several hundred yards from the Texas School Book Depository on November 22, 1963—the date of Kennedy's assassination. A few blocks away, a Dallas police officer named Marvin Wise was responding to a burglary when a dispatcher ordered him "to report code three to the intersection of Elm and Houston." Wise suspected the shooting of a fellow officer, so he hurried, driving straight toward the horrific chaos and parking his car outside the main entrance to the book depository. A sergeant told him to grab his shotgun and "guard the building," where he set up a post near the loading dock. Wise was guarding the exits when another superior ordered him and four additional officers to walk over to the railway tower, west of the book depository.

The controller of the tower had seen three suspects running down the tracks. Several hundred yards away, they jumped into a convoy of parked coal cars. Wise and the four officers ran out of the tower, holding their shotguns as they sprinted, accompanied by a locomotive engine on an adjacent track. The driver of the engine pointed the suspects out and Wise climbed inside the coal car to find three filthy hoboes in hiding. They were placed under arrest and led back to the book depository at gunpoint.

Two Dallas journalists photographed the men as they were led across Dealey Plaza and over to the sheriff's office. The first man in the series of pictures, the one with a sharp nose, walks purposely and pensively, framed by a distinct concrete pattern in the depository's ground-level architecture. In another image, he comes off as more menacing, a man of action. His coat is furled open and it seems as if he is walking in haste, his severe eyes trained on the cop immediately ahead. Wise took down each man's information on a sheet of paper that he kept in his hat, then dropped them off at the sheriff's department. A year later, the Warren Commission interviewed Wise about the arrests, but nothing came of it. In 1966, he cleaned out his locker and threw away the piece of paper identifying the three hoboes.

On April 10, 1968, six days after King's assassination, an artist for Mexican Police Headquarters named Sergio Jaubert released a sketch of the suspect being hunted day and night by the FBI. It looked identical to the photograph of the sharp-nosed hobo being escorted through Dealey Plaza in November 1963. The AP claimed that Jaubert's sketch was "based on information supplied by the Federal Bureau of Investigation." Hundreds of newspapers around the country reprinted it, side-by-side with a similar sketch released by the *Commercial Appeal*. The latter was based on "a description given by a man living in the building where the shot was fired." It was from Charles Stephens, the rooming house eyewitness who described the suspect this way: "He was clean shaven and had a long, sharp nose. He had normal eyes and a square chin, thick hair at the front and receded on each side."

In New Orleans, Garrison and his investigator, a former FBI agent named William Turner, held a press conference in early May 1968 to make the case for conspiracy. "The sharp, pointed nose, the wide mouth and thin lips, the firm set of the jaw. I remembered something—the photograph of a suspect being taken into custody by two shotgun carrying Dallas policemen," Turner announced. Later in the month, as Ray made it to London on a forged Canadian passport, another group of conspiracy peddlers, the Kennedy Assassination Inquiry Committee, held a press conference at the Taft Hotel in New York "seeking the identity of two of three men photographed in police custody in Dallas." Adamant and vocal, the group demanded that the FBI investigate whether Oswald and Ray were connected to the three penniless hoboes rounded up in that infamous Dallas dragnet.

The FBI doubled-back, but no identification of the three men showed up in bureau files. Nor could Dallas police locate the official arrest records. Agents also noted, internally, that Jaubert had

received no information from the FBI, and it became Hoover's
opinion, though not publicly, that Jaubert relied exclusively on the
Dealey Plaza photographs in preparing the sketch. The story went
away until Huie revealed the alias of Ray's co-conspirator, Raoul,
in late October. Now conspiracy peddlers had a name. The next
step was to put Ray and the hobo in the same room. As the new
year approached, Huie was in a panic to do so. Judge Battle would
not allow him to see Ray, so he gave the photos to Foreman. As Ray
later recalled, "Mr. Foreman described one of them in the picture
as an 'anti-communist' Cuban refugee who was arrested at the time
President Kennedy was shot. 'The arrest took place in Dallas,' I was
told. I was asked if I would identify the man if he was brought to
Memphis. I said no, although he did look similar to the man I was
involved with."

Huie's editors at *Look* thought Ray was hedging. They wanted
something more definitive, but Huie could not confirm Raoul's existence. The leads in Canada and Birmingham were burned out, Huie
claimed, so the entire premise of conspiracy now centered on Ray's
mysterious trip from L.A. to New Orleans on December 15, 1967.
Huie's editors dispatched him to the Big Easy in hopes of finding
someone who could remember seeing Ray and Raoul in the same bar
or hotel room. It had only been a year.

>>> >>> >>> ««« ««« «««

As with the Dealey Plaza photos, Huie was not the first journalist to investigate Ray's trip to the French Quarter. Two weeks after
Jaubert's sketch ran in the AP, journalist Louis Lomax, writing for
the North American Newspaper Alliance on April 24, claimed the
conspiracy involved "a mysterious Hollywood blonde and a New
Orleans industrialist." His reporting, if you could call it that, relied
almost exclusively on the drug-fueled recollection of Charles Stein,
who accompanied Ray to New Orleans. Lomax recreated the trip
with Stein, who claimed that Ray pulled over at a gas station near
San Antonio, Texas, to contact "a cash man" with "an Italian sound-
ing name." Along the way, they located the Texas phone booth where

the call was made. Lomax declared victory: "The solution to the assassination of King, then, now lies in the hands of God and the telephone company," the article read. But the telephone company soon reported to the FBI, not Lomax or the general public, that it had found no evidence of such a call.

When Huie arrived in New Orleans, Garrison's upcoming trial of Clay Shaw had the city abuzz. The businessman would become the first "conspirator" ever tried in the JFK assassination, and reporters were crowding outside Garrison's Tulane Avenue office and carousing in the French Quarter's finest haunts. On December 18, Garrison told them that the assassinations of Jack Kennedy, Bobby Kennedy, and Martin Luther King Jr. were "all accomplished by the same force and that they were all intelligence assassinations." Jurors would soon hear Garrison talk about an "assassination party" in the ritzy Monteleone Hotel that Shaw supposedly attended with Oswald hours before the president's murder.

William Monteleone, owner of the famous hotel with a carousel bar, was chairman of the Crusade to Free Cuba Committee. Garrison believed the plot was connected all the way up to New Orleans mafioso Carlos Marcello, a Sicilian mobster and bitter enemy of President Kennedy. Garrison planned to show that David Ferrie, the pilot who trained Oswald in the Civilian Air Patrol, worked for Marcello and had played a mysterious role in the Bay of Pigs invasion. Had Ferrie not killed himself, Garrison would have proven Ferrie's part in the greatest conspiracy since the Dreyfus affair.

Huie was caught up in the intrigue. At 611 Canal Street, he spotted Le Bunny Lounge and eagerly stepped inside. Ray had told Huie that he drove clear across the country to meet Raoul at this seedy, little bar with little memory or tradition. Over drinks, Raoul had revealed the final job to Ray. "Three hours after I got to New Orleans I was ready to leave," Ray wrote to Huie. "Raoul just wanted a report on what I had been doing. He said we had one more job to do, and we'd do it in about two or three months. Then we'd be finished, and, for sure, he'd give me complete travel papers and $12,000 and help me go anywhere in the world I wanted to go."

Huie thought somebody might remember the encounter. He asked around the bar and flashed the Dealey Plaza photographs. But it soon became apparent that two men meeting for a drink was not a memorable event in the French Quarter. Next he tried the Hotel Provincial on Chartres Street. The clerk was helpful, providing records showing that Ray stayed from December 17 to 19, but there was nothing about Raoul. With no more leads to track down, Huie's reporting turned into tourism. He took a stroll down Exchange Alley, where Oswald once lived, past the Monteleone Hotel, where Clay Shaw's "assassination party" supposedly took place and where ransomed pilots involved in the Bay of Pigs were allegedly treated like kings. New Orleans seemed to Huie like a revolving door of conspiracy, a place where a man's very presence seemed grounds for opening an investigation. "If you are in New Orleans on a cold Saturday night," Huie later wrote, "walking through the French Quarter with the ghosts of assassins, you find it easy to believe in conspiracy."

》》》 》》》 》》》 《《《 《《《 《《《

No closer to the truth than when he arrived, Huie traveled on to Mexico, where he found more dead ends. During three days of reporting, he surveyed Ray's favorite hotels around Acapulco and Puerto Vallarta. He met a prostitute, a photographer, and a bartender, all of whom recalled different qualities of the tight-lipped American who tipped so poorly. All three spent time alone in Ray's presence, some more intimately than others, but none could remember anything about a person named Raoul. Huie left Mexico in possession of hotel receipts and petty rumors that Ray may have trafficked a small quantity of marijuana into California. But overall, he was no closer to identifying the tramp of Dealey Plaza.

30

The Bay of Hubris
Birmingham, January 1969

Back home in Hartselle for Christmas, Huie dialed up Hanes in Birmingham and asked him to rendezvous at Aeromarine Supply, the sporting goods store where Ray purchased the murder weapon. It's unclear exactly why Huie continued to associate with Hanes, but the most likely reason concerned Hanes's refusal to turn over his investigative files to Foreman until he received more money. Hanes also knew the owner of Aeromarine while working for more than a decade across the street at Hayes Aircraft. When Huie and Hanes arrived, owner Don Wood made it clear that he'd been ordered not to talk, lest he suffer the wrath of Judge Battle's contempt order. To loosen his tongue, Huie took out a wad of cash and asked for the same kind of rifle that killed King. Wood brought it out, a brand-new Remington 760 Gamemaster, and he mounted the scope and explained how to "bore-sight" it. Huie paid cash, $265.85, and left on US 78 bound for Memphis.

Immersed in reenacting Ray's last days before the King assassination, Huie left Hanes in Birmingham and drove northwest until he reached Memphis. He pulled in just outside Bessie Brewer's rooming house, which was now a crime scene, and made his way into Room 5-B carrying the rifle. He took the gun from the box and walked over to the community bath, where Ray stood nine months earlier, leveling the Remington on the windowsill, forging his aim on Room 306 of the Lorraine Motel, its second-floor balcony just two hundred feet away in a direct line of sight. Huie lowered the rifle and shook his head. "When I stood in that rooming-house bathtub, in Ray's footprints," he later wrote, "and looked down at where Dr. King had stood, I said: 'My god, how easy it was!'" Later, back in Alabama, he test-fired the gun from a similar vantage. "I hadn't fired a rifle in twenty-three years," he claimed. "But with a rifle and scope exactly like Ray's, and duplicating the distance and angle of the shot, I put ten straight shots in a circle the size of a silver dollar. Any twelve-year-old boy reasonably familiar with a .22 rifle, could have killed Dr. King from that bathroom window with the rifle that Ray used."

》》》 》》》 》》》 《《《 《《《 《《《

As the New Year began, FBI informants at *Look* reported the existence of a third article that would serve as an ending to Huie's series on Raoul and a primer for *They Slew the Dreamer*, which would be released right after the trial. Hoover learned that *Look* "has decided to go ahead with the third article rather than wait until Ray's trial starts, which is scheduled for March 3, 1969."

That report came on the heels of a strange Birmingham FBI dispatch on Huie's search for Raoul. It emerged on January 3 when a retired army colonel named Larry Persons walked into the FBI's Birmingham field office carrying a book, *The Bay of Pigs*, written and vanity published by his brother Albert under the imprint Kingston Press. Colonel Persons claimed Swalley Printing Company, a small Birmingham press, printed the first and only edition in 1968. Because of the book, Colonel Persons told the FBI that he received a call around Christmas from Tad Holt, a respected national broadcaster from Birmingham. Holt wanted Albert's phone number to give to Huie. "One or two days later Huey contacted his brother and asked him to work with him on the James Earl Ray case," the FBI report read, spelling Huie's name incorrectly.

Colonel Persons was worried about his brother but apparently did not articulate why. He just said that an oil distributor close to Wallace's speechwriter, Asa Carter, put up $10,000 to have Albert's book printed by Swalley. According to the FBI's report, "[Colonel Persons] stated that he is of the opinion that there is a possible conspiracy between Carter and Ray in the killing of Martin Luther King." Colonel Persons said the plot must have originated in Birmingham, and he believed that his brother's book had something to do with exposing the plot laid out in Huie's *Look* articles, which like his brother's book "contains numerous Spanish names." The agent either didn't see the connection or didn't document it. Despite Colonel Persons's insistence, the agent simply thanked him for coming in—for betraying his own brother—and stowed the book away in a dark closet. The FBI's two-page report of the incident ended thusly: "No action is being taken on the above and it is being furnished only as a matter of information."

The FBI may not have understood the context of what Colonel Persons was trying to say, but Huie knew that the timing of the Bay of Pigs invasion ran parallel to Birmingham's segregationist rebellion. While Hanes ran for mayor in early 1961, the CIA was recruiting sixty national guardsmen to train Cuban freedom fighters how to fly the B-26, an old twin-engine bomber still patrolling in just two places: Birmingham and Cuba. Nearly all of the Americans picked for the air operation grew up in Birmingham or Bessemer, attended Woodlawn or Tarrant High School, and served in World War II or the Korean War. Nearly all of the recruits worked as pilots or mechanics for Hanes's former employer, Hayes Aircraft. They signed up to fight Castro as Hanes fought to "Keep Birmingham White."

In reading Albert Persons's book, Huie learned that General Reid Doster, commander of the 117th Tactical Reconnaissance Wing of the Alabama National Guard, handpicked all of the Birmingham recruits, including Persons. The boys from Birmingham turned Cuban rebels with little flying experience into functional fighter pilots. The failed invasion, so poorly planned and executed, became so dire in April

1961 that ten pilots were finally ordered into the fight at the eleventh hour. A CIA telegram gave the order at midnight on April 19, 1961. "Cannot attach sufficient importance to fact that American crews must not fall into enemy hands," the telegram read. "In event this happens, despite all precautions, crews must state hired mercenaries, fighting communism, etc.; US will deny any knowledge." That same day four of the ten pilots—Riley Shamburger, Thomas "Pete" Ray, Leo Baker, and Wade Gray—were shot down. None survived and the CIA covered up the circumstances of their demise. The true story of their deaths did not surface for nearly two years, until Albert Persons revealed Birmingham's role in the Bay of Pigs in an article for the *Chicago American*. Albert's disclosures prompted President Kennedy to try to neutralize the leak at a February 3, 1963, press conference. "Let me say this about these four men. They were serving their country," Kennedy admitted. "The flight that cost them their lives was a voluntary flight and that while because of the nature of their work it has not been a matter of public record, as it might be in the case of soldiers or sailors, I can say that they were serving their country."

An ardent segregationist, Persons turned his anti-Communist outrage against the civil rights movement. In March 1965, he took an assignment from Congressman William Dickinson, a Montgomery politician famously elected to the US House of Representatives as an Alabama Republican, the first of many political districts flipped to the GOP during Lyndon Johnson's tenure. On March 30, 1965, after the Selma–Montgomery march, Dickinson stood on the floor of the House and claimed to have evidence that "drunkenness and sex orgies were the order of the day in Selma, on the road to Montgomery, and in Montgomery." Religious observers who were actually there expressed outrage at the bogus allegation, and hundreds of participants issued statements calling Dickinson a racist and a liar.

The congressman responded by hiring Albert Persons to gather harmless pictures of white women and black men walking together on the road to Selma, including images of Liuzzo and Moton. Dickinson and Persons then pieced it together in a vanity magazine titled *The True Selma Story: Sex and Civil Rights*. By the summer of 1965, just before Klonsel Murphy's death, Huie called it "the best-selling magazine in Alabama," even though it contained no sex, just harmless images of white women in the company of black men. Nor was the writing all that persuasive. Albert's first chapter, "Black Knight of the Civil Rights Movement," was a typical example of segregationist propaganda. "In ten short years, Martin Luther King has risen to a position of leadership and political influence never before approached by a Negro in America," Albert wrote. "Many people in both races today question his assertions and his ultimate goals. Down what road is King leading his race in the United States—is it toward freedom, or is it back into slavery?" Persons went on to author some of the most disturbing propaganda of the civil rights movement, including Sheriff Jim Clark's memoir, *I Saw Selma Raped*, and another magazine called *Riot! Riot! Riot!*, a racist examination of Watts and other riots that benefitted politicians like Wallace.

》》 》》 》》 《《 《《 《《

Huie never spoke publicly about his reasons for hiring Albert Persons, except to say, ten years later, that he thought Asa Carter could have plausibly met up with Ray during his time in Birmingham. But a closer examination of Huie's line of inquiry, as well as his testimony in court, reveals something much more explosive and controversial. In his desperation to unravel a conspiracy, Huie may have hired Persons to investigate whether General Doster of the Alabama National Guard played a supporting role in King's assassination. Huie's basis for this investigation appears to be the fact that Ray purchased the murder weapon across the street from Doster's headquarters at the Birmingham airport.

Unlike Huie and Hanes, General Doster played only a minor role in the upheavals of the late sixties. In 1967, he created a riot control unit to protect Alabama from the lawlessness that destroyed parts of Los Angeles, Newark, and Detroit, the kind of disturbances documented by Persons in *Riot! Riot! Riot!*. As sensational headlines predicted "civil war" in American streets, soldiers like Doster stood on a war footing. In June 1967, as Ray worked as a dishwasher in Chicago, the US Supreme Court voted 5–4 to uphold a 1963 contempt of court citation against Dr. King. The incident in question occurred amid the Project C demonstrations in Birmingham, when King disobeyed restraining orders forbidding mass protests on Good Friday. The Supreme Court's decision forced King to serve five days in a Birmingham jail and pay a $5,000 fine for ignoring what the court admitted was an illegal order.

Doster prepared for riots when King's jail sentence began on Tuesday, October 31, 1967. A tense peace prevailed, and upon his November 4 release, King applauded the crowd of three hundred peaceful supporters and condemned rioting as counterproductive: "My slogan is not 'Burn, Baby, Burn,' but 'Build, Baby, Build.'" Segregationists thanked Doster, not King, for the reprieve. In Tuscaloosa, the Rotary Club honored Doster, who milked the spotlight by calling King and his supporters "rabble rousers." He cited speeches "made elsewhere in which it had been advocated that Birmingham 'be burned down.'" That wouldn't happen on his watch, Doster vowed. "We hope by taking care of snipers, looters, and arsonists on the spot, we will prevent another Detroit," he said. "And if it comes down to taking a human life, maybe it will be one or two instead of forty-two."

Six months later, King's assassination made the threat of rioting even more real. But as Washington, Chicago, and Memphis erupted in violence and arson, Birmingham remained calm—that is, until news of the murder weapon leaked out. Huie could not have known it, but on April 9, Doster phoned the Birmingham FBI to ask whether the rifle that killed King had really been purchased in Birmingham. Hoover did not respond immediately, so Doster, in something of a panic, sent his adjutant to the Birmingham FBI's field office to point "out that the National Guard had the responsibility for the overall security in the State and a tense racial situation might develop if it is true that the rifle used in the killing had been purchased in Birmingham, Alabama." Headquarters instructed the Birmingham field office to "advise the General of the Alabama National Guard for his confidential information that it appeared that a rifle found near the scene of the shooting was in fact purchased in Birmingham,

Alabama; that the FBI if asked about this will neither confirm nor deny." Doster was not told, however, that the rifle was purchased across the street from his headquarters.

There's no evidence the FBI investigated Doster in the King assassination. But after Ray's capture, it surely must have occurred to Hoover that Doster shared his airport with Hayes Aircraft, where Hanes served as chief of security for nearly ten years. It was also no secret, at least in Birmingham, that Hanes and Doster remained the best of friends. They both played football at Woodlawn High School and never grew apart. Nor would it have been the first time Doster found himself in hot water for illegal activities. Over the years, as he racked up medals and leadership honors, the general "was up to his bushy eyebrows in Alabama politics." As one Birmingham veteran of the failed invasion later put it, "There was a lot of rotten stuff going on in the guard after the Bay of Pigs."

In October 1965, Alabama attorney general Flowers, a courageous enemy of Governor Wallace, accused Doster of illegally flying $21,000 worth of tax-free liquor into the state from New Orleans. Doster defended himself and got off the hook by saying that his "personal friend" Governor Wallace approved the trip. That same year, Congress uncovered evidence, but did not release it publicly, that Doster may have also used a state plane in 1964 to help fly a Klansman to a North Carolina hospital after a fall at Birmingham's Tutwiler Hotel during the Klan's annual meeting, better known as Klanvocation. According to a confidential source, "Matthew Murphy, Imperial Counsel, made contact with Al Lingo, head of the Alabama Bureau of Investigation, requesting that the injured Klansman be flown by State plane to North Carolina. Murphy's request was granted and the injured Klansman was flown to North Carolina in a State National Guard plane. It is unknown whether the state billed the Klan for the expenses of transporting the injured Klansman to North Carolina; however, during the meeting of September 6th, the sum of $384.00 was collected to pay the expenses of the injured Klansman from Birmingham, Alabama, to an unknown destination in North Carolina."

Doster was not the only person at the Birmingham airport with ties to Wallace and the Bay of Pigs invasion. On November 15, 1968, just three days after Ray changed lawyers, a *New York Times* reporter named Martin Waldron revealed, somewhat nonchalantly, that Hanes too served as a CIA asset. Waldron worked on the article for weeks, but his scoop ultimately amounted to just one line: "Mr. Hanes is a former agent of the Federal Bureau of Investigation and a one-time contract employee of the Central Intelligence Agency." In the caverns of Langley, those twenty-two words caused something of an uproar. Hanes's outing in the *Times* was first reported to the CIA by Birmingham attorney Thomas McDowell, "who has been utilized" by the CIA "in matters concerning the Birmingham widows" of the four American pilots killed during the Bay of Pigs invasion. CIA director Richard Helms, a longtime hand in the CIA's operations division before and after the Bay of Pigs, dashed off a handwritten note banning Hanes from the CIA for life. In all caps, it read: "SUBJECT IS NOT TO BE USED AGAIN BY THE AGENCY."

Waldron was wrong. Hanes could not be described as a one-time contract employee. Far from it. He spied for the CIA for most of the ten years he worked at Hayes Aircraft. An internal CIA summary explained the scope of his service.

> Arthur Jackson Hanes is a former FBI agent (1949 to 1951) who is known personally to a number of officers in the Office of Security. When he was considering resignation from the Federal Bureau of Investigation in 1950 because he felt chances to rise were too limited in the bureau, he submitted an application for employment to the Agency but his file reflects that his application was withdrawn a week later.
>
> Mr. Hanes served as a confidential correspondent of the Office of Security from May 1952 to February 1959. He terminated this service due to the pressure of his regular employment. At that time, he was employed by Hayes Aircraft Corporation in Birmingham, Alabama (his employment with this firm was from August 1951 to November 1961.)
>
> He was elected Mayor of Birmingham in 1961 but was in office for only a year. He was granted a covert security clearance

in August 1961 by the Office of General Counsel on their Cleared Attorneys Panel. In addition, he was instrumental in recruiting several Alabama National Guard pilots during the Bay of Pigs incident, several of whom lost their lives.

At the time he terminated his relationship with this Office in February of 1959, he had displayed an unhealthy tendency toward becoming a segregationist and in later years he might well have been termed a racist. For this reason, we were not too unhappy with his decision to sever his relationship with us. Nonetheless we have always considered him pro-agency and his statements regarding the agency are somewhat surprising.

What Hanes actually did for the CIA from 1952 to 1959 as a "confidential correspondent" and a "contract administrator" remains an agency secret. Huie most likely never knew, unless Hanes confided, that Ray's first choice as lawyer had been added to the FBI's "Confidential Correspondents" list in March 1961—just weeks before the Bay of Pigs invasion. Huie could also not have known that Birmingham's former mayor had once acquired a "covert security clearance" and served on the "Cleared Attorneys Panel," even after severing ties with the CIA in 1959. Whether Hanes remained on the "Cleared Attorneys Panel" when Ray reached out to him in June 1968 has never been revealed by the CIA.

31

An Educated Bluff
Memphis, February 1969

Huie received a legal summons on February 4, but it was not, to his surprise, for the contempt of court citation he received back in November. The state of Tennessee had convened a grand jury to investigate the possibility of a conspiracy in the King assassination. Prosecutors, eager to address public concerns stemming from Huie's *Look* articles, decided not to wait for answers to emerge in Huie's book. "You are hereby commanded to summon William Bradford Huie and bring with him writings, or all of the aforementioned, under his control concerning the slaying of Martin Luther King Jr., including but not limited to those writings furnished by James Earl Ray and/or his agents," the subpoena read.

Huie realized it might be time to make a deal. Though hardly a champion of journalism ethics, he viewed the subpoena as a violation of his First Amendment rights. Serious constitutional issues were at stake, such as the government's right to subpoena journalists to solve crimes, but now was not the time to protest, not with a looming deadline and pending contempt charges. Instead, Huie volunteered to testify while also offering something much more valuable, something prosecutors could not get with a subpoena: Huie believed he could convince Ray to plead guilty and turn state's evidence. Doing so would save the people of Tennessee tens of thousands of dollars. For prosecutors, it would eliminate the possibility of an acquittal.

Three days before Huie's grand jury appearance, Attorney General Canale arrived at Huie's suite, Room 1108, at the Holiday Inn Rivermont. Canale went to deliver the subpoena, and his team of prosecutors tagged along to make sure Huie told a consistent story when put on the stand. Having that conversation today would give Canale a baseline to measure Huie's truthfulness tomorrow. For that reason, one of Canale's lieutenants took notes during the meeting, and Huie talked first, saying he viewed Ray's story as a business opportunity and nothing more. "He further stated that his only other interest other than business in that matter was an earnest desire to get and expose other co-conspirators of Ray," the notes read. If Judge Battle could be convinced, Huie would visit Ray in his cell and talk some sense into the boy. Foreman, whom Huie claimed to have known for some time, had supposedly taken the case by mistake and now wanted out.

What Huie didn't seem to know is that the prospect of a plea emerged as early as December, almost as soon as Foreman entered the case. To Canale, Huie was trying to mortgage what he didn't own. If the state wanted to trade horses, it would do so directly with Foreman, not with Huie or *Look*. To Canale, it quickly became clear that Huie did not have any tangible proof of a conspiracy, nor the holy grail of Ray's written confession. Instead, Canale drilled him with questions about Ray's segregationist motive. "Did Ray leave Montreal and go to Birmingham in August 1967 because of having committed a crime in Montreal, or could his interest in Birmingham have been caused by his admiration of George Wallace?" Canale asked.

Despite weeks and weeks of downplaying Ray's racial motive, Huie showed sympathy for the premise while remaining adamant that the conspiracy overshadowed Ray's individual role. "Ray and his brothers were 100 percent convinced that Wallace was going to be elected president of the United States," the notes quoted Huie as saying, "and that we knew that Ray was politically motivated toward

Wallace because of his activities in Los Angeles. He further related that Ray is very disappointed at this time in that Wallace was not elected and that he didn't receive the support from the people that he thought he was going to receive by killing King." Huie did not stop there. He suspected that Ray might have met an accomplice in Birmingham before getting back to Atlanta at dawn on April 5. It seemed likely that someone else rode in the Mustang, Huie believed, because Ray didn't smoke, and yet the Mustang's ashtray contained at least one cigarette butt, though not an "overflowing" ashtray of butts as some journalists erroneously reported.

More to the point, the purchasing of the rifle so close to the Birmingham airport pointed to something much more nefarious. "Mr. Huie further related that it struck him as peculiar that Ray did make trips to Aeromarine Supply which is in the vicinity of the airport in Birmingham and that also in that location was the headquarters of General Doster," the notes read. "He stated that Doster assembled the pilots that participated in the Bay of Pigs Invasion. He also stated that it was a known fact that people could come and go there in General Doster's headquarters who were of the like character as Ray." For some inexplicable reason, Huie said nothing about Hanes and his recently disclosed ties to the CIA, not to mention Hanes's friendship with Doster. But the implication was obvious: if Doster entered into a conspiracy with Ray, then Hanes, whom Ray handpicked as his attorney, must have also been a co-conspirator. After all, Hanes, much more than Doster, had a clear motive in wanting revenge on King.

Despite those obvious inferences, nothing in the FBI or attorney general's records suggests that Hoover or Canale entertained the idea that Doster, Ray, and Hanes entered into a conspiracy. Canale, like Judge Battle and Hoover, was fed up with Huie. He pointedly asked whether the journalist had interviewed "even one person who has seen Ray in the presence of Raoul." The answer, of course, was no. Huie did not have "any facts or evidence or proof in his possession." Rather, he had drawn his conclusions from "suppositions and inferences." And his gut told him that Ray's brother Jerry clearly played some role in the assassination. He also felt the circumstances surrounding

Ray's hasty trip to New Orleans—not to mention the parallels with President Kennedy's assassination—could not be ignored.

> He then related that Oswald had lived in Exchange Alley in back of the Monte Leon [sic] Hotel and that at that time the Monte Leon family had as their guests, pilots who had been ransomed from Cuba who had participated in the invasion of the Bay of Pigs.
>
> Huie related that Ray on his trip to New Orleans with Stein had met unknown, unnamed parties in a bar from which diagrams made by Ray, Huie concluded was across the street from the Monte Leon. Huie started relating about John F. Kennedy not supporting the invasion of Cuba and that because of that there was such resentment for the Kennedy family among the rescued participants of the invasion of Cuba.

Canale refused to go down that dark, murky road. He served Huie the subpoena and left. His executive assistant, James Beasley, hurried back to the courthouse and typed up an eight-page memorandum while an agent from the Memphis FBI hovered over his shoulder as he punched the keys. By the time Huie stepped in the grand jury room three days later, Hoover would already know what he was going to say.

32

A Simple Story
Grand Jury Room, Shelby County
Courthouse, February 3, 1969

The checkbook journalist from Hartselle, Alabama, took center stage in the grand jury room at 10:55 AM. A note on the transcript described the witness as having evidence "concerning a possible conspiracy in the assassination of Dr. Martin Luther King Jr." The deposition started out civil but grew more contentious over time. Huie entertained the jurors with long soliloquies about the origin of his association with Ray, about his many book projects, and about the rationale behind checkbook journalism. He made it clear that he did not believe in Ray's innocence. "I have never had the slightest doubt that Ray and Ray alone killed King."

That, of course, did not mean that Ray acted alone. The prosecutors wanted Huie to explain this strange position, particularly the statements he made to the press about the existence of "black and white" co-conspirators. Huie obliged: "[Ray] has never given me any other names other than the name Raoul. This is an uncommon name here but not in Canada. He said he was a Latin man, a French-Canadian, approximately thirty-five years old. He described him as blond but after I had written it Ray told me he was more red headed than blond."

Huie expressed certainty that Jerry Ray knew about his brother's master plan. He speculated that Jerry might have helped execute the assassination, but provided no evidence. Despite Huie's wild speculation three days earlier, Canale did not ask him about General Doster of the Alabama National Guard. Instead, he let Huie pontificate about the tramp of Dealey Plaza.

> There is an enormous amount of interest in the American assassination in Europe which states that the assassination of Dr. King was planned by the CIA and that Ray was let out of prison for this reason. The point is this: There are photographs; there is a man who many people; there is a very large number of Americans that think there is a connection between the killing of John F. Kennedy and Martin Luther King and there are a couple of places where the same area of New Orleans is involved.
>
> There are photographs; there is a photograph of two men who were arrested thirty minutes after the assassination of John F. Kennedy at Dealey Plaza. One of those men is a French-Canadian who meets the description that Ray gives of Raoul. That photograph has been shown to Ray and he says it looks like him but he doesn't have the same type of clothes on. The man that was arrested in Dallas had French cut clothes on.

Canale brought up the fact that Huie investigated the Kennedy assassination in 1963. He knew that a London publisher offered Huie $250,000 to author the first conspiracy allegation, but Huie simply couldn't deliver it. "I went to Dallas and worked for ten days and got everything I could," Hue admitted. "I knew Robert Kennedy at that time but I concluded that Jack Kennedy was shot by Lee Harvey Oswald and I concluded that Ruby never knew Lee Harvey Oswald so I didn't support all these reports about a conspiracy. I think Garrison is crazy. I think that all these assassinations being linked together is a most dangerous assumption." But again, that didn't mean he was giving up the conspiracy angle. Huie still believed that the King assassination "is a simple story not involving a great conspiracy. I think the maximum that knew would have been maybe three or four."

When Huie stepped off the hot seat, he also surrendered. Judge Battle ordered him arrested for contempt of court while on the premises. As he'd done to Hanes, Battle then refused to order sentencing—a maximum penalty of ten days in jail and a fifty-dollar fine—to avoid giving Huie a drawn-out appeal. Battle's admonishing lasted only a few minutes, but the beleaguered judge made no effort to hide his personal contempt for the journalist: "I sent Mr. Huie copies of all orders issued in this case and requested him not to publish anything. But his first story in *Look* came out two weeks before the trial was set and second came out the day of the trial. Frankly, I don't trust Mr. Huie not to violate these orders in the future."

The grand jury met twice to consider the evidence Huie and others presented. Jurors needed to decide whether to charge Ray's brother Jerry with conspiracy or to book Huie with obstruction of justice for not handing over his notes. In the end, no charges were handed down. Huie stayed out of jail, but at a cost to his credibility. One news report put it bluntly: "The Shelby County Grand Jury apparently has not been much impressed with the testimony of William Bradford Huie, the Alabama author who claims to have information that a conspiracy was involved in the slaying of Dr. Martin Luther King Jr."

Ray became furious when he learned of Huie's grand jury testimony. From that moment forward, he began building a legal case against the journalist that would drag on for a decade. "I think the attorney general knows it," Ray wrote to the court, "but the main reason I ask Mr. Hanes to withdraw was that he was working for Mr. Huie to my detriment and Mr. Huie from his statements had ceased to be an impartial reporter but intends to aid the state to convict me."

33

Guilty, Not Racist
Memphis, February 1969

The fact that Ray hired Percy Foreman, the most expensive attorney in the country, did little to calm conspiracy peddlers who were already riled up by Huie's *Look* articles. Foreman's fees were so high he usually walked out of court owning the client. A city worth of storage sheds in Houston housed all of the possessions he'd taken from bankrupted clients in lieu of money. Writing to Judge Battle shortly after becoming Ray's lawyer, Foreman spelled out his compensation strategy, with a few twists in logic. "I am appalled at the publicity attended upon the publication of *Look* magazine's so-called life story of James Earl Ray," Foreman claimed. "I will have no part in any such endeavor. [But] I realize from the importunities heaped on me by reporters, writers and broadcasters since my name was mentioned in the case that it is possible the life story of James Earl Ray may have some financial possibilities in the future. If so, I shall undertake to recoup whatever I may have expended for my time. I will also undertake to collect from any such potential source a reasonable fee."

Despite Foreman's assurances, he and Huie finalized a new publishing deal at the Huntsville International Airport. For weeks thereafter, the two men ate long dinners together at Justine's in Memphis—on Huie's dime. As Huie later claimed, Foreman would always say, "Now, you know, of course, I'm depending on you for my fee. So tote that bale, boy! Get to work!" To help defray legal expenses, Foreman also filed a motion to auction pictures of Ray to magazine photographers for $15,000 or more. Ray also wrote to Judge Battle and asked that the white Mustang and the murder weapon be assigned to Foreman. Judge Battle gave Foreman the Mustang but turned down everything else, opting instead to provide Foreman with public defender Hugh Stanton to help speed up trial preparations.

Stanton soon became Ray's lead attorney because Foreman nearly died from a winter bout with pneumonia. Ray's lawyer did not leave the bed for several weeks, but Judge Battle refused to reschedule the March 3 trial date. Ray smelled a rat: "[Foreman] is still and will remain chief consul as far as I am concerned regardless of what the court, attorney general, or press has to say, or what Mr. Huie may desire through the attorney general's office."

What Ray did not realize is that Huie's betrayal was not so absolute. On January 25, he paid Hanes a final sum of $5,000 to turn over one hundred and fifty pages of work product. Huie may have also been the one who persuaded Hanes's private investigator, Renfro Hays, to provide the defense with a list of witnesses and depositions. Fortuitously, Foreman beat his bout with pneumonia and returned to Memphis in late January. Looking flushed and exhausted, he resumed his all-night work sessions inside the Peabody Hotel while paying daily visits to Ray's cell.

At 3:00 AM on January 31, Foreman decided to phone public defender Michael Eugene in London regarding a key piece of evidence that Hanes still refused to disclose. Foreman could not get it from the state through discovery because the document in question originated in London's Bow Street Magistrate Court during Ray's extradition hearing. Foreman pleaded for Judge Battle to intervene. "The only records of any [British] proceedings furnished me by Mr. Hanes," Foreman wrote, "were delivered to me on Tuesday, January 28, 1969, by William Bradford Huie, who stated that he had obtained them from Arthur J. Hanes Sr. on Saturday afternoon, January 25, 1969." What Foreman needed was a copy of "the testimony of FBI

Fingerprint Expert George Bonebrake," testimony Eugene claimed to have sent Hanes in late October at the cost of $285. Huie told Foreman that Hanes "advised him that he had never seen the affidavit and testimony of Bonebrake." After several weeks of bickering with Hanes, Foreman called London and took copious notes while Eugene read "excerpts from the Bonebrake affidavit and testimony."

Foreman considered it devastating evidence, to say the least. Bonebrake proved that Ray's fingerprints were all over the boarding house windowsill, the rifle, and the bundle dropped outside the staircase. A Klansman might ignore Ray's fingerprints on the murder weapon, his purchasing of the rifle, and his registration at the boarding house, but betting on a single racist to ignore a smoking gun seemed cavalier. As Wallace and Nixon's "Law and Order" campaigns showed, people wanted justice, for blacks and whites. Foreman knew the prosecution would exploit the FBI's exhaustive investigative reports and put at least two African Americans on any jury through voir dire.

Without Raoul, the best Ray could hope for was a hung jury. But from the work product Huie secured, Foreman learned that Hanes believed he could put Raoul in Memphis at the time of the murder. Intrigued, Foreman sent investigators to check hotel registries at the Ambassador, the Tri-State, the Clark, and the Pontotoc. Hanes had planned to show "that a blond male, white 25 to 30 years old stayed one or two nights in one of these hotels under the name Willard or Sneyd, an alias alleged to have been used by James Earl Ray. This man was alleged to have stayed sometime between April 1, 1968 and April 5, 1968." If confirmed, Foreman could ask the jury a simple question: Why would Ray book two rooms for one night's lodging?

Foreman's investigators returned empty-handed. "The above mentioned hotels reveal that no such man checked into any of these establishments about that time," the report read. To make matters worse, the defense's eyewitness, Harold "Cornbread" Carter, turned out to be a notorious wino and a known liar. The entire "bushman" theory—the idea that the shot was fired from the bushes below the rooming house—was ridiculous. After putting it all together,

Foreman could not convince himself that a public trial would spare Ray's life.

))))))))) (((((((((

On February 13, Ray enjoyed a lunch of hamburger patties in gravy, creamed potatoes, green beans, Jell-O, bread, and iced tea. Guards on duty did not notice anything out of the ordinary, except Ray's excessive pacing. "After getting up [Ray] shaved, and at 12:00 noon, Mr. Percy Foreman entered A Block and talked with Ray until 12:40 PM," the report read. "After Mr. Foreman left Ray walked in the block for thirty minutes, and then swept and mopped the block. At 2 PM he was given two empirin." What really happened was more dramatic. Foreman pulled a note from his breast pocket that read:

> I write this letter to put of record my analysis of your case, my judgment concerning the probable outcome and my recommendation as to the course of action we should explore in your behalf. I also write it for my own protection. Because I anticipate the coming of a time when it will be needed for reference.
>
> I have spent several weeks reviewing the nature of the case the State of Tennessee has against you. I have surveyed the jury sentiment in this country and jury verdicts in other recent cases. And I have come to this conclusion:
>
> In my opinion, there is a little more than a ninety-nine percent chance of your receiving a death penalty verdict if your case goes to trial. Furthermore, there is a 100 percent chance of a guilty verdict. Neither I nor any other lawyer can change the overwhelming evidence that has been assembled against you. The above analysis of your chances would still obtain without the *Look* articles.

Ray was in near disbelief. The great attorney was abandoning him. Foreman showed no sympathy or second thoughts, insisting that Ray sign a statement acknowledging, not agreeing with, his advice. Five days later, on February 18, Foreman returned to Ray's cell, and guards noticed that the prisoner subsequently lost his appetite: "At 9:50 AM Mr. Foreman entered A Block and talked with Ray until

11:40 AM. At the time Mr. Foreman left a lunch of chicken gizzards and rice, pinto beans, bread, and iced tea was served. Ray did not eat but walked in the block and listened to the radio until 1:30 PM." Having thought about it for five days, Ray gave up that morning. Pleading guilty would save his life, which was the whole point of hiring Foreman in the first place. By taking the years, Ray could now bet his chances on another escape.

> You has asked me to put in writing my authorization to you to negotiate a plea of guilty in the murder case pending in Shelby County, Tennessee (Memphis) in which I am indicted for the murder of Martin Luther King. That is the purpose of this letter.
>
> I appreciate the fact that you have stated you are willing to contest this case through the trial court and the appellate courts of Tennessee; and, if necessary, to the Supreme Court of the United States. But you have told me that an appeal is not necessarily synonymous with a reversal, and I already knew that.
>
> We have, together, analyzed the evidence against me and both of us have concluded that it is impossible to controvert certain incriminating fingerprints, identification, and other circumstances. We both believe that, ultimately, a trial or trials will result in a final conviction, and that the alternative punishments will be either life, ninety-nine years in prison or death in the electric chair.
>
> Therefore, this is my authority to you to negotiate a plea of guilty on my behalf for any term of years, but with a waiver of the death penalty. If you are successful in doing so, I will enter such a plea at the convenience of the Court and all concerned. You have guaranteed me that if I do enter such a plea, that the death penalty needs must be waived and that I will not be sentenced to death.

》》》 》》》 》》》 《《《 《《《 《《《

When Canale received Foreman's overture, he immediately called Coretta Scott King's lawyer, Harry Wachtel, in New York. The state had spent tens of thousands of dollars and probed into every possible lead, but if a man wanted to take a plea, Canale felt an obligation to respect his choice. King's widow felt the same way, Wachtel told Canale, but on different grounds. Her slain husband abhorred the death penalty as much as any segregation ordinance. He spoke out against capital punishment for the same reason he refused body-guards: violence begets violence. Foreman and Ray did not seem to understand that it would have been an insult to execute King's killer. Of course, the state had no obligation to respect the King family's wishes, but politically, the execution of King's killer would have been a human rights faux pas.

So with the King family's backing, Canale accepted Foreman's offer and prepared a list of "material facts which the state would prove in the course of the trial." It covered everything from the safe deposit box in Birmingham to plastic surgery in Los Angeles. It noted Ray's purchase of the rifle and his firing of the fatal shot. It contained fifty-six assertions of fact. Annoyed by the long list, Ray apparently signed off without much forethought. But later, he took the time to study each allegation in detail, and the first sixteen he read without objection. Then there was number seventeen: "That in December, 1967, defendant drove to New Orleans with Charlie Stein and brought Rita Stein's children back to Los Angeles after having taken Charles Stein, Rita Stein, and Marie Martin to George Wallace headquarters in Los Angeles for purpose of registering for Wallace."

Ray assumed he could plead guilty and protect his motive. Now, he was caught unawares, and it put him in a frenzy. He dashed off a poorly spelled letter to Foreman threatening to kill the plea over "Wallace," a word that clearly conjured up notions of racism. Other assertions, such as those stipulating his execution of the crime, remained acceptable.

> I don't want the Wallace part in for the following reasons . . . what is said in court will not be what the papers print, they have been harping on the Stein-Wallace thing in Calif. for sometime now and I no from past experience that after the papers have me convicted they will start on someone else. Now I have signed this cop out and it will look like I did sign it just to save myself at someone else's expense. They had some reason for useing the

word 'Wallace' since their is no Wallace Party, it's the Amer. Ind. Party. If Mr. Canale wants to he can call Marie Denno and she will tell him I told her if she wanted to get a political lawyer to help her boy friend out of jail she should rec. with the Democrat or Rep which she did. Also I don't want to become involved in any of these cheap political tricks. But if they want to at the trial, I have a few names myself. . . . On this guilty plea it seems to me that I am taking all the blame which is all right with me, but if Canale insists on playing politics I will go to trial.

Ray's umbrage over stipulation number seventeen was fascinating to contemplate: If his passion for Wallace played no role in his reasons for killing King, why then would he only begrudge that statement? Why would he care if people thought he did it for racist vengeance? After all, anyone charged with killing the leader of the civil rights movement should be assumed to be prejudiced against African Americans. The reason, it seemed to Foreman, was that Ray felt naked having the world know why he did it. He thought he could kill King, plead guilty, but keep something for himself.

Canale let Ray have it. The Wallace reference had little to do with proving that Ray fired the rifle that killed King. The defendant was agreeing to a ninety-nine-year sentence, which in Tennessee was much more severe than life in prison. Under a life sentence, Ray could have possibly been paroled in twelve years. Assuming good behavior, he was now agreeing to serve at least forty-eight years behind bars. The Wallace omission would be the state of Tennessee's only concession.

34

The Last Supper
Shelby County Courthouse,
March 10, 1969

The Saturday, March 8, papers had reported "developments" in the Ray case, and since that time, planes were landing every few minutes at the airport, as newspapermen and broadcasters occupied the city on short notice. Inside the Shelby County courthouse on March 10, a venire of thirty prospective jurors now understood that at any moment they might be called to deliver justice in the Ray case even though their term ended on March 11, many weeks before the delayed April 7 trial date.

Inside Judge Battle's windowless court, the journalists who cleared security entered at 8:30 AM on James Earl Ray's forty-first birthday. Wearing suits and topcoats, they sat thirty-eight strong in hard theater seats on the right side of the courtroom, impatient and expecting, cooling their heels for history. As the Western Union clock ticked away, some craned their necks over the rail, as if to peek inside the giant mass covered in bedsheets that sat on the table. Ray's two brothers, the first to arrive, sat in the third row.

Just before 9:00 AM, Percy Foreman strutted into court wearing a houndstooth fedora and a dark tailored suit with a gray and blue tie. He palmed his hat and bowed dramatically to the women seated in the courtroom. During the previous two months, dozens of Memphis journalists attended his scotch-and-soda sessions at the Claridge and Peabody hotels, and most of them went away seduced by his personality. One reporter called Foreman a "rough-hewn courtroom tactician" who could "sell horse collars at a hot rodders' picnic." But as the great attorney took a seat, it became clear this wasn't his show. Everyone's attention was drawn to the mass of blankets, soon accompanied by a "long shotgun box, a large red and black checkered suitcase, and small blue valise"—all taken from either the rooming house or the bundle dropped on the sidewalk.

Foreman's client had not yet appeared, but clerks continued to heap evidence on the table as if preparing for an auction. Foreman stood up to peek inside the sheet. "Looks like the last supper," he said, just as Ray appeared through a rear door escorted by five deputies. The accused wore a blue-and-brown sport coat, "a tattle-tale-gray white shirt," a blue tie, and black shoes. The hearing began when Foreman stood to announce that Ray was prepared to change his plea. He would admit his guilt and assume a sentence of ninety-nine years in prison. The audience groaned loudly, but Judge Battle was not surprised. He'd been preparing for this moment for several weeks.

"James Earl Ray, stand. Have your lawyers explained all your rights to you and do you understand them?"

"Yes."

Battle then carefully walked Ray through the standard voir dire for a guilty plea. He told Ray that he was waiving his right to a trial by jury and in doing so would waive his right to appeal. The burden of proof would be on the state of Tennessee, not the defendant, if he reconsidered and allowed the trial to take place. However, if he continued to demand a guilty plea, he would never have a trial, which meant he would have no grounds to appeal.

"You are entering a plea of Guilty to Murder in the First Degree as charged in the Indictment and are compromising and settling your case on agreed punishment of ninety-nine years in the State Penitentiary. Is this what you want to do?"

"Yes."

Judge Battle continued asking variations of the same question, and each time Ray responded in the affirmative. At that point, the clerk picked out thirteen names—twelve jurors plus an alternate. They walked into the court forming a slow line, orderly taking their seats in the jury box on the left-hand side. They were all men, eleven white and two black. Each member of the jury was asked whether he could accept the plea agreement and the ninety-nine-year sentence. While staring at Ray, they all nodded, and prosecutors suddenly removed the bed sheeting to reveal two meticulously designed models of the Lorraine Motel and the boarding house. "Damn things must have cost us $20,000!" Foreman exclaimed.

At 10:00 AM Canale began laying out the state's case. He explained the severity of the sentence and the jurors' role in approving it. The elephant in the room was conspiracy, and Canale promised vigilance if new evidence emerged. "There have been rumors going around that Mr. James Earl Ray was a dupe, a fall guy, or a member of a conspiracy," Canale said. "We have no proof other than that Dr. Martin Luther King Jr. was killed by James Earl Ray and James Earl Ray alone." When the state was done, Foreman followed up, praising Canale for not trying to put "scalps on his belt" by going to trial. He called Judge Battle "a compassionate and humane judge" as he approached the jury with a bow. "I never expected, hoped, or had any idea that I could accomplish anything but saving this man's life," Foreman swore. To each juror, he asked the same question: "Are you willing to effect the punishment that His Honor and General Canale and the attorneys for the defense have agreed upon in this case, ninety-nine years?" All twelve agreed.

It was nearly over when Ray suddenly spoke directly to Judge Battle, who was perplexed.

"Your honor, I would like to say something. I don't want to change anything that I have said, but I just want to enter one other thing. The only thing I have to say is that I can't agree with Mr. Clark."

"Mr. Who?"

"Mr. J. Edgar Hoover. I agree with all these stipulations, but I am not trying to change anything."

"You don't agree with whose theories?"

"Mr. Canale's, Mr. Clark's, and Mr. J. Edgar Hoover's about the conspiracy. I don't want to add something on that I haven't agreed to in the past."

Ray had signed an agreement with Foreman that he would not do this in court. But now he'd reneged in a big way, and Foreman stood up to save the guilty plea.

"I think that what he said is that he doesn't agree that Ramsey Clark is right or that J. Edgar Hoover is right. I didn't argue that as evidence in this case. I simply state that—underwriting the statement of General Canale—that they had made the same statement. You are not required to agree with it all, Jim."

Everyone in the court could sense how bad this looked. It got even more uncomfortable watching Battle try to clarify Ray's statement. Weeks earlier, Sirhan Sirhan, Robert Kennedy's assassin, attempted a similar plea in Los Angeles, but the judge refused to allow it for this very reason. Battle, on the other hand, forced Ray to keep talking.

"You still—your answers to those questions that I asked you would still be the same? Is that correct? There is nothing in these questions that I have asked you and your answers to them—you changed none of them at all? In other words, you are pleading guilty to and taking ninety-nine years."

"Yes, sir."

"I think the main question that I want to ask you is this: Are you pleading guilty to murder in the first degree in this case because you killed Dr. Martin Luther King under such circumstances that it would make you legally guilty of murder in the first degree under the law as explained to you by your lawyer? Your answer is still yes?"

"Yes, sir."

》》 》》 》》 《《 《《 《《

The nation was outraged by Ray's guilty plea. The *Commercial Appeal* ran a political cartoon depicting a lengthy book whose final page reads, "Guilty Plea, 99 Years, The End" next to an epilogue that asked, "What was the motive? How was he financed? Any answers?"

The *New York Times* was less diplomatic. It called the plea "a shocking breach of faith with the American people." Neither conservatives nor liberals could accept the idea that Ray acted alone without seeing all the evidence. Congressman James Eastland of Mississippi, a diehard segregationist, was so outraged he started his own conspiracy investigation. Coretta Scott King and other King lieutenants openly blamed the FBI for King's murder despite approving Ray's guilty plea.

More speculation emerged when it became public that Foreman could receive up to $165,000 for two months of work. What was never fully understood is that Foreman owned all royalties that Ray might receive from Huie's book, and journalists were reporting that film producer Carlo Ponti had negotiated for the dramatic rights, which could be worth hundreds of thousands of dollars. Despite this, Foreman agreed to cap his earnings at $165,000, so that Ray could take what was left over. If the movie was a success, the assassin could potentially make more than Foreman's $165,000.

Judge Battle was offended by the negative reaction to the sentencing. In a local interview, he conceded doubts that Ray acted alone but noted that a trial would not have revealed the scope of the plot. It was a tough call for sure, accepting the plea, and he too must have thought twice about it when an unexpected letter from Ray arrived three days later: "I wish to inform the honorable court that that famous Houston Att. percy Fourflousher is no longer representing me in any capacity. My reason for writing this letter is that I intend onto file for a post conviction hearing in the very near future and don't want him making any legal moves unless their in Mr. Canale behalf." [sic]

Battle read this juvenile nonsense and went on vacation. When he returned to his chambers on the last day of March, another letter from Ray had arrived. This one demanded a reversal of the ninety-nine-year sentence and nullification of the guilty plea. Related or not, Battle broke at the strain. He suffered a massive heart attack and died right there in his chambers. Prosecutor Dwyer, who would have made the state's case at trial, found Battle several hours later—deceased. His forehead was resting on Ray's angry letter.

PART VII

»»» »»» »»» ««« ««« «««

Though It Hath No
Tongue, 1969–1986

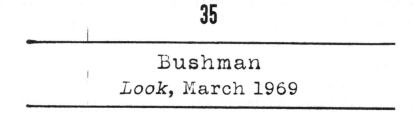

35

Bushman
Look, March 1969

The final *Look* article, WHY JAMES EARL RAY MURDERED DR. KING, hit newsstands dead on arrival in late March. Huie conceded that Raoul did not exist. Falling for Garrison's hubris cost him tremendously, starting with $25,000 for the final magazine piece and $30,000 in guaranteed book royalties; the payout was contingent on Ray going to trial. Huie's personal investment, now more than $70,000, would never return a profit because the book, slated for galleys any day, was hastily renamed *He Slew the Dreamer*. Removing the *T* and the *y* eroded hundreds of thousands of dollars in sales, and as a mea culpa, Huie repaid *Look* the entire advance.

Ray's guilty plea had already killed the movie deal because film producer Carlo Ponti, husband to Sophia Loren, backed out. After all, Huie was no longer making an original argument. Another assassination book—*The Strange Case of James Earl Ray*—was already out and losing money. Ponti understood that the masses were not interested in a story about a petty criminal from Missouri. They wanted the dark heart of conspiracy, the one Huie had primed them for since November! Neither Huie nor his editors apologized for their false statements and outright lies in the first two installments. Instead,

Look bought its way out of trouble by paying Foreman and Hanes $1,000 to disclose their conflicting views of the crime.

Having been criticized for pleading Ray guilty and assuming all of his royalties, Foreman was gracefully defiant. "If, in the dead of night, I ever summon a physician, and he arrives at my bedside and asks, 'Are you sick?' I shall use my remaining energy to leave my bed and throw the man out of my house," Foreman wrote. "So when a man accused of murder sends for Percy Foreman, I show him the courtesy of assuming he is guilty and that he hopes I can save him from excessive punishment. Else why would he be preparing to divide his worldly goods, or hope of same, with me?" Foreman was convinced of Ray's guilt. He never took the case seriously because he quickly found the common link between Ray and Oswald: they killed for ideological purposes. "I think Ray believed Dr. King was a Communist; that his crusades had opened the Pandora's box of riot; and that, though he preached nonviolence, by indirection he created Black Muslims, Black Panthers, and Invaders," Foreman wrote. "Ray thinks that the war between the races is imminent, and he wanted to fire the first shot. The shooting of Dr. King, to him, was the Pearl Harbor of that war. He didn't tell me any of this: it is what I believe he thinks."

>>> >>> >>> <<< <<< <<<

Hanes took a more complicated view. Under the heading "For Conspiracy," he sketched out the legal argument he so desperately wanted to share with an all-white jury. His central point was that the FBI failed to match the ballistics of the shot. He conceded that the rifle linked Ray to the boarding house, but not the bullet. Ray's presence at the boarding house diverted attention away from the real killer, Hanes wrote.

> Twenty feet below the bathroom window from which the shot is alleged to have been fired, there is a vacant lot, which at the time was covered with bushes twelve to fifteen feet high. Dr. King's chauffeur, Solomon Jones, told reporters a few minutes after the shooting that 'just after the shot was fired, a man

with a sheet over his head ran out of the bushes heading south.'
Another witness, [Harold] 'Cornbread' Carter, said that he saw
'the man' fire the shot from the bushes and then 'take off.'

From a concealed position in a firehouse just south of Bessie
Brewer's rooming house, police were watching the area of Dr.
King's room, trying to protect him from what they thought was
the most serious threat to him: possible attack by Negro militants. A Negro policeman who could recognize the most dangerous of these militants was at a peephole and actually saw Dr. King
fall. Both firemen and policemen who were in the back of the fire
station heard the shot, and they all thought that it came from the
bushes, not from any window twenty feet above the bushes. So I
find the 'bushman theory' of this shooting hard to dismiss.

Speculation had already emerged that Hanes might resume his
duties as Ray's lawyer. After Foreman's firing, he received "a very nice
letter from Mr. Ray" but told reporters, "I don't have any firm plans
to go to Nashville, however. I never had any intentions of getting back
into the case in an active way, although I thought, of course, I would
like to talk to him." Whether Hanes did or not is unknown, but hours
after the guilty plea, he appeared on NBC's *Huntley-Brinkley Report*
and "made reference to having information and names concerning
organizations connected with this case which he had offered on several occasions and no one had accepted his offer or seemed interested."

This vague accusation led the assistant US attorney in Birmingham,
Macy Taylor, to confront Hanes. Taylor called the Frank Nelson Building and offered to set up a three-way conference among Hanes, himself,
and the Birmingham FBI. Instead, Hanes went back on national television—this time NBC's *Today* show—to sell conspiracy. He shared the
stage with Reverend Joseph Lowery, cofounder of the Southern Christian Leadership Conference. Hanes told millions of viewers that rioting
black militants were responsible for King's death, offending Lowery,
who rejected the idea as fantastic and conspiratorial. After all, King
met with the Invaders, the militants responsible for sabotaging the first
march, just hours before his death; he confronted them face-to-face
and sent them home crestfallen. In short, Hanes could present no evidence to conclude that black militants or bushmen killed King.

36

The Bushy Knoll
Memphis, April–September 1969

As Hanes continued his crusade of disinformation, another Memphis "conspiracy" file emerged. It was from Russell X. Thompson, a respected Memphis criminal lawyer who defended many of the city's undesirables, including the Invaders. A forty-one-year-old white man, Thompson also worked for the NAACP despite the ostracism he received from his white colleagues in the Tennessee bar. After Ray's extradition from London in July, Hanes briefly hired Thompson to take the racial edge off his participation in Ray's defense. When the criticisms relented, Hanes released Thompson of his duties because "too many cooks spoil the broth." Like any good lawyer, Thompson gave his files to Foreman when prompted, but not before making copies.

What Hanes did not know when he hired Thompson proved valuable to the defense Ray cooked up. Six days after King's murder, on April 10, 1968, Thompson received a call at home from a man who said he needed counsel, on the spot.

"Can you tell me what this pertains to, generally?" Thompson asked.

"It pertains to murder," the stranger replied.

The next morning at 8 AM, a blond Latin about thirty-five years old, a man who called himself Tony Benevetta or Benevitas, entered

Thompson's office inside the Home Federal Building. Benevetta said he'd come to Memphis from Chicago on behalf of his roommate, a man from Denver. "The party responsible for Dr. King's death is my roommate," Benevetta said. "That shot didn't come from the window in that rooming house, in the bathroom window—I can tell you that. It came from the wall behind the rooming house." He then claimed to have Klan contacts in Brownsville, Texas; Thompson took that as another allusion to his complicity in the assassination.

"Are you prepared to tell me why he shot Dr. King?" Thompson asked.

"He's a professional hired gunman." Benevetta said.

"Are you the man?" Thompson asked.

"No, Mr. Thompson. I'm telling you that it was my roommate."

Benevetta later asked for help making Klan connections in Memphis, but Thompson could not oblige. They chatted for several more minutes, and Benevetta left, refusing to touch the door handle for fear of leaving a print. The encounter shook up Thompson, who'd just lost a son in Vietnam. The assassination had turned Memphis lawless, snipers had taken to the streets, and the FBI had not yet identified Ray as the suspect. Despite his sacred respect for attorney-client privilege, Thompson immediately contacted the Memphis field office and asked for agents to visit his office.

The FBI believed Thompson's story because he wasn't the only victim. Two local ministers, Reverend James M. Latimer and Reverend John Baltensperger, had just dined with a drifter at Jim's Steak House. This time he called himself J. Christ Bonnevecche, not Benevetta or Benevitas. He claimed to be a runner for the mafia out of St. Louis who stole $300,000 in counterfeit traveler's checks before arriving in Memphis. When asked by the ministers if he killed Dr. King, Benevetta said no but provided more specifics of the conspiracy, even a name. He said a man named "Nick" was paid "$20,000" by a "well-known fraternal order." Nick, the killer, came to Memphis "disguised as a black man with the help of theatrical makeup." Bonnevecche kept talking. He talked about participating in several murders and various heists. Though supposedly flush with $300,000, he asked to be dropped off at the Greyhound station to catch a bus for Brownsville.

On May 7, 1968, the FBI showed Thompson pictures of a suspect from Denver. The man did not resemble Benevetta, so the FBI wrote him off as another kook. But the encounter bothered Thompson for some time, especially when Huie's Raoul character emerged in *Look* in late October. It bothered him more when Ray pled guilty in March 1969 but played coy about the possibility of a conspiracy. On March 14, Thompson decided to go public. He flew to New York to deliver his file to the NAACP, leaked the story to the press, and framed it as a conspiracy allegation.

Hoover was angered by the stunt. Thompson appeared to be pulling a publicity hoax at the bureau's expense. But after several "miscommunications," Thompson called the Memphis FBI on March 26 to apologize and explain. He denied the way the story was framed in the papers and claimed he'd been misquoted. He admitted having no proof of a conspiracy. Nor was he persuaded that one existed. The simple reason he wanted to speak with the bureau was to remind them of Benevetta because the man who came into his office six days after the assassination seemed eerily similar to Huie's Raoul.

There was something else too. The FBI report read,

Thompson also advised that during the initial stages of the James Earl Ray case he did assist Attorney Arthur Hanes, Sr. of Birmingham, Alabama, and he did tell Hanes about this blond Latin who had called on him. Thompson speculated that Hanes had told Ray about this blond Latin and possibly on that basis Ray had come up with the Raoul character. Thompson further said, of course, there was a possibility that Hanes himself might have manufactured the character Raoul, based on the data he had furnished about a blond Latin.

In other words, Thompson believed that Hanes and Ray morphed Benevetta into a "bushman" shooter named Raoul and propped him up with statements from King's chauffeur Solomon Jones,

"Cornbread" Carter, and District Attorney Jim Garrison. In doing so, the defense effectively fabricated a second grassy knoll.

》》》 》》》 》》》 《《《 《《《 《《《

Thompson's conspiracy file emerged just as Ray returned to his happy place: the state penitentiary. Despite a barrage of appeals, escape attempts, and futile lawsuits, he would remain caged in a maximum-security prison for the rest of his natural life. But before leaving Memphis, he passed his guards a letter addressed to J. B. Stoner. "I suppose you have read the results of the trial," Ray began, "since it is over it is now alright with me if you file those libel suits that is if you still want to." On March 21, Stoner officially became Ray's attorney of record. Instead of pursuing libel claims, the NSRP hired two Tennessee criminal attorneys and released this statement in Ray's name. "In the spring of 1968, I was working with agents of the Federal Government, including Raoul," the statement read. "They told me that I was helping them to supply arms and guns to Cuban refugees to overthrow Castro and the Communists in Cuba. The reason I made trips to Mexico was in regard to helping the agents of the Federal Government to supply arms to Cuban refugees there to overthrow Castro. The federal agents led me to believe that I was in Memphis in April for that same purpose."

Talking to the *New York Times* on April 1, Hanes gave a nearly identical statement. When asked why Ray ended up in the boarding house on the day of King's assassination, Hanes's answer, which was not a joke despite coming on April Fools' Day, inspired this headline: EX-ATTORNEY LINKS RAY TO RIFLES FOR CUBAN EXILES. Hanes said he believed that Ray was ordered to Memphis by someone in Louisiana, mostly likely in New Orleans, "to try and sell rifles to Cuban exiles. . . . The only show of emotion, apprehension or concern which Ray showed was when he went over the list of state's witnesses from Louisiana. He was terrified."

For six months, Hanes let go of the Ray case to continue his representation of the Klan. In the summer of 1969, he defended seventeen Klansmen accused of shooting at black protesters and causing a riot in Hyde County, North Carolina. The FBI investigated his new assignment when Hanes stood in open court on July 18 and claimed that someone bugged the telephone in his Washington, North Carolina, Holiday Inn hotel room. The judge refused to enter the accusation into the record, but after the hearing Hanes held a press conference and exhibited the "bug" to skeptical reporters. The FBI's sources believed that Hanes fabricated the entire episode to create a red herring, though it didn't work. All twelve men pled guilty, and the *Washington Post* later reported that the Klan fell into turmoil over his attorney's fees. Hoover took note. "The Bureau is familiar with the fact that Hanes is very closely allied with the Klan and previous information has been furnished to the Bureau that he received a sum of $12,500 as an attorney for Klan members in North Carolina, and also met with Klan officials recently in Tuscaloosa, Alabama."

Upon his return to Birmingham in September 1969, Hanes injected himself back into the King assassination saga. He approached assistant US attorney Macy Taylor about the Cuban gunrunning conspiracy that he and Stoner mentioned back in the spring. This time the word *evidence* came out of his mouth. Hanes said he could almost prove the plot to kill King originated out of Birmingham. He was even prepared to turn over his file to the FBI. When the news reached Washington, Hoover fired off an "airtel" with specific instructions:

> You should interview Arthur Hanes for all details he may have relative to alleged gunrunning conspiracy involving James Earl Ray as outlined in airtel 9-26-69, in order that appropriate action can be taken to run out such allegations. Hanes should be thoroughly pinned down for specifics. For your additional information you will recall that only one bullet slug was recovered from King's body which was mutilated to the extent that it could not be identified as having been fired from the suspect gun although it was the type of projectile which could have been fired from such weapon.

On the sixth floor of the Frank Nelson Building, where he'd received Ray's overture, Hanes finally got an audience with his former employer. Birmingham FBI agent Henry Snow, sent to interview

Hanes on October 10, must have noticed the portrait of Confederate general Robert E. Lee that hung on the dark-paneled wall, or
nearby, the framed picture of Wallace and Hanes standing shoulder
and shoulder for segregation. When the conversation began, Hanes
said he had two theories on the assassination: the first involved the
CIA and the second involved black militants. Agent Snow asked for
the second, and Hanes told a tale of Birmingham conspiracy that
centered on the petty theft of silver and shotguns from a residence in
suburban Birmingham on December 18, 1968, just a few weeks after
Ray fired Hanes as his lawyer.

Hanes represented one of the culprits, an African American man
from Birmingham, and convinced the man to turn state's evidence.
In doing so, Hanes's client fingered the owner of a Cadillac as an
accomplice. The accomplice was from Memphis, Hanes explained.
Together they robbed the house for the guns because "weapons such
as these had been intended for black militant groups in Memphis,
who might have intended to use them in King's Assassination." Hanes
then named three ostensibly African American suspects: his client,
another suspect from Birmingham, and the Cadillac owner from
Memphis. He wanted the FBI to interrogate the Cadillac owner while
he remained in the custody of the federal Alcohol, Tobacco, Fire-
arms, and Explosives division. Ask him about Ray, Hanes suggested.

Agent Snow must have thought there was more to it. He
reminded Hanes that he was talking about "shotguns, not rifles," as
well as events that occurred eight months after the assassination. A
rifle, not a shotgun, killed King. Hanes apparently didn't know what
to say. He tried to free himself by entering "into a lengthy discourse
of his theories concerning the James Earl Ray case and stated that
although Ray undoubtedly was involved, it was his theory that Ray
had been led or instructed in his actions by other unknown individuals." Agent Snow went back to his office and drafted the following
report: "Hanes furnished no information to tie this burglary in with
the gun running theory, and it is noted that King was shot 4-4-68,
eight months before the burglary occurred. . . . The information he
related as far as gunrunning would appear to in no way relate to

James Earl Ray, and for that reason, Birmingham suggests no further action in this matter concerning information furnished by Hanes."

Nor would the FBI ever open a full investigation into Hanes's ties to the Klan despite intelligence that he appeared to be attending Klan board meetings in Tuscaloosa. For all intents and purposes, Hoover wrote off Hanes as a black sheep whose connections to the Klan and the CIA, as well as King's assassin, were more of an embarrassment than a conspiracy worth pursuing.

37

Belated Justice
Birmingham, 1977

Seven years later, Hanes got his final chance to free a racist killer, but the defendant was not James Earl Ray. In the fall of 1977, Alabama's young attorney general, Bill Baxley, convinced a Birmingham grand jury to indict seventy-three-year-old Klansman Robert "Dynamite Bob" Chambliss on the charge of first-degree murder. After fifteen bitter years, someone would finally have to answer for bombing the Sixteenth Street Baptist Church. Baxley promised a full accounting. "It's just a start. We've got a long way to go toward getting there," he announced.

That September, a state judge ordered Chambliss held on $200,000 bail—$50,000 for each child killed in the blast. Some whites saw the bail as excessive, and the head of the Alabama Klan was so appalled that he promised to lead a march through Birmingham the following weekend in protest. "It's ridiculously high for a man his age," the grand dragon told a reporter. The news that Hanes would serve as Chambliss's attorney also raised a few eyebrows. He and his son, Art Jr., quickly secured the necessary property bonds—more than $400,000—for Chambliss's bail. Like Matt Murphy in the Liuzzo case, Klonsel Hanes refused to disclose who put up the money.

Fourteen years had passed since Hanes's secret participation in the charade that occurred in October 1963, when Wallace's state troopers arrested Chambliss for the bombing. Hanes was present in the St. Francis Hotel on the night that Shelton and Lingo brokered Chambliss's arrest. Hanes was also present at the trooper outpost when Murphy arrived and told Chambliss to remain silent. The cover-up that Wallace sanctioned that night took fifteen years to undo, yet now it was a Wallace-backed attorney general bringing the murder charges. What on earth had changed in Alabama? the media asked.

The answer was simple. Wallace mellowed his racial prejudices to stay in power. Now that African Americans could really vote in Alabama, the governor could no longer use the same racist rhetoric. Token investigations of white crimes were suddenly good politics because they helped win over black voters and white moderates. Perhaps more to the point, Wallace became a sympathetic figure after he cheated death during the 1972 presidential campaign. Assassin Arthur Bremer shot him five times in a Maryland parking lot, leaving the governor paralyzed from the waist down.

Having lost another presidential election, Wallace returned to Alabama, where black and white voters elected him to serve two additional terms. But under Alabama law, he could not run again until 1982, which meant that his endorsement for the 1978 gubernatorial campaign was something Attorney General Baxley, a candidate, desperately needed. For Hanes and son, that presented an obvious opening in their defense of Chambliss. They could attack Baxley as an ambitious politician eager to throw voters some red meat. But doing so would also be a direct insult to Wallace, Hanes's longtime friend and ally.

The trial began in late November, seventeen years after Hanes took over as Birmingham's mayor. It moved fast. A jury of nine whites and three African Americans—eight women and four men—heard the case and delivered a verdict in one week flat. The trial began with fireworks. On the first day of testimony, Baxley put Elizabeth Cobbs, Chambliss's niece, on the stand. In an outraged and confident tone, she recounted how Chambliss read in the paper about a young

African American man who was charged with cutting a white woman with a knife. "He said if he'd been there that man would have never gotten away with it," she testified. "'You wait until after Sunday. They'll beg us to let them segregate.'" When Cobbs returned to her uncle's house after the bombing, Chambliss was sitting at the television making excuses. "'It went off at the wrong time,'" she quoted Chambliss as saying. "'No one was suppose to get hurt.'"

The next witness was an African American woman from Detroit who was visiting a friend in Birmingham on the weekend of the bombing. Her friend lived across the street from the church, and when they returned to her home at 2:00 AM on Sunday, September 15, she saw white men parked across the street. One of them stood out. Later, she would pick him out of a stack of photographs shown to her by the FBI. His name was Robert Chambliss.

Hanes's son, Art Jr., did most of the work for the defense. He put twelve witnesses on the stand but never went for the jugular like his father might have done. He never attacked Baxley's political ambitions, nor did he claim, as his father did in nearly every case, that the bombing was the product of an international Communist plot. Instead, Art Jr. reminded the jury that "rough talk doesn't make murder." He described the state's case as "the same old stuff that got Bob Chambliss in this court fourteen years ago and acquitted." The decision went to the jury on the birthday of Denise McNair, the murdered child whom Huie profiled after the bombing. No sudden verdict emerged. A single juror refused to relent, and by nightfall, the 11–1 impasse seemed impossible to break. It appeared to be another Klan special—a hung jury held up by a committed racist. But the next morning, after sleeping it over, the holdout relented and word spread that a verdict had been reached.

At 10:30 AM on Friday, October 18, Chambliss was found guilty. Amens broke out across the scarred city of Birmingham. When order was restored, the judge asked Chambliss if he would like to make a statement before sentencing. "God knows, your honor, I never in my life bombed anything in my life," Chambliss pleaded. "And I was not down at the Sixteenth Street Baptist Church." The judge sentenced

Chambliss to life in prison, and editorials called it "Birmingham's Finest Hour." Others dubbed it "Belated Justice." Hanes Jr. viewed it differently though. "What a shame to put that whole thing on a 73-year-old man," he said. "I hope the verdict was reached for the right reasons. People wanted to believe in a new case. They wanted and hoped it would be solved."

Hanes Sr. stayed out of the limelight, except to appeal for a new trial. The hearing came on March 3, 1979, and that morning Hanes informed the judge that an anonymous caller threatened his life. Someone called his office and promised to blow his "fucking brains out" during that afternoon's hearing. With beefed-up security in the courtroom, the defense called Chambliss a "scapegoat to purge the collective consciousness of the people," though to no avail. Chambliss lost his appeal on May 22, 1979, and six days later the angry bomb-maker wrote to his wife, Flora. In a handwritten note, he claimed that Hanes and Connor, Birmingham's mayor and commissioner of public safety, knew "all about the Bombing" of the Sixteenth Street Baptist Church.

>>> >>> >>> ⫷⫷ ⫷⫷ ⫷⫷

The same Birmingham grand jury that indicted Robert Chambliss also brought charges against Stoner—but for a different church bombing. In 1958, a Klan informant approached Stoner about dyna-miting certain synagogues and churches affiliated with the civil rights movement. Eight days later, Mr. X and other Klansmen bombed Fred Shuttlesworth's church—the nerve center of the Birmingham move-ment—in expectation of a $2,000 payoff. Now, twenty years later, Stoner would finally be held accountable for the crime. As the trial began, Stoner lashed out from Georgia, where he continued to fight extradition to Alabama. In a remarkable piece of theater, he sud-denly went public with the Klan's dirty laundry, announcing that the same informant who approached him about bombing Shuttles-worth's church also offered him a bounty for taking King's life. "He insisted that I find a good marksman to kill King," Stoner claimed. "They wanted it done by rifle."

No one took Stoner seriously except for Congress. Testifying in secret before a congressional committee, Stoner later revealed that a high-ranking Klan official named William Hugh Morris—the informant who ratted Stoner out—offered Asa Carter and himself $25,000 for King's assassination. For $5,000 up front, Stoner told Morris that he would kill King with a bomb, but Morris declined. It had to be by rifle, Stoner testified. Morris was now an elderly man, but Congress dragged him to Washington for an explanation. He'd been in the Klan since 1924 but swore to have never commissioned a single act of violence. He described Stoner's accusation as retribution for his testimony in Stoner's upcoming trial. Asa Carter seemed to support Morris, not Stoner, testifying that threats on King's life were "commonplace," though he refused to provide specifics. Congress combed back through secret FBI files and discovered some disturbing parallels between Stoner's accusation and statements attributed to Morris during 1961, the year of the Bay of Pigs and the Mother's Day Riot.

> Nevertheless, in its review of the FBI files concerning Morris, the committee found several FBI intelligence reports, based on informant information, that indicated Morris, at an October 1961 Klan meeting, had said southern racial problems could be eliminated by the murder of Dr. King. Morris then apparently boasted that he had a New Orleans underworld associate who would kill anyone for a price. Under oath, Morris denied making these statements.

For undisclosed reasons, the committee dropped its inquiry into Stoner and Morris's feud because the allegations in question preceded the assassination by seven years. The only justice that came out of Morris's cooperation with law enforcement was Stoner's ultimate conviction for the 1958 church bombing. Ray's other Klan attorney received ten years in prison but only served three and a half.

38

The Grapevine
St. Louis to Washington, 1978

In 1977, the same year Robert Chambliss and J. B. Stoner were charged in the Birmingham bombings, James Earl Ray broke out of Brushy Mountain, a fortress high in the Appalachian Mountains of eastern Tennessee. The manhunt took ten National Guard helicopters, combing dangerous Appalachian ravines, and a pack of eager bloodhounds, hunting through the dense cover of hardwoods and rock outcroppings. No one had scaled those fifteen-foot walls in the prison's seventy-five-year history, but Ray and five others climbed over using a makeshift ladder made of miscellaneous piping. A guard in the tower shot the last man, but the rest squeezed underneath a two-thousand-volt electric fence to freedom.

The brazen escape drew scare headlines all across the nation, and two days into the hunt, Ray still had not been found. Some speculated that he might have fled the state or crossed the border into Mexico or Canada. Others believed he would finally make it to Rhodesia and join the white resistance. But on the third day, bloodhounds tracked him to a pile of leaves less than five miles from the penitentiary. He was hiding in nature's refuse, like "a pig wallowing in a sty." Authorities put him in handcuffs and stowed him away in solitary. The state then added three more years to his original ninety-nine.

Ten years had passed since Ray's escape from the Missouri State Penitentiary. The timing could not have been more precise. After years and years of futile court appeals and unsuccessful libel actions, Ray found himself with no other recourse. He was in the crosshairs of a multimillion-dollar congressional investigation tasked with getting to the bottom of the Kennedy and King assassinations. Public hearings would not come for more than a year, but Ray had already been deposed five times. Moreover, *Playboy* was soon to reveal the results of his voluntary lie-detector test. It showed that Ray killed King and acted alone.

The House Select Committee on Assassinations, as this new inquiry was called, picked up where previous investigations left off. Editorials described it as an inquisition of dregs—a replay of Garrison-like deceits that seemed to never die. It was more troubling, some pundits wrote, that the committee would seal its investigative materials after issuing a final report. Living journalists and historians could never question the findings. Had nothing been learned from the Warren Commission or Watergate?

A small crew of investigators combed through ten years of competing conspiracy allegations. They conducted major investigations in Memphis, New Orleans, Birmingham, Louisville, Miami, Texas, and New York. They investigated the Klan, the Minutemen, the NSRP, the CIA, the FBI, and an array of black militant groups. Hundreds of people received subpoenas and dozens testified in executive session—including Hanes. Only a select few (not including Hanes) would be brought back for public hearings that were set to begin in the summer of 1978. It seemed clear that the committee would simply drag Ray to Washington, give him the spotlight, and spend a week trying to debunk his lies. But then something no one could predict—a twist in the plot—emerged. A novel lead out of St. Louis, the city where Ray learned his criminal trade, changed the course of the conspiracy investigation.

〉〉〉 〉〉〉 〉〉〉 〈〈〈 〈〈〈 〈〈〈

It started with the heist of Frederic Remington's statue "Bronco Buster" in January 1978. A group of armed men broke into the St. Louis Art Museum—a freestanding marble masterpiece in the city's biggest park—twice in less than a month, only to escape each time with precious statues. Citizens wanted them returned, but the trail went cold for weeks, until late one February evening. That's when veteran St. Louis detectives Robert Downey and Larry Layton stormed into a rundown brownstone and arrested one of the burglars. After an interrogation, the suspect led them to a ranch-style home in suburban St. Louis, where a suspected hitman named Russell Byers lived. The house was raided and agents recovered a treasure trove of stolen art. The statues were recovered shortly thereafter.

That March, as the assassinations committee checked out conspiracy leads across the country, the St. Louis FBI was asked to check its holdings for dirt on Byers, a longtime suspect in high-profile heists and at least one murder. The FBI was under strict orders to send any assassination-related reports to Congress, and on March 13, a memorandum on Byers ended up in Washington by the end of the day. It had nothing to do with statues yet everything to do with King's murder. It originated from a routine informant's report on Byers from March 1974.

> Byers talked freely about himself and his business, and they later went to informant's house where Byers told a story about visiting a lawyer in St. Louis County, now deceased, not further identified, who had offered to give him a contract to kill Martin Luther King. He said that also present was a short, stocky man, who walked with a limp. (Later, with regard to the latter individual, Byers commented that this man was actually the individual who made the payoff of James Earl Ray after the killing.) Byers said he had declined to accept this contract. He did remark that this lawyer had Confederate flags and other items about the house that might indicate that he was a 'real rebel.' Byers also commented that he had been offered either $10,000 or $20,000 to kill King.

Extensive further research in the St. Louis indices and files failed to reveal this information was in any way disseminated and the information simply reposes in the informant file.

The proposition Byers described to FBI informant and art dealer Richard O'Hara, a business partner of sorts, occurred in the spring of 1967 as Ray escaped the state pen. No one had ever investigated the lead, even though the attorney referenced in the reports was a longtime St. Louis resident named John H. Sutherland. A Virginia transplant, Sutherland worked as a patent attorney for big midwestern corporations and government contractors. On the weekends, he enjoyed dressing up like a Confederate colonel at his riverside home in St. Louis County. He was an original member of the John Birch Society who played bridge with the son of founder Robert Welch. A hard-line segregationist, Sutherland started St. Louis's first White Citizens' Council after Congress passed the Civil Rights Act of 1964. At the first meeting, he announced to one hundred and twenty-five people that he wanted to bring Wallace to speak in St. Louis. "It's not exactly definite yet," Sutherland told his supporters, "but I am making every effort to have him here."

When Wallace couldn't make it, Sutherland settled for Selma sheriff Jim Clark and future Georgia governor Lester Maddox. Three years later, in 1967, Sutherland personally bankrolled Missouri's American Independent Party, Wallace's political arm, and got the candidate registered on Missouri's 1968 presidential ballot in record time. To acknowledge Sutherland's support, Wallace campaigned in the Show-Me State twice during the fall of 1967, making stops in Kansas City, Smithville, and two trips to St. Louis. Famously, Wallace spoke to the St. Louis Rotary Club, an organization Sutherland once served as president in twenty years of membership, and came away gloating, "They really liked me!"

Committee investigators pounced on the lead. They soon discovered that Ray's brother Jack and sister, Carol, might have a connection to Sutherland. In 1968, they were running a corner tavern in South St. Louis called The Grapevine. The name referred to the underground communication network criminals use to solicit and commission new crimes. When it opened in the winter of 1968, The Grapevine became what Huie—who had no knowledge of the Sutherland bounty—described as an "unofficial Wallace-for-President headquarters." Across the street lived the treasurer of the Missouri American Independent Party, a woman who worked closely with Sutherland. She held meetings at her home and patronized The Grapevine with other canvassers in the Third District.

The bar might have been an "unofficial" headquarters of the Wallace for President movement, but it was also an "official" distribution point for American Independent Party literature. More troubling, the day before Ray's escape, his brother Jack drove from The Grapevine to the state penitentiary in Jefferson City for a rare visit. The next morning, Sunday, April 23, Ray escaped prison just as Wallace announced his presidential candidacy on *Meet the Press*. After the assassination, reporters asked Jack about the timing. It seemed like a hell of a coincidence, and the ex-con just grinned. "He and I are both strong supporters of George C. Wallace," Jack told the press, "so maybe we talked about him a little."

⋙ ⋙ ⋙ ⋘ ⋘ ⋘

The problem with The Grapevine investigation was that Sutherland and John Kauffmann, the stocky bald man who supposedly gave Ray the payoff, both died in the early seventies. Sutherland's wife was alive, but when investigators confronted her with the allegation, she stood by her man. Sure, he might have been the brains and bank behind a plethora of segregationist causes in Missouri—including the NSRP and the St. Louis Property Owners Association, which brought Stoner to Missouri in 1964—but he was not a killer. Nor was he in the Klan, she pleaded.

That put the committee in the awkward position of trying to confirm Byers's story without access to the lead suspects. It got harder in July 1968, when two *New York Times* reporters appeared at Byers's home in Rock Hill asking about the Sutherland bounty. Having already testified in executive session, Byers would only speak to one of them because he wanted to be able to deny the conversation later if Congress held him in contempt. The story appeared on the front page of the *Times*, and on the record, Byers confirmed being offered "$50,000," not ten or twenty thousand, for killing King.

Almost immediately, the FBI denounced the story as "hearsay three times removed," likely fabricated to finger FBI informant Richard O'Hara. That criticism became less persuasive when a local judge, Murry Randall, and a St. Louis defense attorney, Lawrence Weenick, backed up Byers's story. On several occasions before 1978, Byers told both lawyers about the Sutherland bounty, but they said nothing because of attorney-client privilege. The committee also interviewed two anonymous sources close to Kauffman, the "payoff" man. These unnamed witnesses described Sutherland's bounty on King as common knowledge. So if Byers was trying to finger the FBI's informant, why would he tell the story to at least three different people? And how could individuals not associated with Byers have heard about it?

In November 1978, Byers was subpoenaed against his will—he tried to fight it—to become the star witness of the public hearings. He was introduced by the chairman of the assassinations committee, Louis Stokes, who noted that the FBI received fifty threats on King's life before the assassination, but the committee narrowed those down to six concrete leads. Only one of the six revealed any kind of legitimate circumstantial evidence. "The conspiratorial allegation that has received the most attention from the committee originated in St. Louis earlier this year," Stokes read, "when the FBI advised it of a memorandum containing information on a concrete offer to pay money to kill Dr. King." With that, Byers took the stage and invoked his right to ban all cameras from the chamber. He cut right to the chase: the encounter with Sutherland occurred at 6:30 PM one afternoon in the spring of 1967, around the time Ray escaped prison. Payoff man Kauffman, a crooked stockbroker who was also running an illegal amphetamine racket that fed drugs to prison inmates like Ray, asked Byers if he would be interested in making $50,000. Byers said absolutely. He assumed it would require an illegal transaction, and together they drove to Sutherland's house on Wolf Hollow Road in Imperial, Missouri, to learn more.

"Mr. Sutherland met us at the door with a pair of like overalls and a hat," Byers testified. "Looked like a Confederate hat, with crossed swords. He took us to a den with a Confederate carpet, Confederate flag, bugles, swords, and all the paraphernalia hanging on the wall."

Sutherland's wife was in the house and Byers was offered a drink.

"Well, we got into it. We got down to business. I said, 'What do I have to do to make $50,000?' He says, 'Either arrange or kill Martin Luther King.' At that point I said, 'Who is Martin Luther King?' I didn't know who he was."

The investigation might have ended right there. Byers was thirty-six years old at the time. He could tell a Rockwell from a Rembrandt but expected the nation to believe that he didn't know the existence of King in the spring of 1967. It was a ridiculous lie. King won the Nobel Peace Prize in 1964 and appeared hundreds of times on television. Yet for some reason, the committee let it go and accepted the broader truth of Byers's testimony. The final report diagrammed four ways that Sutherland's bounty might have reached Ray in prison. The most convincing was the notion that it passed through his brother's Third District tavern, The Grapevine.

》》 》》 》》 《《 《《 《《

The HSCA's final report also cited a handful of prisoner interviews completed by the FBI *after* the assassination. Several of these prisoners claimed that Ray obsessed over killing "Martin Lucifer Coon." One alleged that Ray expected $10,000 to $100,000 for taking King out from "a businessman's association" or "Cooley's gang." But as with Byers's story, no proof was offered, and all of the committee's sources—especially the prisoners—were nothing if not questionable.

Ray himself made multiple public appearances but failed to crack under oath. For months he milked the spotlight and seemed as comfortable lying to congressmen as to his own attorneys, even after investigators caught him by surprise when they raided his brother's hotel room and found a sketch of Ray's newest escape plan. Overwhelmingly,

Ray won the publicity battle. Between appearances, he drew attention away from the hearings by marrying an eccentric courtroom artist named Anna Sandhu. The Reverend James Lawson, the same Memphis preacher who asked King to lead that final march in Memphis, united Ray and Sandhu in matrimony, and the *National Enquirer* offered Ray thousands of dollars for exclusive photos of the wedding.

This disturbing charade took emphasis off other compelling witnesses. Though conspiracy was never proven, Ray's racial motive became more apparent. The testimony of Scotland Yard detective Alexander Eist was particularly damaging. Eist had never spoken publicly about what he knew, so his sudden appearance proved meaningful. Eist was the only person to befriend Ray while in British custody. He earned Ray's trust by helping him acquire eating utensils and magazines during confinement. Over time, Ray relaxed, and so did his tongue. "He never really told me he pulled the trigger or anything like that," Eist testified. But Ray did admit that "he panicked and threw the gun away."

Eist also attested to Ray's guarded racism. He noted that when the American spoke of blacks he called them "niggers," and "he told me that he tried to get into Africa at some stage—he said to kill more of them." Eist noted that Ray repeatedly contacted a British journalist who covered white mercenaries for the *Times* of London. Ray called the reporter on multiple occasions asking for contacts in Rhodesia. He also flew to Portugal for the sole purpose of boarding a ship to white Africa, but it didn't pan out. While in Lisbon, he contacted the Rhodesian Diplomatic Mission and the South African Embassy, and a few weeks later, at the moment of his Heathrow capture on June 8, Ray was two flights away from Salisbury, Rhodesia, by way of Brussels.

Ray, of course, denied everything, including a long-standing rumor that he and his brothers robbed the Bank of Alton during the summer of 1967. Such a finding would have explained how Ray financed the assassination and why he immediately opened that safe deposit box in Birmingham. It would explain how he could afford the Mustang and the hotel rooms. By the end of the year, as the public hearings ended, committee investigators were begging for more time to nail down Ray's connection to Sutherland and his source of money. Unfortunately, Washington's patience had run out. The dual inquiries—there was also one conducted on Kennedy's assassination—cost $5.4 million and created twenty-seven volumes of published material.

The Kennedy report—686 pages in length—concluded that a conspiracy also existed in the president's assassination. Using a previously unknown audio recording, investigators hired experts who determined that at least four shots were fired as the president's motorcade passed through Dealey Plaza. Oswald only fired three, the evidence clearly showed, and a host of witnesses took the stage to claim that additional shots came from the grassy knoll, not the book depository. The bottom line: both the Kennedy and King assassinations "likely" resulted from well-executed conspiracies involving politically motivated criminals.

39

Walking It Back
Hartselle, Alabama, 1977–1978

The assassinations report was a slap in the face to the FBI. A year earlier, the bureau publicly released its first internal investigation of what it called the MURKIN case since Hoover's death in 1972. The impetus for the investigation came from public statements made by William Sullivan, one of Hoover's top lieutenants, who described the FBI's counterintelligence program against King, dubbed COINTELPRO, by saying that "no holds were barred." Hoover zealously sabotaged any person or organization suspected of Communist or terrorist sympathies, including the civil rights movement and the Klan. Thousands of people were targeted, but perhaps only Fidel Castro—whom the FBI and CIA repeatedly tried to kill—received worse treatment than King.

Internal FBI files show that Hoover used techniques reserved for "Soviet agents" to discredit and neutralize King. In fact, Attorney General Bobby Kennedy authorized Hoover to tap King's phone in October 1963, just weeks after the Sixteenth Street Baptist Church Bombing. Kennedy approved the measure because the FBI suspected that King's closest white associate, a car dealer named Stanley Levison, was really a Soviet spy with long-standing ties to the Communist Party. By 1964, Hoover convinced himself that King himself was a Communist, if not a Soviet spy. Subsequently, the FBI investigated King's private life and mailed Coretta proof of his many infidelities. As insurance, Hoover acquired a fifteen-reel sex tape, a recording so salacious that a federal judge later put it under seal for fifty years. The tape revealed an "uproarious party" at the Willard Hotel, a stone's throw from the White House, where FBI microphones captured King making drunken, "ribald" comments, before picking up sounds of people having sex in the same hotel room. As if the Klan threats on King's life weren't serious enough, the FBI joined in by sending King threatening letters, one of which urged him to commit suicide.

》》》 》》》 》》》 《《《 《《《 《《《

Scrutiny of governmental conspiracies in the King and Kennedy assassinations opened a window of opportunity for Huie. He was eager to recover what amounted to nearly $100,000 in losses—travel expenses and legal fees—on the Ray case. Instead of becoming the true-crime bestseller of a generation, *He Slew the Dreamer* was enjoined by a judge in the spring of 1969. When the book was finally printed in May 1970, it flopped, grossing less than $5,000 in sales. Huie had not published much nonfiction since. A trilogy of "serious" novels was in the works, but Huie also wanted to reestablish himself as a journalist on the national stage, and he viewed these congressional witchhunts as an opportunity to recoup his losses. Unfortunately, the layoff killed his platform, and ultimately, he could only convince a Nashville, not New York, publisher to rerelease *He Slew the Dreamer* under a more salacious title: *Did the FBI Kill Martin Luther King?*

Ninety-nine percent of the book was a reprint of *Dreamer.* The only new part consisted of an introduction in which Huie retold the origin of his friendship with King, how during the Montgomery Bus Boycott he sat in a pew at the Dexter Avenue Baptist Church, put money in the collection plate, and came to know one of history's great change-agents. "In all I must have spent six hours in one-on-one conversation with him. . . . We discussed strategy for the movement," Huie claimed.

The fact that King penned a preface for *Three Lives for Mississippi* proves the relationship. However, Huie may have invented a key scene that had suddenly become topical. Huie recalled sitting in a pew when an anonymous parishioner, an older woman, approached him with some disquieting gossip. She said that King was turning out to be "something of a rounder." Troubled by the news, Huie brought it to his friend's attention. "It was not until our last conversation that I mentioned sex," Huie wrote. "I told Reverend King what I had heard and when he offered no comment I said, 'I'm not insisting that this is any of my business, but I'll say what we both know is true: if you continue to . . . to forage among the sisterhood . . . you'll be vulnerable to your enemies.'"

King apparently did not respond but became pensive at Huie's cold turkey.

"Don't you do it?"

"Yes. I do a modest amount of it. But then I'm not a reverend."

Huie assured his readers that Hoover had nothing to do with King's murder. To promote this "new" book, he wrote an article for *Atlanta Magazine*—the lucrative contracts with *Look* and *Esquire* were no longer an option—and claimed to have never considered the idea that Ray acted as part of a conspiracy. Instead, he compared Ray to Byron De La Beckwith Jr., killer of NAACP field officer Medgar Evers, then conveniently omitted that his book on Ray was originally titled *They Slew the Dreamer*. Huie also invented an appropriate reaction from one of his editors on the night of the assassination. "Around 7:00 PM on April 4, 1968, I was called again," Huie wrote. "'They've killed Dr. King!'" Huie, ever sober-minded and cautious, warned the unnamed editor from New York about going headlong down the road of conspiracy. "'Not *they* but *he*,' I said. 'He's another Beckwith. He thinks he'll be an international hero. So you can be sure he left plenty of calling cards.'" The editor called back sometime later to confer on Huie the crown of righteousness, citing evidence that, miraculously, had not even been made public. "'Did *he* leave calling cards! Not only the fingerprinted rifle, scope and binoculars, but even his transistor radio with his prison number carved into it!'"

》》》 》》》 》》》 《《《 《《《 《《《

Another article in the April 1977 issue of *Skeptic* found Huie engaging in a one-sided argument with an unidentified member of the assassinations committee: "An 'investigating' congressman tells us on television, 'We must remember that Ray quickly *rescinded* his guilty plea!' You think that's significant, do you, Congressman? You think Ray's rescinding his plea justifies an expensive new investigation? Nonsense." But Huie's hostility toward Congress did not deter investigators from arriving in Hartselle to threaten him with a subpoena. Huie had already been interviewed once in 1977, and in April 1978, a six-hour interrogation ensued.

The investigators' notes reveal that Huie discussed some leads that he withheld from the Memphis grand jury in February 1969. The most notable was his now-admitted interest in Klansman Asa Carter, who had since reinvented himself as a bestselling author of *The Education of Little Tree*, a touching Native American "memoir" that Carter invented out of whole cloth. Wallace's speechwriter now lived in Texas and called himself "Forrest Carter," a tribute to Ku Klux Klan founder Nathan Bedford Forrest. Based partly on Huie's remarks, Carter would be interviewed in executive session by committee investigators, but no transcript of his testimony would ever reach the public. Notes from the interview with Huie simply read: "He also tried to find some connection between Ray and Ace Carter, Wallace's chief speech writer, but was unsuccessful."

Huie could not have known in 1969 or 1978 that the FBI found Carter hanging out with Stoner in Jackson, Mississippi, weeks after King's assassination. In a brief, tense interview, Carter was blunt:

> He mentioned that he would cooperate with the FBI if he obtained information that communists or other subversive elements were responsible for any of the bombings and violence which have occurred in the southern states in recent years; however, if he knew or felt that the violence or bombings were perpetrated by local people acting emotionally and through frustration, he would not cooperate with the FBI.

Why Huie gave up on Carter is unknown. But ten years later he still wondered whether someone in Birmingham helped Ray, though he mentioned nothing of Albert Persons, General Doster, or the Bay of Pigs angle. Nor did he cast suspicion on Hanes, whom he credited with revealing that Ray "stopped in Birmingham for an hour and a half on the way back to Atlanta after the assassination," though he did not explain how Hanes could have reached this conclusion. The investigator's notes provided little explanation: "Hanes did not ask Ray any questions about the stop, and evidently Huie did not instruct Hanes to ask him. Huie tried to locate someone in Birmingham who could substantiate the stopover, but he was unsuccessful." After years of reflection, Huie now felt that Ray " 'could' have met with Stoner in Birmingham in 1967. Again he has no evidence," the notes read.

Huie said his relationship with Hanes was professional but never close. "Huie figures that he knew everything Hanes knew since this full exchange of information was what the contracts signed by Hanes, Huie, and Ray stipulated," the notes read. Huie said Hanes "knew that the FBI had tape recordings of some of King's sexual affairs. Although Hanes did not have the tapes in his possession, he intended to get them and use them in the trial to show that a jealous husband may have had a better reason for killing King than Ray had." Moreover, Hanes told Huie that Ray test-fired the rifle in Mississippi hours before the killing. "As far as Huie knows, Hanes never asked Ray why he fired the rifle if he had no intention of killing King," the notes read. "In fact, Huie minimizes the amount of investigation Hanes did for the case. Hanes was interested in defending Ray, not in finding the truth."

Huie felt embarrassed by his failure to find a conspiracy. Going down that New Orleans rabbit hole wasted time that he should have spent in Birmingham. "For about one week during 1968 or 1969," the notes read, "Huie thought that the FBI might arrest a Greek in New Orleans who frequented Le Bunny Lounge." When the intrigue of conspiracy wore off, Huie convinced himself that Ray "had a racial motive for killing King." That's why the assassin bought the rifle in Birmingham, Huie believed. "Ray would have preferred to kill King in Alabama because of Wallace. Ray thought Wallace might be willing to pardon the murderer of a famous civil rights leader." In documenting the six-hour conversation, investigators never mentioned the name "John H. Sutherland," the man in St. Louis they believed was offering a bounty for King's head.

For cooperating, Huie would not be subpoenaed to testify in executive session or during the public hearings. He was getting off easy, but not cheap. His second attempt to sell the anticonspiracy of James Earl Ray flopped as bad as the first.

40

The Klan?
Washington, 1978

Hanes must have wondered what the hell it was all about. On June 7, 1978, he too received a subpoena to testify in executive session before the assassinations committee. There was no way to fight it without going to jail because Ray waived Hanes's privilege. Unlike Huie, Hanes would have to go to Washington; Washington was not coming to him. Any doubts that he might have harbored about the line of questioning disappeared on arrival. The committee put him in a queue alongside his Tuscaloosa clients, Imperial Wizard Shelton and former grand dragon Melvin Sexton, who made consecutive congressional appearances in as many decades.

None realized that a Klansman using the alias George Wilson, described as "a former midwestern leader of the Klan," had come forward and told the committee that Shelton paid $10,000 to Ray's defense "under the pretense of paying for Hanes's legal representation of a group of North Carolina Klansmen." Wilson said the money was really a payoff to Hanes, but he did not, however, suggest that Hanes played a role in any type of conspiracy. To confirm Wilson's allegation, investigators found "two documents in the FBI file covering the murder of Dr. King" which "indicated that two sources independently corroborated some of Wilson's information." Source A said

Shelton planned to "review the jury list" for Ray's trial, and Source B said Hanes attended a Klan board meeting in Tuscaloosa to discuss his $12,000 fee in the North Carolina case. The report said Hanes left the meeting early, and the grand dragon of Alabama "allegedly commented on the King assassination and said he had a piece of paper for Hanes pertaining to the Ray case." Though no record of Hanes's testimony was made public, the final report makes clear that he vigorously denied these allegations. His Tuscaloosa buddies did the same, and finding the truth ten years later was all but impossible.

Still, it naturally led to much bigger questions. Congress simply could not answer why Hoover did not dig deeper on Hanes during the assassination investigation: "The committee was unable to locate any FBI documents indicating that the Bureau attempted to interview Hanes, Shelton, [Grand Dragon Melvin] Sexton, or other principals concerning cooperation between the Klan and Hanes during Ray's trial. . . . While the committee was unable ultimately to resolve all conflicts in the evidence, it found no indications of an agreement between the Klan and James Earl Ray prior to Dr. King's assassination. The committee concluded that there was no evidence that Ray and members of the United Klans of America entered into a conspiracy to assassinate Dr. King."

More importantly, finding one connection between patent attorney Sutherland and Hanes would have raised plenty of eyebrows, but no arm of government made an attempt to do so. It may one day prove to be a fatal oversight because Hanes and Sutherland had several attributes in common. Both identified themselves as Wallace loyalists and served as Wallace's presidential electors, Hanes in 1964, Sutherland in 1968. Both held leadership roles in the White Citizens' Council and in sensitive governmental roles at various points in their careers, Sutherland as a patent attorney and Hanes as an executive at Hayes Aircraft. Both lived respectable lives as attorneys and took great pains to disguise their racism with respectability while actively investing both money and time to stop integration and Communism.

In its zeal to prove a conspiracy, the assassinations committee failed to grasp the deep connections between the Wallace apparatus and the

Klan. Some basic research would have shown that Wallace personally ordered Imperial Wizard Shelton and Klan speechwriter Asa Carter to canvass the Midwest—Sutherland's turf—during the 1968 election. It would have been nice to know if those four men ever showed up together at the same function. Putting Sutherland, Shelton, Carter, and Hanes in the same room would have been difficult, but a closer look at press reports from 1967 gives plausibility to the possibility. On the night of January 16, 1967, for example, Lurleen Wallace was inaugurated as Alabama's first female governor, but she held no ball because of the war in Vietnam. Still, segregationists from all over descended on the capital of the Confederacy to congratulate Alabama's new governor, and a select few—two dozen leaders from four "Southern" states—met secretly inside Woodley Country Club in Montgomery to start planning Wallace's third-party run for the presidency. Those present received personal invitations from Asa Carter and Sheriff Clark. Whether Hanes and Sutherland were there remains unknown. But one thing is clear. Not everybody at that meeting was from a "Southern" state because Floyd Kitchen, who soon began receiving his $600 per month salary directly from Sutherland, was in the room that night.

Kitchen ran Missouri's American Independent Party, and he did more than just run the St. Louis effort. As the 1968 campaign progressed, Kitchen was promoted to Wallace's "national staff," and in this new role, he "directed the candidate's 1968 campaign tour of Florida." It was Kitchen, not Sutherland, who greeted Wallace on the tarmac in St. Louis during a campaign stop, and like Sutherland, he also served as a Wallace elector in Missouri. He did this all while living less than two miles from Ray's sister Carol, owner of The Grapevine tavern.

Today, Kitchen lives in a very modest home in suburban St. Louis. Despite multiple entreaties, he refuses to discuss his relationship with Wallace and Sutherland. In a cryptic letter, he writes that he "can't help." Ask details concerning the Woodley Country Club conference of 1967, or anything else regarding the Wallace for President campaign, and you'll learn that the one man who might have credible information about a conspiracy to kill Martin Luther King Jr. is working on a book about the 1968 election "when I get time."

41

Full Circle
Alabama, 1980s

Huie died over his typewriter in November 1986. He dedicated the last years of his life to an ambitious and unfinished trilogy of novels. Collectively, the three works would explain how the greatest generation in history could so quickly "blow it." In 1975, a subsidy of *Look* published the first book, *In the Hours of the Night*, a revisiting of his investigations of the Eisenhower administration through the eyes of a hero named Frank Castleton. The other two books were never published, but the second one, *The Adversary*, exists in Huie's original draft. In short, the Castleton character becomes appalled at the immoral behavior of a thinly disguised President John F. Kennedy. One critic, to whom Huie provided a sneak preview, described the novel's plot this way: "Castleton discovers a lying, laying, America-betraying President John F. Kennedy whose cowardly bungling of the CIA's Bay of Pigs project is only a prelude to the bloody inflationary mess into which he and his Wall Street banker counselors lead the nation."

The manuscript shows that Huie created a major character named "General Reed" and pitted him against President Kennedy. The two engage in a bitter disagreement regarding the lack of air cover during the failed Bay of Pigs invasion. Amazingly, it appears that Huie evolved from accusing General Doster of being complicit in the King assassination to making him a sympathetic figure in a war novel. The inspiration likely came from his association with Albert Persons and Art Hanes in 1968 and 1969. "Now I knew why General Reed was protesting on Thursday," Huie's manuscript reads. "Kennedy had ordered him to send only nine bombers on Thursday. But why? Castro had ten warplanes, including two jets. He had six fields on which one or more of those planes might be hidden. . . . Then why, on the crucial first strike, had Kennedy restricted General Reed to nine bombers?"

This obsession with Birmingham's link to the Bay of Pigs makes Huie's partnership with Hanes, a lifelong friend of Doster, more enigmatic. A closer look at their association in the Ray case reveals at least one major contradiction that should have easily been resolved by Congress. Both Hanes and Huie always claimed their partnership began when Huie picked up the phone, called Hanes, and brokered the deal. Only once did the story line change. In August 1979, an interviewer for the PBS documentary *Eyes on the Prize* quoted Huie making an important contradiction. "Art Hanes got in touch with me, 'cause he'd never been to London and he didn't have the money," Huie said. "And, I gave Hanes $10,000 and helped him go to London and made a deal with Ray then, and Hanes for Ray to tell me the truth about whether or not he killed Dr. King. And that's how I came to write a book called *He Slew the Dreamer*, which cost me an enormous amount of money."

The accuracy of this statement is suspect at best. Huie may have just been continuing his revisionist campaign to cover up his authorship of the Raoul canard. But a harder look by Congress would have cleared up any doubt or speculation that Hanes pinned Huie as the foil in a grander scheme. Think about it. If Hanes—an FBI agent, CIA asset, and Klan lawyer—was involved in a conspiracy with Ray, his partnership with Huie would have made the crime nearly perfect. Imagine a better premise: the foremost critic of Wallace is hoodwinked into paying for the assassination of Martin Luther King, Wallace's number one enemy.

》》》 》》》 》》》 《《《 《《《 《《《

Huie saved his strangest writing project for last. He saved it for Wallace, the devil he could never slay. As some African Americans in Alabama graciously accepted the governor's apology, Huie continued to harangue the paralyzed governor without remorse. That is until Wallace approached Huie, in the early eighties, with an olive branch.

> I went in to see Wallace. I met him for the first time. I sat right close to him at the desk because his hearing is impaired. And good lord, with all his hangers on listening Wallace and I talked for close to four hours. We talked about a lot of things. . . . Wallace stunned his own lawyers, who were present there, by announcing that if anyone made a television film about him that he wanted me to write it.
>
> He was later chastised by his lawyers, his wisdom was questioned, and his lawyer said to him in effect, "What the hell do you want that son-of-a-bitch to write the story for? He's never been anything but your most effective enemy. He's never done anything but denounce you publicly during the forty lectures a year he delivers across the country, he's always treated you with contempt."

Huie and Wallace did indeed forge a deal to write a screenplay for television. To flesh out the details, Wallace called Huie's home "12 or 15 times." Each time the phone rang, Huie's "90-year-old mother" answered the call. "My mother acquired a high regard for the governor because of the way he talked with her," Huie said. "We would be talking two-and-a-half hours later and so I talked to George Wallace perhaps a total of thirty hours. . . . As unbelievable as it may sound, I listened and found what the governor told me was interesting."

One person who did not care for the idea was Wallace's second, much-younger wife, Cornelia. Having recently divorced the governor, she sued Wallace and Huie for cutting her out of the screenplay, which she claimed was her idea. And that's essentially how Huie's journalism career ended, in a lawsuit with his fast friend and codefendant, George Corley Wallace. They were strange bedfellows indeed.

EPILOGUE: MEMPHIS, 1993–1999

Art Hanes lived until May 1994, long enough to see his bushman theory of the King assassination go mainstream. Any chance to field calls from journalists, lawyers, and would-be sleuths was a chance to sanitize his legacy and to argue Ray's innocence. He was not a defeated man, but to the end of his life, he fought for the defeated cause of segregation. Wallace may have begged African Americans for forgiveness, but Hanes made it clear that he would never apologize for what happened on his watch as mayor of Birmingham. "I'll buy anybody a double-breasted Kuppenheimer of his choice if he can prove anybody had their skin broken by a police dog here," Hanes said. "Actually, the situation wasn't handled too badly. We didn't turn any automatic weapons on those black folks. We used the fire hose, but that was just to cool them down a little bit."

It must have satisfied him immensely when, the year before his death, HBO began filming a "mock trial" in the modernized Memphis courthouse where Ray pled guilty in 1969. This $3 million media spectacle was sold to the public as Ray's first rendezvous with justice, and its well-paid participants included a former federal judge, a former US attorney, and PBS host Charlayne Hunter-Gault, the first African American woman to integrate the University of Georgia. This Hollywood saga, entitled *Guilt or Innocence: The Trial of James Earl Ray*, started in late January 1993, presented dozens of key witnesses, and lasted ten days. The verdict remained secret for two months, in anticipation of Sunday, April 4, the twenty-fifth anniversary of King's assassination.

Ray was now sixty-five years old. In 1981, he survived a savage attack by black inmates who stabbed him twenty-two times inside the Brushy Mountain library. That near-death experience allowed him to transfer to the Riverbend Maximum Security Institution in Nashville, where he participated in the HBO trial by testifying remotely. Not surprisingly, he sold the mock jury—a diverse pool of jurors from all over the country—the same old medicine. Wearing thick glasses and sporting something of a crew cut, Ray spoke with a strange intonation, pitching his words in quick, plainspoken phrases that seemed rehearsed. Mostly, he stammered along by playing the part of a patsy and putting the blame on Raoul, whom the jury was later told hired Ray to traffic guns to Cuban rebels out of New Orleans. Ray said he purchased the rifle in Birmingham for that purpose and rented the apartment in Bessie Brewer's rooming house on those instructions. Hours before the assassination, Raoul had kicked him out to conduct some confidential business; Ray said he spent the afternoon drinking beer in Jim's Grill, directly below the rooming house. He was sitting there at 6:01 PM when someone, possibly Raoul, fired the shot.

The prosecutor's cross-examination did little to establish a racial motive. Wallace was mentioned just once, Hanes not at all. Competent witnesses like FBI agents George Bonebrake and Neil Shanahan, as well as Memphis detective N. E. Zachary and ballistics expert Donald Champagne, established Ray's guilt beyond a reasonable doubt, but the defense team led the jury astray by questioning the ballistics and putting the FBI's well-documented harassment of Dr. King on trial. As Hanes had long argued, an alternative narrative involving black militants and an unidentified bushman shooter with possible CIA connections could generate some reasonable doubt.

In support of that narrative, *New York Times* reporter Earl Caldwell, who was staying at the Lorraine Motel the night of the assassination, suddenly claimed to have also seen a mysterious figure in the bushes just seconds after the shooting. His surprising testimony—which contradicted his original account—gave yet another voice to what was becoming the grassy knoll of Memphis. To add texture, the defense deposed a Memphis police officer who claimed to have identified a fresh footprint in the bushes on the night of April 4. Before it could be cast, the jury was told, workers for the Memphis Public Works department showed up the morning of April 5 and cut down the bushes, contaminating the crime scene.

Never mind that such "evidence" had no basis in fact. The bushes weren't cut down for six months, but after all, entertainment is not justice. And on the evening of April 4, 1993, HBO subscribers tuned in for the drama, not truth. The marathon trial was pared down to three hours, allowing the show to move quickly. After closing arguments, the jury, which had deliberated for ten hours in February, delivered its unanimous verdict: not guilty. Back in Birmingham, Hanes must have celebrated proudly. The defendant's testimony, which Hanes would have never allowed in a real trial, ironically saved the day.

》》 》》 》》 《《 《《 《《

The architect of Ray's mock trial was William Pepper, an American lawyer with a British accent. During the Vietnam War, Pepper visited various medical centers around Saigon to document what was happening to "The Children of Vietnam," as his article in the January 1967 issue of *Ramparts* magazine was titled. The photographs and reporting touched Dr. King immensely, sparking a friendship that culminated in King's controversial antiwar speech at Riverside Church on April 4, 1967—exactly one year before the assassination. "Somehow this madness must cease," King spoke. "We must stop now. I speak as a child of God and brother to the suffering poor of Vietnam. I speak for those whose land is being laid waste, whose homes are being destroyed, whose culture is being subverted."

Pepper could not accept the coincidence. He convinced himself that someone in the intelligence community killed King for his opposition to Vietnam. In February 1979, as the assassinations committee sealed its evidence, Pepper showed up in Birmingham to begin his own inquiry. One of his first sources was Hanes, who gladly explained the intricacies of the bushman theory. Seven years later, in 1985, Pepper succeeded Mark Lane, a notorious peddler of CIA complicity in both the Kennedy and King assassinations, as Ray's top lawyer. Pepper's genius was to take conspiracy out of the courts, Lane's specialty, and into the media. By 1989, he'd convinced the BBC to produce a disingenuous documentary called *Inside Story: Who Killed Martin Luther King?* It came complete with a self-described CIA assassin and a litany of schizophrenic diatribes. Pepper and Lane followed that up with Ray's first book, *Who Killed Martin Luther King? The True Story by the Alleged Assassin.* Reverend Jesse Jackson, who witnessed King's death, wrote the foreword, claiming "I have a strong sense that there was a government conspiracy to kill Martin Luther King Jr."

From lawyers in his past, to judges in his future, Ray's book slandered everyone involved with his Memphis prosecution—everyone except for Hanes, the one stakeholder who actually worked for the CIA. It was a mysterious oversight, or a remarkable show of restraint, especially considering that the *New York Times* had exposed Hanes's participation in the Bay of Pigs in November 1968. Focusing on Hanes's ties to the FBI and CIA, not to mention the Klan, would have created a much more compelling case of conspiracy. But Ray's duplicity, his most apparent trait, simply did not extend to Hanes.

The book was still on shelves in 1993 when HBO ran its three-hour exoneration. Subsequent publicity fueled a media blitz that brought out a dark and bountiful crop of new bushman allegations. No matter how unreliable the source, Pepper and Ray found a way to incorporate the lead into an evolving, throw-it-against-the-wall narrative of CIA-backed conspiracy.

And yet, the most compelling of these post-HBO allegations actually held a grain of truth. In the spring of 1993, Stephen Tompkins, a reporter for the *Commercial Appeal*, established as fact that soldiers from the 111th Military Intelligence Group, based in Atlanta, monitored King's ill-fated sanitation workers demonstration of March 28, 1968. To help Memphis police prepare for a possible riot, several of these soldiers stayed in town through the assassination. That much was true, but Tompkins didn't stop there. Using anonymous sources and no attribution, the story alleged that a secret Green Beret unit—Operation Detachment Alpha 184—had also been dispatched to Memphis before April 4. This "A-team" of the 20th Special Forces Group, a Birmingham outfit, had "often spied on King and other black Americans during the 1960s, military records and interviews show," Tompkins reported.

Pepper seized on this lead and hired Tompkins to walk it out. In 1995, they released *Orders to Kill*, which included a pivotal chapter exposing Alpha 184. Readers were told that this elite Birmingham unit had completed lethal missions in American cities like Los Angeles, Detroit, Washington, and Chicago and had quietly assassinated black militants engaged in Communist-style rioting. So it was no coincidence, Pepper surmised, that Alpha 184 arrived in Memphis at 4:30 AM on April 4, 1968. They spent the day scouting the area for the right vantage, and by 6:00 PM, everything was in place. "Down near the railroad tracks," Pepper wrote, "a two-man 'recon' unit met with a 'spook' (army slang for CIA)" that led them "to a tall building that dominated that downtown area and loomed over the Lorraine." Pepper continued: "On the order, they were to shoot to kill—'body mass' (center, chest cavity)—Dr. Martin Luther King, Jr., and to my surprise, the Reverend Andrew Young . . . They were shown 'target acquisition photos' of the two men and the Lorraine Motel."

It took two years for anyone to scrutinize this suspicious claim. After all, the railroad reference should have conjured up memories of the three tramps captured in Dealey Plaza's rail yard. On multiple occasions, Pepper brazenly repeated his libel on national television, but interviewers like Montel Williams never penned him down on the proof. Justice finally came in June 1997, when ABC's *Turning Point* located former members of the 20th Special Forces Group and flew them to New York. Pepper was ambushed, live, and confronted by the unit's commander, Billy Eidson, whom Pepper had slandered as a racist and written off as dead. "I think you may owe the American people an apology," journalist Forrest Sawyer declared, after proving that documents and sources on which Pepper and Tompkins based their account were forgeries.

Perhaps the most remarkable part of the Alpha 184 fabrication is the reluctance by Ray and Pepper to exploit an angle on Birmingham, home of the 20th Special Forces Group, the Alabama Air National Guard, General Doster, Albert Persons, Matt Murphy, Gary Thomas Rowe, or Art Hanes. It must have occurred to Ray that Birmingham's unique history of white terrorism and Cold War intrigue set the perfect scene for a thriller of violent revenge and conspiratorial denouement. Why Hanes and Birmingham remained off-limits to Ray's destructive imagination and general vindictiveness remains a mystery.

>>> >>> >>> <<< <<< <<<

Like his hero Jim Garrison, Pepper abided no shame. In his world, ABC's takedown simply proved that the conspiracy had more layers. King's family shared the sentiment, and under Pepper's intoxicating influence, Dexter King, the youngest son, confronted Ray in Nashville on March 27, 1997, the year before the prisoner's death.

"I want to ask for the record: Did you kill my father?" Dexter asked.

"No, I didn't, no, no," Ray replied.

"I believe you, and my family believes you, and we will do everything in our power to see you prevail," Dexter vowed, shaking Ray's hand for the cameras.

Ray's liver was failing, and shortly thereafter he was admitted to intensive care. In April 1998, thirty years after the assassination, he went into a coma and died. The announcement of his death, combined with Pepper's conviction in his innocence, spawned a final push to prove Ray's innocence. Coretta Scott King had always believed in a giant conspiracy, so she asked President Bill Clinton to conduct a final investigation. The Civil Rights Division of the Justice Department accepted the charge, but as its inquiry began, Pepper filed a civil suit on behalf of the King family's estate for the tort of murder. The defendant's name was Lloyd Jowers, owner of Jim's Grill in Memphis.

Months after the HBO trial in 1993, Jowers confessed to King's murder on national television but few took him seriously. Intoxicated by the prospect of making millions, Jowers contradicted twenty-five years of his own testimony and suddenly claimed to have been recruited by a Memphis grocer named Frank Liberto, a known racist with a loud mouth, to complete a $100,000 contract on King's life. It took five more years—and the ruination of innocent people's lives—for Jowers to get his story straight, but he finally settled on an intricate plot involving the brass of the Memphis police department and a killer named Raoul. However, Jowers still could not identify Raoul.

That soon changed when a Tennessee woman named Glenda Grabow approached Jowers's lawyer with a lead. Grabow, forty-nine years old, had grown up in Houston, and she claimed to have slept with Percy Foreman, Jack Ruby, and a man she called Dago, who subsequently raped her. Grabow said that Dago and Ruby—and possibly Percy Foreman—were in a conspiracy with Lee Harvey Oswald to kill President Kennedy. After Ruby rubbed out Oswald, Dago pursued King, whom he killed in 1968. Grabow said that Dago's real name was Raul, not Raoul. She described him as an underworld figure who sold guns and passports on the black market. Naturally, William Pepper embraced Grabow with open arms. On her word, his investigators fingered a Portuguese immigrant who had lived in New York state for decades. His name was Raul. When shown a lineup that included his picture, Grabow identified the man as Dago; Jowers reviewed the same lineup and identified the same man.

》》 》》 》》 《《 《《 《《

As if Jowers's bogus confession and Grabow's sudden epiphany weren't a big enough headache, the Justice Department's investigation would also have to look into a new lead out of Atlanta. In March 1998, Pepper, Dexter King, and Andrew Young, former US ambassador to the United Nations, began applying pressure on Justice to investigate the explosive claims of a former FBI agent named Donald Wilson. On April 11, 1968, Wilson was working for the bureau's Atlanta field office when Ray's Mustang was located at Capitol Homes, a public housing project. Thirty years later, in March 1998, Wilson confessed to stealing an envelope and five pieces of paper that fell out of the passenger-side door during a search of the vehicle.

Wilson met with Justice in September 1998 and handed over two cryptic documents that ended up costing taxpayers thousands of dollars to verify. The first was a torn-out page from the *H* section of a 1963 Dallas telephone directory for individuals with the last name "Hunt." After Watergate, conspiracists like Jim Garrison began to argue that the third tramp arrested in Dealey Plaza looked exactly like E. Howard Hunt, a former CIA agent and one of Presidents' Nixon's convicted "plumbers."

Wilson's allusion to the tramps of Dealey Plaza did not end there. Penciled handwriting in the top margin of this same directory page depicted an encircled *J* followed by "LA84775" and "Raul-214." The *J* likely stands for Jack Ruby because "LA84775" was the number to Ruby's infamous Vegas Club. "Raul-214" is the beginning of what is assumed to be the Dallas phone number for the mystery man who assassinated both Kennedy and King. It's incomplete because the right edge of the page, where the number must have continued, is torn away. The second document, which was even more cryptic, contains only one meaningful phrase: "Raul."

Investigators professionally analyzed the documents and concluded that they contained no apparent code—or credibility. In the end, Justice decided that Wilson never actually searched the Mustang back in 1968 and therefore, never found any envelope. He had joined the FBI in 1962, but on April 11, 1968, when the Mustang was found, Wilson spent the day searching through money orders at Western Union. He quit the FBI after ten years of honorable service "because of personal values and career objectives" but never found his niche as a businessman. Subsequent research confirmed that he'd come forward under a certain amount of financial duress. "After leaving the FBI, Wilson established several small businesses, all of which failed," the final report read. "His most recent business dissolved in 1998. At the time he made his allegations, he was a teacher in a community high school and still professed a deep and continuing commitment to civil rights."

≫≫ ≫≫ ≫≫ ≪≪ ≪≪ ≪≪

Neither Donald Wilson nor the New York State Raul would testify during *King v. Jowers*—they were outside the court's civil jurisdiction. But that didn't prevent either side from mentioning their names throughout the seventeen-day Memphis trial. When proceedings began in November 1999, Pepper pulled out the stops. He introduced Tompkins's "reporting" into the record, deposed a plethora of CIA-obsessed kooks, and talked incessantly about Jowers and Liberto's connections to New Orleans mobster Carlos Marcello—David Ferrie's former employer and Jim Garrison's infamous foil. Pepper connected it all together with this closing statement.

> Part of the evidence in terms of the military involvement is contained in a lengthy article that we put into evidence that appears in March of 1993 in the *Commercial Appeal* by Steve Tomkins, and that article indicated that there was a high-ranking general who had been charged and imprisoned for aiding and abetting the trading in stolen weapons. That deal meant what he was involved in was the theft of guns from arsenals, armories and camps, like Camp Shelby in Mississippi, the theft of weapons from those places that went to—were trucked to—a Marcello property in New Orleans, and from the Marcello property in New Orleans were shipped around the coast into Houston, Texas, where they were taken off. And that is where Raul and his crowd came into the receipt of those weapons before they went into Latin and South America.

The trial ended on December 8, 1999. The King family rejoiced when the jury found Jowers liable for the murder of their patriarch. Ray's culpability, not to mention his racial motive, was crushed to the earth as an inconvenient fact. In June 2000, the DOJ's *Investigation of Recent Allegations Involving the Assassination of Martin Luther King, Jr.* poured cold water on the Jowers confession, the Raoul fantasy, and Hanes's black militant farce. Not surprisingly, Clinton's administration stood by the FBI's original investigation but delivered no additional evidence regarding Ray's racial motive: "Ultimately, we found nothing to disturb the 1969 judicial determination that James Earl Ray murdered Dr. King or to confirm that Raoul or anyone else implicated by Jowers or suggested by the Wilson papers participated in the assassination."

⋙ ⋙ ⋙ ⋘ ⋘ ⋘

The most significant part of the Jowers show trial was the testimony of Art Hanes Jr. For the previous fifteen years, he had served as a circuit judge in Birmingham. His father's hero and ally, Governor Wallace, appointed him to the bench. On November 22, the twenty-seventh anniversary of Kennedy's assassination, Hanes Jr. took the stand in *King v. Jowers* to continue the family tradition of conspiracy. "In 1968 on the eve of trial, the State was absolutely confined to a theory of one man: James Earl Ray, acting alone, killed Dr. King," Hanes Jr. testified. "Our view of it was that the evidence and testimony was inescapable that that was an impossible result both factually and it was an impossible result at the trial. We were absolutely confident that the case would be won."

Hanes admitted that he and his father could find no one at Jim's Grill to corroborate Ray or Raoul's presence on the day of the assassination, but that didn't really matter. The killer, whoever it was, must have had help, Hanes told the jury, and the place to look is not Memphis or Birmingham. "Ray told us the reason the rifle was in Memphis was that it was part of an operation to bring guns from Mississippi down to New Orleans to Cuban revolutionaries," Hanes testified. "We wanted to go to New Orleans. We thought it was very, very strange that James Earl Ray refused to allow us to go to New Orleans. He instructed us that no matter what happens, to do nothing to investigate that connection."

Defending Ray's innocence is just one part of Hanes Jr.'s attempt at an ancestral whitewash. In 2013, he told the *Birmingham News*—with a straight face—that his father secretly tried to broker a compromise that would have allowed Birmingham to integrate without violence in 1962. He cites Thomas Jefferson and James Madison, not the ideology of segregation, as the motive for trying unpopular cases involving racist killers. He keeps "Exhibit A" on the wall of his law office: an aerial photograph of the Memphis crime scene. He hopes to one day shed light on Ray's innocence by revealing new evidence that he's held back for nearly fifty years. "It's important in the sense that it accounts for what [Ray] was doing that day," Hanes said in 2013. "It's the explanation of how did your gun get there, how did this happen. It's just an interesting link to the puzzle. I'll share it some time."

ACKNOWLEDGMENTS

I lost my father just before completing this book. Like Ray, he too was a Wallace supporter in 1968. Thankfully, those racist politics were no match for his kind heart and generous spirit. A pharmacist for nearly forty years, my dad showed great compassion for the sick—white, black, or brown—and maintained the highest degree of integrity in all his dealings. This book is a symbol of my appreciation for his unyielding love and relentless faith in my future. As I said at the time of his passing, Larry McMichael was my dreamcatcher. I dedicate this work to his memory.

A nonfiction book is no good without sourcing and editing. Senior editor Yuval Taylor improved both. He showed great skill helping me to clarify the book's thesis and title, as well as simplify the storyline without skipping over important facts. His careful eye, candid opinions, and thoughtful suggestions made this book better, all around.

I have tried to rely almost entirely on documented facts and public records, but where the trail ran cold, I was able to lean on the generous memories of the following individuals: former Alabama governor John Patterson, artist Martha Huie, Professor Don Noble, author Warren Trest, lawyer Russell X. Thompson, writer Randy Sparkman, congressional investigators Pete Baetz and Michael Eberhardt, as well as Birmingham natives Albert Persons Jr., Laura Williams, W. Edward Harris, and Judge Art Hanes Jr. I would also like to give a sincere thanks to Sysco vice president and general counsel Mike

Nichols. Who would have ever believed such a stash of Birmingham history was hiding in your childhood closet in that enchanting part of Atlanta?

I must also thank an army of archivists, librarians, and Freedom of Information specialists who worked magic for me over a long period of time. Getting access to important historical records can prove to be nearly impossible, but after much prodding by journalists and historians like me, Tom Leatherwood of the Shelby County Register of Deeds should be applauded for finally putting a gigantic trove of primary source material related to the King assassination online. I have come to know that we have an economy of good people like Leatherwood who dedicate their lives to transparency and discovery. My list includes Mary Kay Schmidt and Kate Mollan of the National Archives, Jim Baggett of the Birmingham Public Library, Norwood Kerr of the Alabama State Archives, Rebecca Jewett of Ohio State, Kathleen Shoemaker of Emory, Kristen J. Nyitray of Stoneybrook, Jacquelyn Sundstrand of Nevada-Reno, Samantha McNeilly of Auburn, Mary Bess Paluzzi of Alabama, Edwin Frank and Brigitte Billeaudeaux of Memphis, Cathy Spitzenberger of Texas-Arlington, and Charlie Brown of the St. Louis Mercantile Library.

My former employer, Georgia College, and mass communication chair Dr. Mary Jean Land supported this project generously with travel funds and research grants. My colleagues in the Department of Mass Communication were always supportive and generous with their ears. Hundreds of students tolerated my rantings, and but for their youthful encouragement, I might not have completed this complex work. Hardworking Georgia College librarians, most especially Jennifer Price, bore the brunt of my incessant Interlibrary Loans requests. A special thanks also goes out to Mass Comm's onetime student worker, Courtney Howell, for a ridiculous amount of photocopying.

I have two very good friends to thank. The first is retired sergeant Robert Downey of the St. Louis Metropolitan Police Department: thank you for answering my call in 2006 and for handing over a fascinating career of files. This book is also for you, Bob! Another dear friend is my former editor Ramsey Nix, professor at Piedmont College. Were it not for our successful forays into America's failed immigration policy, I might never have revisited this exhausting project. Thank you for putting my voice in print and for being a constant source of optimism in the cruel business of journalism.

Last, I must also mention family. My mother, Melanie Carey McMichael, taught me much about empathy, humility, and resilience. Today she is the phoenix who rose from my father's ashes. I'm also grateful for the friendship I have with my older brother, Alex, and his wife, Lilia. Their beautiful children, Jack and Mila, have brought joy and wonder to my life and made our close-knit family infinitely stronger.

This book taught me one valuable lesson: racism is hereditary but tolerance is a state of mind. To put it another way, we must all choose to rise above our innate prejudices; we can't wait on government to do it for us. My beautiful wife, Marlene Roldán McMichael, is the most tolerant person I know. In our time together, while traveling in Mexico or working into the night, we have shared something fearless and sacred that no amount of modifiers can illuminate. Thank you for accepting my love and for making the coffee.

NOTES

Abbreviations for Frequently Occurring Citations

AP:	Associated Press
BAPBOMB:	Refers to the FBI's investigation of the Sixteenth Street Baptist Church bombing in September 1963
BN:	*Birmingham News*
BPH:	*Birmingham Post-Herald*
BPL:	Birmingham Public Library Department of Archives and Manuscripts; individual collections and folders are cited as needed
FOIA:	Freedom of Information Act request
HSCA:	Final Report, volumes, and appendices of the House Select Committee on Assassinations, 1979, cited by volume and page number
HUAC:	Investigative files, by state, of House Un-American Activities Committee's investigation of the Klan; a finding aid called "Records from the 1965 Investigation of the Ku Klux Klan" can be acquired from the National Archives (Washington)
HUIE:	William Bradford Huie Papers, Rare Books and Manuscripts, Ohio State University
Klan:	United Klans of America
LAT:	*Los Angeles Times*
MCA:	Memphis *Commercial Appeal*
MIBURN:	Refers to the headquarters file, 44-25706, on the murder of three civil rights workers in Neshoba County, Mississippi, during the summer of 1964

MPS: *Memphis Press-Scimitar*

MURKIN: Refers to the FBI's exhaustive investigation of Martin Luther King's murder. The case file number, 44-38861, is cited by page number only. Field office files without a 44-38861 page stamp are cited individually. Maintained by the NARA, College Park, Maryland. Accessed there in person, but also for a fee at http://maryferell.org/mlk

NYHT: *New York Herald Tribune*

NYT: *New York Times*

SCRD: Shelby County Register of Deeds maintains an extensive collection that it calls "Dr. Martin Luther King, Jr. Assassination Investigation." All files cited from this collection use this abbreviation and cite various sections of the collection as needed. The collection is maintained online: http://register.shelby.tn.us/media/mlk/

TNR: The *New Republic*

UPI: United Press International

WP: *Washington Post*

Prologue

"The Revealing Story" "The Revealing Story of a Mean Kid," *Life*, vol. 64, no. 18, May 3, 1968, 1, 20–29.

"As a thief" "Nation: Ray's Odd Odyssey," *Time*, June 21, 1968, 22–23.

Alton Drew Pearson and Jack Anderson, "Conspiracy Theory Exploded in King Assassination Case," *Washington Merry-Go-Round*, July 31, 1968.

Inquest Edward Jay Epstein, *Inquest: The Warren Commission and the Establishment of Truth* (New York: The Viking Press, 1966).

Garrison Peter Kihss, "Photos Cited by Research Group in Kennedy Death," *NYT*, May 24, 1968. "Picture Parallel: Theory of 'Double' in Assassinations," *San Francisco Chronicle*, May 6, 1968, 1, 26.

Part I: The Deal, 1968

1. A Pretty Fair Country Lawyer

"Get in touch" MLK Exhibit F-93, *Investigation of the Assassination of Martin Luther King, Jr.*, HSCA, 95th Cong., vol. 3, 255–263. The letter is dated June 10, 1968.

Monday morning This account of Ray's arraignment and contact with British lawyer Michael Eugene comes from the MURKIN files, as well as Gerold Frank, *An American Death* (New York: Doubleday, 1972), 202–205. Frank's book is one of the best and most accurate accounts of the assassination investigation. This account was supplemented with news clippings from the *London Times, NYT,* and *MCA.*

"the Martin King case" MLK Exhibit F-93, *Investigation of the Assassination of Martin Luther King, Jr.,* HSCA, 95th Cong., vol. 3, 255–263.

Born 10-19-16 MURKIN, 4564 and 4602.

"I've never heard of Ray" "Ex-Birmingham Mayor to Defend James Ray," *UPI,* June 18, 1968. "Won't Fight Extradition, Says Ray Attorney," AP, June 19, 1968. The author has chosen to attribute news service articles directly to the newswire. Some newswire articles accessed by the author were found online through Google News's archive search. Others came from mountains of news clippings in the author's possession.

"Hanes is a former" MURKIN, 4564.

"absolutely no good" MURKIN, 4564.

"pretty fair country lawyer" Alvin Shuster, "A Lawyer for Ray Arrives in London," *NYT,* June 21, 1968, A18.

Hoover shared MLK Exhibit F-511, *Investigation,* HSCA, 95th Cong., vol. #7, 88–94.

"Dear Mr. Sneyd." MURKIN, 4727.

2. Extradition

Bonebrake "Ray Tells Court He Is Not Guilty in Dr. King Death," *NYT,* June 28, 1968.

702nd Hampton Sides, *Hellhound on His Trail: The Stalking of Martin Luther King, Jr. and the International Hunt for His Assassin* (New York: Doubleday, 2010), 321.

"I feel so trapped" "Ray Plans Appeal After Futile Bid to Avoid Return," *MCA,* July 3, 1968.

"taking into totality" Teletype, "TO DIRECTOR FROM LEGAT LONDON NO. 85," MURKIN (file number unknown), July 2, 1968, accessed at: http://maryferrell.org.

July 4 MURKIN, 4771.

wire screen Karl E. Meyer, "Attorney Sees Ray, Plans a Not Guilty Plea at Trial," *WP,* July 6, 1968.

"austere and severe" Karl E. Meyer, "'Black Plot' Defense Hinted in Ray's Case," *WP,* July 7, 1978.

"His face reddening" Scott B. Bruns, "Hanes Meets Ray, Leaves Beaming, Fuming," *UPI,* July 6, 1968.

"conspiracy masterminded" Karl E. Meyer, "'Black Plot' Defense Hinted in Ray's Case," *WP,* July 7, 1978.

"I am beginning" "Hanes has 'fruitful' interview with Ray," *BN,* July 6, 1968.

"Lord R.G. Sneyd" MURKIN, 4855.

"any member" MURKIN, 4923.

"No sir, I will not." "Won't Fight," AP, June 19, 1968.

"for the purpose" MURKIN, 4852.

Imperial Wizard MURKIN, 4936.

"He will probably" MURKIN, 4852.

"a very unusual request" MURKIN, 4923.

"high-class person" J. Edgar Hoover, "Memorandum for Mr. Tolson," MURKIN (file number unknown), July 16, 1968, accessed at: http://mary ferrell.org.

"Klan infiltration" MURKIN, 4884–85.

"the unprecedented, libelous" Karl E. Meyer, "Ray's Attorney Protests Flight Plans," *WP*, July 18, 1968.

3. The Memphis Gag

Operation Landing The account of Ray's extradition to Memphis was reconstructed using Frank, *American Death*; "Trials: A Very Important Prisoner," *Time*, July 26, 1968. "Report," Shelby County Sheriff's Department, October 11, 1968; Attorney General File, SCRD.

"Tank" The description of the jail's security apparatus, as well as the account of Ray's first meeting with Hanes, comes from "Summary of 'A' Block Daily Log for July 20, 1968," Daily Activity Reports of James Earl Ray, Ray Jail Activity Logs, SCRD. Also, Henry P. Leifermann, "Foreman Expected to Demand Privacy for James Earl Ray," *UPI*, Dec. 8, 1968; Charles Thornton, "Ray and Defense Attorney Meet in First Long Session," *MCA*, July 21, 1968; Frank, *American Death*, 235–240.

"I don't want to alarm you," Frank, *American Death*, 248.

bizarre routine Frank, *American Death*, 235.

"one pocket comb" "Summary of 'A' Block Daily Log for July 20, 1968," Shelby County Sheriff's Department, Daily Activity Reports of James Earl Ray, Ray Jail Activity Logs, SCRD.

arraignment MURKIN, 4959. Frank, *American Death*. "Arraignment of James Earl Ray," Audio Files, SCRD.

drinking problem Charles Thornton, "Ray and Defense Attorney Meet in First Long Session," *MCA*, July 21, 1968; Frank, *American Death*, 214.

Sheppard Sheppard v. Maxwell, 384 US 333, 1966.

"No cameras" Tennessee v. Ray, "Order on Courthouse and Courtroom Procedures AND Publicity," July 18, 1968; "Trial Press Gag Order," Court Records 1, SCRD.

4. Giant Conspiracy

"advised that" MURKIN, 4934.

"thrust" MURKIN, 4940, 4955.

refused the bait MURKIN, 4955.

dragnet "The Greatest Manhunt in Law-Enforcement History," *Reader's Digest*, August 1968, 63–69.

"any changes" MURKIN, 3266.

O'Leary Ibid.

"in light of the many unfactual" "HSCA Press Release of 27 November 1978 Staff Report on Performance of DOJ and FBI," HSCA, Nov. 27, 1978. Accessed at: http://maryferrell.org. Search with quotes.

"I was appalled" MURKIN, 5058

"to assure you" Ibid.

"In my judgment" Charles Thornton, "Hanes Says Ray Helpless Victim in Red Conspiracy to Kill King," *MCA*, July 28, 1968.

"The Reader's Digest" "Summary of 'A' Block Daily Log," July 29, 1968, Daily Activity Reports of James Earl Ray, Ray Jail Activity Logs, SCRD.

"I had a gun" Roy B. Hamilton, "Hanes Carried Pistol to Shelby Jail on Visit to Ray," *MPS*, July 29, 1968.

"Neither Mr. Hanes" Ibid.

"No formal complaint" MURKIN, 4952.

"contempt committee" Charles Thornton, "Possible Publicity Violations in Ray Case to Be Studied," *MCA*, July 29, 1968.

"It's like something" Roy B. Hamilton, "Judge Goes Along With Bar Report," *MPS*, July 30, 1968.

fair way Charles Edmundson, "Battle Issues 5-Point 'Fair Trial' Order," *MCA*, July 31, 1968.

"Just my name" "Hanes Quiet After Order on Publicity," *MPS*, July 31, 1968.

"After supper" "Summary of 'A' Block Daily Log," July 31, 1968, Shelby County Sheriff's Department, Daily Activity Reports of James Earl Ray, Ray Jail Activity Logs, SCRD.

5. The Checkbook Journalist

"I'm interested" William Bradford Huie, *He Slew the Dreamer* (New York: Delacorte Press, 1970), 1.

royalties William Bradford Huie to Arthur J. Hanes, July 8, 1968, HSCA, 95th Cong., vol. 2, 162.

approached the FBI MURKIN, 5158, 5167, 5169.

grand jury MURKIN, 5174.

$10,000 bonus "Book Fees Pay Ray's Defense, Huie Declares," *MCA*, Sept. 11, 1968; Also, MURKIN, 5171.

"pervasive and widespread" Brown Alan Flynn, "Attorney Seek Dismissal for Ray: Claim 'Prejudicial Publicity,'" *MPS*, Aug. 16, 1968.

bloody images "Summary of 'A' Block Daily Log," Aug. 27, 1968, Shelby County Sheriff's Department, Daily Activity Reports of James Earl Ray, Ray Jail Activity Logs, SCRD.

clandestine operation MURKIN, 5193.

Stoner Martin Waldron, "A Klan Organizer Made Visit to Ray," *NYT*, Oct. 3, 1968.

Part II: Strange Bedfellows, 1954–1963

6. Little Mencken

"Whenever I try" Huie, "The South Kills Another Negro," *American Mercury*, vol. 53, November 1941, 535–545.

Birmingham Post David Campbell, "William Bradford Huie: Founding Alabama Magazine," Folder 424, Box XL, HUIE.

"turned fascist" Miscellaneous promotion for *Mud on the Stars*, William Bradford Huie folder, Ala-Authors Vertical File, Tutwiler Collection of Southern History, BPL.

Mud on the Stars Huie, *Mud on the Stars* (New York: L.B. Fisher Publishing, 1942).

Gloria Swanson Gloria Swanson to William Bradford Huie. December 15, 1950. Correspondence file, Michael Dorman Papers, Special Collections and Archives, Stony Brook University.

Normandy Huie, "The Navy's Seabees: They Build Roads to Victory," *Life*, Oct. 9, 1944. Huie, *Can Do! The Story of the Seabees* (New York: E.P. Dutton, 1945).

Mamie Stover Huie, *The Revolt of Mamie Stover* (New York: Duell, Sloan and Pearce, 1951).

Longines Chronicles "Representative John F. Kennedy (D-MA) interviewed by William Bradford Huie and Donald I. Rogers," *Longines Chronoscope*, March 12, 1952, NARA, 200LW68. "Senator Joseph R. McCarthy (R-WI) interviewed by William Bradford Huie and Donald I. Rogers," *Longines Chronoscope*, June 25, 1952, 200LW114.

bleeding cash "The Press: Trouble for the Mercury," *Time*, Dec. 8, 1952.

deep flaw Ibid.

enduring work Huie, *The Execution of Private Slovik* (New York: Duell, Sloan and Pearce, 1954).

secret key Huie, interview by Blackside Inc. for *Eyes on the Prize: America's Civil Rights Years (1954–1965)*, August 1979, transcript, Henry Hampton Collection, Film and Media Archive, Washington University Libraries, St. Louis.

Zora Neale Hurston C. Arthur Ellis Jr., "Zora Hurston and the Strange Case of Ruby McCol.um" (Lutz, FL: Gadfly, 2009).

"was gonna be gover:ior, sure" "The Press: Case of Ruby McCollum," *Time*, Oct. 25, 1954.

"you shoveled out" Ibid.

fugitive "Writer's Gt.ilt Upheld," *NYT*, May 21, 1955. Huie, *Ruby McCollum: Woman in a Su:vannee Jail* (New York: E.P. Dutton, 1956).

7. Wolf Whistle

pivotal moment Brov/n v. Board of Education, 347 US 483 (1954).

Mississippi lawyers Neil R. McMillan, *The Citizens' Councils: Organized Resistance to the Second Reconstruction 1954–64* (Champaign: University of Illinois Press, 1994), 17–18.

George W. Lee "Neg:o Aide Shot, Accuses Whites," AP, Nov. 26, 1955.

wolf whistle Simeon Wright, with Herb Boyd, *Simeon's Story: An Eyewitness Account of the Kidnapping of Emmett Till* (Chicago: Chicago Review Press, 2010), 51.

"Crazy nigger" Howell Raines, *My Soul Is Rested: Movement Days in the Deep South Remembered* (New York: Penguin Books, 1983), 389.

$4,000 cash Huie, "The Shocking Story of Approved Murder," *Look*, vol. 20, Jan. 24, 1956, 46–50; Raines, *My Soul*, 425–433; Gene Roberts and Hank Klibanoff, *The Race Beat: The Press, the Civil Rights Struggle, and the Awakening of the Nation* (New York: Knopf, 2006), 101–107.

Fordham Graduate Huie, interview, *Eyes on the Prize*.

inaccuracies Wright, *Simeon's Story*, 133–136.

"Admit that you've gone off half-cocked" Roberts and Klibanoff, *Race Beat*, 105.

back to Alabama Don Noble, "Introduction," in Huie's *Mud on the Stars* (Tuscaloosa: University of Alabama Press, 1996), xxiii.

Huie made the trek Huie, *Did the FBI Kill Martin Luther King?* (Nashville, TN: Thomas Nelson, 1977), 210.

Nat King Cole Dan T. Carter, "The Transformation of a Klansman," *NYT*, Oct. 4, 1991.

Judge Edward Aaron Huie, *Three Lives for Mississippi* (New York: Signet Books, 1968), 12–22; "Deputies Get Confessions in Negro's Sex Mutilation," *BN*, Sept. 7, 1957.

"In 1957, on learning" Huie, *Three Lives*, 12–22.

8. Birmingham's New Mayor

Salisbury Harrison Salisbury, "Fear and Hatred Grip Birmingham," *NYT*, April 12, 1960.

beloved evangelist James Oscar Hanes, *Five Years on the Firing Line* (Nashville, TN: House M.E. Church, 1913).

"A colored minister" James Oscar Hanes, *Aggressive Evangelism* (Nashville: Cokesbury Press, 1935), 53.

"Chicken" Le Revue, Birmingham-Southern College, 1938, 95–99, 127.

El Paso Arthur J. Hanes, personnel file, FBI file 67-HQ-17592.

MacArthur Jerry Norris, "Hanes Does Not Like to Hear City Knocked," *BPH* (exact date unknown, but early 1961). Found in "Birm-Bios-Hanes," vertical file, Tutwiler Collection, BPL.

Surigao Strait Ibid.

PT-525 Robert J. Buckley, *At Close Quarters: PT Boats in the United States Navy*, Washington, DC: Naval History Division, 1962, 393–397, 433, 478.

quit Arthur J. Hanes, personnel file, FBI file 67-HQ-17592.

CIA "Subject: Arthur Jackson Hanes," Director of Security to Mrs. Elizabeth Dunlevy, 20 November 1968, CIA, Record Series 104-10117-10304, Record Series JFK, Agency File Number 80T01357A, JFK Assassination System Identification Form, NARA, College Park.

Citizens' Council "Citizens' Councils Impact Seen Ebbing," *Christian Science Monitor*, May 22, 1956, 4.

Mayflower Diane McWhorter, *Carry Me Home: Birmingham, Alabama: The Climactic Battle of the Civil Rights Revolution* (New York: Simon & Schuster, 2002), 180–181.

two sermons Norris, "Hanes Does Not Like," *BPH*, Tutwiler, BPL.

Tommy Langston Raymond Arsenault, *Freedom Riders: 1961 and the Struggle for Racial Justice* (New York: Oxford University Press, 2006), 108.

"Keep Birmingham White" Michael Cooper Nichols, *Cities Are What Men Make Them: Birmingham, Alabama, Faces the Civil Rights Movement, 1963*, Brown University, 1974; McWhorter, *Carry Me Home*, 196.

dirtiest trick William A. Nunnelly, *Bull Connor* (Tuscaloosa: University of Alabama Press, 1991), 93–95.

"You may be assured" Glenn Eskew, *But for Birmingham: The Local and National Movements in the Civil Rights Struggle* (Chapel Hill: The University of North Carolina Press, 1997), 166.

9. No Summertime Soldier

"A divided city" "Birmingham's Decision," *BN*, May 31, 1961.

Hobart Grooms "Nation: That's What'll Happen," *Time*, Dec. 22, 1961; "Birmingham Acts Early in Park Tiff," AP, Dec. 10, 1961.

"You're realistic, Mayor" "Nation," *Time*, Dec. 22, 1961.

"If they integrate" "Mayor Hanes Steadfast on Closing Parks," *BN*, Dec. 12, 1961; "Pros, Cons Heard on Parks Closing," *BPH*, Dec. 12, 1961; Nunnelly, *Bull Connor*, 116.

"This letter acknowledges" Lou Isaacson, "Hanes gives two Negro ministers curt answer on petition," *BN*, Feb. 7, 1962; "Segregation Plea 'Filed' in Ashcan in Birmingham," AP, Feb. 8, 1962.

surplus food "Southern Mayor Decries Boycott," *NYT*, April 5, 1962, 19.

disgusted Pitts "Birmingham Officials Refuse Negro College Permit to Solicit," press release, April 7, 1962, provided to the author by Michael Nichols.

quick glance McWhorter, *Carry Me Home*, 294.

"ultimatum" "King Makes Four Demands on City, Issues 'Ultimatum,'" AP, Sept. 28, 1962.

punched "Rev. King Attacked by Nazi at Parley," AP, Sept. 30, 1962.

10. Project C

Citizens for Progress Nunnelley, *Bull Connor*, 127.

rig the jury Nunnelley, *Bull Connor*, 128.

lawsuit Arthur J. Hanes, Eugene 'Bull' Connor, and J. T. Wagoner, "Statement of the Commissioners of The City of Birmingham," April 7, 1968, *BN*, advertisement.

stalemate David J. Garrow, *Bearing the Cross: Martin Luther King, Jr., and the Southern Christian Leadership Conference* (New York: HarperCollins, 1986), 173–230.

"sic the dogs" Nunnelly, *Bull Connor*, 121.

"Congolese mob" Michael Dorman, *We Shall Overcome* (New York: Delacorte, 1964), 178.

Birmingham jail Martin Luther King Jr., *A Letter from Birmingham City Jail*, April 16, 1963.

"If you take part" Eskew, *But for Birmingham*, 266.

AP *photographer* Bob Carlton, "Birmingham 1963: Photographers were on the front lines to capture the civil rights movement," *BN*, Aug. 4, 2013.

"An injured, maimed, or dead" "Statement by Attorney General Robert F. Kennedy," Department of Justice, May 3, 1963. Accessed through the John F. Kennedy Presidential Library and Museum at http://civilrights.jfklibrary.org/.

"capitulation by certain" Irving Bernstein, *Promises Kept: John F. Kennedy's New Frontier* (New York: Oxford University Press, 1991), 92.

"Man in Red" Charles S. Porter, "Klan Meeting Dull in Spite of Crossburning," *New York Herald Tribune News Service*, May 13, 1963.

police escort McWhorter, *Carry Me Home*, 436.

"Martin Luther King is a revolutionary" Claude Sitton, "50 Hurt in Negro Rioting After Birmingham Blasts," *NYT,* May 13, 1963.

"to be sponsored by the Klan" Belmont Memo to Rosen, "Bombings in Birmingham," May 15, 1963, Birmingham file 157-881-102.

"If I were a Negro" "Ruling Ends Long Careers for Two Men," *BN,* May 23, 1963.

11. A Rotten Harvest

Asa Carter Dan T. Carter, *The Politics of Rage: George Wallace, Origins of the New Conservatism, the Transformation of American Politics,* Second Edition (Baton Rouge: Louisiana State University, 2000), 106–107.

"In the name of the greatest" George C. Wallace, "The Inaugural Address of George C. Wallace," Jan. 14, 1963, Montgomery, AL, Jan. 14, 1963, transcript accessed through State of Alabama Archives, http://digital .archives.alabama.gov/cdm/singleitem/collection/voices/id/2952/rec/5.

"hell on niggers" Carter, *The Politics of Rage,* 126–127.

"fawning and pawing" Carter, *The Politics of Rage,* 157–158.

KBI Testimony of Ralph Roton, Feb. 8, 1966, *Activities,* HUAC, Part 4, 3187–3224.

*"with missile bases"*Richard Allen Pride, *The Political Use of Racial Narratives: School Desegregation in Mobile, Alabama, 1954–1967* (Champaign: University of Illinois Press, 2002), 39–40, 263.

Graysville armory "Hanes Lashes Out Again in Two Hour Talk," *BPH,* Aug. 17, 1963.

"resistance forces" Claude Sitton, "Alabama Tension on Schools Rising," *NYT,* Sept. 1, 1963.

"Don't Let Wallace" "Don't Let Wallace Seize the Schools," *BN,* Sept. 2, 1963. "Violence Must Not Have Its Way," *BN,* Sept. 4, 1963.

Redmont Hotel Carter, *The Politics of Rage,* 173; McWhorter, *Carry Me Home,* 503; *Montgomery Advertiser,* Sept. 8, 1963.

"I'm happy to see my friend" Ibid. Wallace had promised to give Bull Connor a state job if not elected mayor. "Alabama News Scope: Going with State?" *BN,* April 14, 1963.

"The untimely death" "City Leaders Express Grief, Shock over Church Bombing," *BPH,* Sept. 16, 1963.

"The innocent blood" Martin Luther King Jr., "Eulogy for the Martyred Children," Sept. 18, 1969.

12. Mr. X

"The Death of an Innocent" Huie, "Death of an Innocent," *Look,* March 24, 1964, 23–25.

secret meeting This document establishes Hanes's attendance at the pre-arrest meeting. "Persons in attendance at meeting in Colonel Al Lingo's room at St. Francis Motel September 29, 1963," Albert Burton Boutwell Papers, File #264.5.7, BPL.

independent investigation See the *New York Times*, which did an exceptional job reporting Wallace's cover-up. "Alabama Seizes Two in Bombings at Birmingham," *NYT*, Sept. 30, 1963; John Herbers, "Alabama Surprises FBI by 2 Arrests in Bombings," *NYT*, Oct. 1, 1963; John Herbers, "Alabama Holds 3 on Charge of Having Dynamite," *NYT*, Oct. 2, 1963.

Matthew Hobson Murphy Jr. "Dynamite Figure Gets 6 Months," *BPH*, Oct. 9, 1963; Carter, *The Politics of Rage*, 189–191.

"Colonel Lingo announced" "Alabama Holds 3," *NYT*, Oct. 2, 1963.

"bought the dynamite" "Birmingham Bars New Negro Talks," UPI, Oct. 10, 1963.

"We then discussed" J. Edgar Hoover, "Memorandum to Mr. Tolson . . . ," Nov. 7, 1963, in BAPBOMB (page number unknown because of poor document quality).

"Stoner has stated" BAPBOMB, 157-1025-41.

patchwork Clive Webb, *Rabble Rousers: The American Far Right in the Civil Rights Era* (Athens, GA: University of Georgia Press, 2010), 159–161; Frederick James Simonelli, *American Fuehrer: George Lincoln Rockwell and the American Nazi Party* (Champaign: University of Illinois Press, 1999), 28.

Gene Roberts Patsy Sims, *The Klan*, Second Edition (Lexington: University of Kentucky Press, 2006), 124.

pickets Webb, *Rabble Rousers*, 167–168.

"The FBI is portrayed" "7th Annual National States Rights Party Convention Report," (transcript compiled by James K. Warner), Redmont Hotel, Birmingham, AL, Sept. 1, 1963. Provided to the author by Michael Nichols.

point a finger FD-302, Oct. 1, 1963, FBI file for Asa Earl Carter, 100-4651-73; FD-302, Nov. 29, 1963, Birmingham FBI BAPBOMB, 157-352-325, 326.

"black devil" BAPBOMB, 157-1025-531; "FBI Bombed Church, Says Rally Speaker," *BN*, Oct. 20, 1963, B-4.

"blue Nash" BAPBOMB, 157-1025-602.

"God fearing" "Matt H. Murphy, Jr. to Defend States Righters" *Thunderbolt*, Feb. 1, 1964; BAPBOMB, 157-1025-647.

criminal indictment US v. Edward R. Fields, CK 63-316, US District Court, Northern District of Alabama.

"Mister X" George McMillan, "The Birmingham Church Bomber," *Saturday Evening Post*, vol. 237, June 6, 1964, 14–17.

"Such articles" BAPBOMB, 157-1025-1027.

free man "Dynamite Trials Are Put Off," *BN*, June 4, 1964.

Part III: The Bloody Road to Selma, 1964–1965

13. A $25,000 Lie

Freedom Summer Stanley Nelson, *Freedom Summer, American Experience*, PBS, June 24, 2014, www.pbs.org/wgbh/americanexperience/films /freedomsummer/.

received a call Huie, *Three Lives for Mississippi* (Oxford, MS: University of Mississippi Press, 2000), 9–10.

"Now I had to sleep" Huie, "A Southerner Goes North," *TNR*, April 25, 1964, 8.

Wallace elector Arthur J. Hanes, personnel file, FBI file 67-HQ-17592.

$5,000 retainer SAC Jackson to Director, July 27, 1964, MIBURN.

"What do we know" Through FOIA, I was able to locate a long-overlooked file on Huie that mostly relates to his reporting for *Three Lives for Mississippi* but also to his earlier career as a magazine writer. The file, FBI file 94-4-6450, details Huie's proposition to the FBI in the summer of 1964. M.A. Jones Memo to DeLoach, Subject: William Bradford Huie, July 6, 1964, FBI file 94-4-6450-23–26, NARA at College Park.

"He is a menace" M.A. Jones Memo to DeLoach, Aug. 10, 1964, FBI file 94-4-6450-26.

one hundred fifty FBI Wayne King, "Mississippi Burning Film: Fact or Fiction in Mississippi," *NYT*, Dec. 4, 1988.

two bodies LaRaye Brown, "Family, Community Recall Men, Still Grieve for Them," (Jackson, Mississippi) *Clarion-Ledger*, Jan. 25, 2007.

shady proposition SAC Jackson to Director, July 27, 1964, MIBURN.

$25,000 SAC Jackson to Director," 27 July 1964, MIBURN.

Clayton Lewis Jerry Mitchell, "Clues on Who Got the 30K to Solve the Mississippi Burning Case," (Jackson, Mississippi) *Clarion-Ledger*, Feb. 16, 2010. Also see SAC Birmingham Airtel to Director, Nov. 14, 1964, FBI File 94-4-64550-19.

"Mr. Johnson said he" Claude Sitton, "Graves at a Dam: Discovery is Made in New Earth Mound in Mississippi," *NYT*, Aug. 5, 1964.

"At dusk" Huie, "The Untold Story of the Mississippi Murders," *Saturday Evening Post*, Sept. 5, 1964, 11–15.

"I think I know his real" Ibid.

glowing profile Huie, "FBI Agents as Missionary," *TNR*, Nov. 21, 1964, 10–11.

George Metz SAC Jackson AIRTEL to Director, Oct. 20, 1964, FBI File
    94-4-64550-27.
"guessing correctly" Ibid.
"By taking potshots" Ibid.
"You've certainly spotted" Huie, Interviewed on NBC's *Monitor,* Nov. 1, 1964.
"technique being used" MIBURN 44-25706-1365. Also, FBI File
    94-4-64550-19.
"characterization" MIBURN 44-25706-1354.

14. Cattle Prods and Plaited Whips

"I believe that wounded" Martin Luther King Jr., "Acceptance Speech," Dec.
    10, 1964, Oslo, Norway, http://www.nobelprize.org/nobel_prizes
    /peace/laureates/1964/king-acceptance_en.html.
"become a symbol of' David J. Garrow, *Protest at Selma: Martin Luther King,
    Jr., and the Voting Rights Act of 1965* (New Haven, CT: Yale University
    Press, 1978), 39.
a jackal from John Herbers, "Dr. King Punched and Kicked in an Alabama
    Hotel," *NYT,* Jan. 19, 1965.
J. B. Stoner Ibid.
"THIS IS SELMA" Martin Luther King, "Letter from a Selma Jail," *NYT,*
    Feb. 5, 1965, advertisement.
"Consider a night march" David J. Garrow, *Bearing the Cross: Martin Luther
    King, Jr., and the Southern Christian Leadership Conference* (New York:
    HarperCollins, 1986), 383.
tear gas Taylor Branch, *Pillar of Fire: America in the King Years, 1963–1965*
    (New York: Simon & Schuster, 1999), 391.
"with plaited whips" Gay Talese, "Burly Sheriff Clark Is Selma Symbol of
    Racism," *NYT,* March 16, 1965, 32.
unruly cattle "Civil Rights: Shades of Bull Connor," *Newsweek,* Feb. 1, 1965,
    21.
symbolic rape "Civil Rights: Black Eye," *Newsweek,* Feb. 8, 1965, 24.
a melee "Trooper's Victim Dies of Wound," *NYT,* Feb. 27, 1965, 2.
"Farewell Jimmie" "Civil Rights: Eulogy for a Woodchopper," *Time Magazine,*
    March 12, 1965, 23B.
Old Testament Taylor Branch, *At Canaan's Edge: America in the King Years,
    1965–1968* (New York: Simon & Schuster, 2006), 9.

15. Bloody Sunday

"This is an unlawful assembly" Roy Reed, "Alabama Police Use Gas and
    Clubs to Rout Negros," *NYT,* March 8, 1965.

"an American tragedy" "An American Tragedy," *Newsweek*, March 22, 1965, 18–20.

one condition David J. Garrow, *Bearing the Cross: Martin Luther King, Jr., and the Southern Christian Leadership Conference* (New York: HarperCollins, 1986), 403.

"This was the first nation" President Lyndon B. Johnson, "Special Message to Congress: The American Promise," March 15, 1965.

"mobs, trained in" Carter, *The Politics of Rage*, 255; Ben A. Franklin, "Wallace Calls on President to Send Marshals to Protect Marchers in Trip to Capitol," *NYT*, March 19, 1965, 20.

countermarch Franklin, "Wallace Calls," *NYT*, March 19, 1965, 20.

"had been responsible for" William Grover Jones, *The Wallace Story* (Northport, AL: American Colonial Printing, 1966), 437.

motorcade FD-362, March 29, 1965, Montgomery FBI file 44-1245, Viola Liuzzo File.

two DC-3s "Dateline US 80," *Newsweek*, April 5, 1965, 82.

binoculars Ibid., 25.

"He is trampling out" Martin Luther King, Jr., *A Call to Conscience: The Landmark Speeches of Dr. Martin Luther King, Jr.* (New York: Hachette, 2001).

16. Baby Brother

"Lookie here" Mary Stanton, *From Selma to Sorrow: The Life and Death of Viola Liuzzo* (Athens: University of Georgia Press, 2000), 50.

blast furnace Gary May, *The Informant: The FBI, the Ku Klux Klan, and the Murder of Viola Liuzzo* (New Haven, CT: Yale University Press, 2005), 162.

accused triggerman Ibid., 159.

defecated Ibid., 170.

"Mrs. Liuzzo went to Alabama"d Charles Mohr, "Bids Congress Act," *NYT*, March 27, 1965.

"a damn liar" John Herbers, "Klan Chief Calls President a Liar," *NYT*, March 27, 1965.

oxygen tank Ben A. Franklin, "4 Alabama Klansman Charged; 3 Released on $50,000 Bond," *NYT*, March 27, 1965.

"Are these men" Ibid.

affidavit May, *Informant*, 175.

"south of the large" Mobile FBI File 44-1245 (no identifying marks).

17. The Klonsel's Stage

full-page ad "A Missing Civil Rights Worker in Mississippi Today Is a Dead Civil Rights Worker," Advertisement, *NYHT*, April 23, 1965, 30.

"The case includes" Fred P. Graham, "3 Are Reported Indicted for Murder in Liuzzo Case," *NYT*, April 22, 1965.

"The Klan" Huie, "Liuzzo Trial: Alabama Klan vs. President," *NYHT*, May 2, 1965.

first dispatch Jimmy Breslin, "Jimmy Breslin," *NYHT*, May 4, 1965.

"close-cropped hair" Ibid.

"Never" Ibid.

Moton May, *Informant*, 196.

toxicologist Ibid., 198.

"Wilkins rolled down" Breslin, "FBI Informant's Story of 100-MPH Death Chase," *NYHT*, March 5, 1965.

"kind of man the" Breslin, "Liuzzo Trial: The FBI Man Vs. Klonsel," *NYHT*, May 6, 1965.

"I most sacredly" Trial Transcript, Alabama v. Wilkins, p. 232, in Box 29, Folder 249, HUIE; May, *Informant*, 206.

"Isn't it true" Trial Transcript, Alabama v. Wilkins, 420–428, in Box 29, Folder 249, HUIE; May, *Informant*, 208–213.

"Niggers are against" May, *Informant*, 218.

Part IV: Krossings in Klan Kountry, 1965–1966

18. I Was a Ku Klux

"expressed a desire" M.A. Jones Memo to DeLoach, "William Bradford Huie Author Request to do Articles on Gary Thomas Rowe," May 11, 1965, FBI File 94-4-6450-33.

"I don't trust" Ibid.

two $75,000 C.D. DeLoach Memo to Mohr, "Eugene Thomas Et Al.," July 19, 1965, FBI File 44-28601.

sympathetic face Ibid.

signing session Huie to Richard Kennedy, July 19, 1965, correspondence file, Michael Dorman Papers, Special Collections and Archives, Stony Brook University.

"It should be understood" Ibid.

"$25,000 for the privilege" Birmingham Teletype to Director and San Francisco, Aug. 18, 1965, 44-28601-43.

"gambling" SAC Birmingham AIR MAIL to Director, Aug. 17, 1965, FBI file 44-28601-432.

"a friend and fellow club" Huie to Richard Kennedy, 28 Aug. 1965, correspondence file, Michael Dorman Papers, Special Collections and Archives, Stony Brook University.

Hartselle Christopher Bell, "Hartselle Klan Rally Told to 'Begin Your Own Fight,'" *Huntsville* (Alabama) *Times*, Aug. 22, 1965; Huie to Richard

Kennedy, Aug. 28, 1965, correspondence file, Michael Dorman Papers, Special Collections and Archives, Stony Brook University.

tragedy "Klan Lawyer Killed in Traffic Crash," AP, Aug. 22, 1965. "Klansmen from 15 States Attend Funeral for Murphy," *UPI*, Aug. 22, 1965.

"A few hours" Huie, "Los Angeles and Hayneville: A Connecting Thread," *NYHT*, Aug. 22, 1965.

"God has a special place" Christopher Bell, "Hartselle Klan Rally Told to 'Begin Your Own Fight,'" *Huntsville* (Alabama) *Times*, Aug. 22, 1965; Huie to Richard Kennedy, Aug. 28, 1965, correspondence file, Michael Dorman Papers, Special Collections and Archives, Stony Brook University.

tears Jane Aldridge, "Art Hanes Will Defend 3 Klansmen," *BPH*, Aug. 27, 1965; M.A. Jones Memo to Deloach, Aug. 24, 1965, FBI File 44-28601. "Funeral of Klan Lawyer," AP, Aug. 24, 1965.

"The citizen-deputy who fired" Huie, "Los Angeles and Hayneville," *NYHT*, Aug. 22, 1965. *Roy* Reed, "White Seminarian Slain in Alabama; Deputy Is Charged," *NYT*, Aug. 22, 1965.

"Huie has advised" Paul Johnston to Gary Thomas Rowe, August 27, 1965, Folders 99.1.8.3.6 and 99.1.8.3.7, Paul Johnston Folders, BPL.

nine stipulations "Agreement between William Bradford Huie and Gary Thomas Rowe, Jr.," Folders 99.1.8.3.6–7, Paul Johnston Folders, BPL.

turned it down Gary Thomas Rowe to Paul Johnston, Sept. 13, 1965, Folders 99.1.8.3.6–7, Paul Johnston Folders, BPL.

"finks" Huie to Paul Johnston, Oct. 4, 1965, Folders 99.1.8.3.6–7, Paul Johnston Folders, BPL.

"Money-wise" Huie to Mike Dorman, Aug. 28, 1965, correspondence file, Michael Dorman Papers, Michael Dorman Papers, Special Collections and Archives, Stony Brook University.

19. The Parable of Two Goats

"From the enclosed" Huie to Richard Kennedy, Aug. 28, 1965, correspondence file, Michael Dorman Papers, Special Collections and Archives, Stony Brook University.

"incensed" May, *Informant*, 235.

"I have never been" Aldridge, "Art Hanes," *BPH*, Aug. 27, 1965.

"Right" Arthur J. Hanes, personnel file, FBI file 67-HQ-17592.

eleven members Huie, "Court Rules: Liuzzo Jury Supremacy," *NYHT*, Oct. 21, 1965.

"Leroy" Ibid.

Rowe's credibility May, *Informant*, 293; Bob Carlton, "Birmingham 1963: Photographers were on the front lines to capture the civil rights movement," *BN*, Aug. 4, 2013; Roy Reed, "Rowe Again Tells of Liuzzo Killing," *NYT*, Oct. 22, 1965.

fingerprints Hoover actually scribbled on a clipping "Why wasn't a finger-print test made?" See FBI file 44-28601-392; "Liuzzo Gun Not Tested for Prints, FBI Says," AP, May 6, 1965; William Chapman, "Jury Begins Deliberating Liuzzo Case," *WP*, May 7, 1965.

"The Parable of Two Goats" May, *Informant*, 233–247.

"Huntsville is too small" Huie, "Football, Sex and the Verdict," *NYHT*, Oct. 24, 1965.

Klansman Huie, *The Klansman* (New York: Delacorte, 1967).

Hubert Strange "LBJ Hails Verdict in Klan Murder," AP, Dec. 4, 1965.

"I would rather" "Ala. Youth Convicted for Slaying Negro Man," *Jet*, Dec. 16, 1965, 9.

Browder v. Gayle Browder v. Gayle, 142 F. Supp. 707 (M.D. Alabama 1956).

bombed Jack Bass, *Taming the Storm: The Life and Times of Frank M. Johnson, Jr. and the South's Fight Over Civil Rights* (New York: Doubleday), 125–126.

flat-footed May, *Informant*, 261.

"Then one of the twelve" Ibid.

"rays of light" "Dr. King Encouraged," *NYT*, Dec. 4, 1965.

"railroaded" Roy Reed, "3 Klansmen Found Guilty in Case of Rights Death," *NYT*, Dec. 4, 1965.

20. The Klokan

Mayflower This interview of Rowe by HUAC has never before been published. All quotes from this section come from Philip R. Manuel to Francis J. McNamara, "Subject: Gary Thomas Rowe AKA Tommy Rowe," Jan. 27, 1968, File: Rowe, Gary, Box 44, HUAC.

recruited May, *Informant*, 4–10. Gary Thomas Rowe, *My Undercover Years with the FBI* (New York: Bantam, 1976).

William Rosecrans Francis J. McNamara to Donald T. Appell, "Subject: . . . William Sterling Rosecrans, Jr., United Florida Knights of the Ku Klux Klan and Bombing on February 16, 1964 of Residence of Iona Godfrey, Jacksonville, Florida," May 24, 1964, File: United Florida Ku Klux Klan, Box 44, HUAC. "Rosecrans Has Lie Test," UPI, March 6, 1964; "Star Witness Links 5 to Negro Bombing," AP, July 4, 1964.

Rosecrans shocked the Klan "Ex-Klansman Testifies on Bomb School," AP, July 3, 1964.

"I'm very happy" "Jury Acquits Four Klansmen of Violating Negro's Rights," UPI, Nov. 27, 1964.

"The Klokan Committee Donald T. Appell to Francis J. McNamara, "Subject: United Klans of America–Realm of Florida," May 21, 1965, File: Roton, Ralph, Box 44, HUAC.

"Rowe stated that J. B. stoner" Ibid.

"The Imperial Klonsel" "The Present Day Ku Klux Klan Movement," *Report of the Committee of Un-American Activities,* Dec. 11, 1967, HUAC, 90 Cong., 1st Session, 112.

21. Klan Kourt

flowcharts Activities of Ku Klux Klan Organizations in the United States, House Un-American Activities Committee, 89th Cong., Oct. 19, 1965, Part 1. *Fifth Amendment* John Herbers, "Klan Head Balks at 73 Questions as Hearing Opens," *NYT,* Oct.20, 1965.

additional accounts "Whiteman's Defense Fund, etc., Birmingham Trust National Bank, Birmingham, Alabama," Box 54, HUAC.

pro bono "Ex-Nazi Links Klan Empress to Plots," AP, Feb. 22, 1966.

"he might hire as his" Louis Russell to Francis J. McNamara, "Subject: Robert M. Shelton," Oct. 14, 1965, File: Shelton, Robert M., Box 45, HUAC.

KBI John Herbers, "Klan Undercover Agent Studied Racial Strife for Alabama Committee," *NYT,* Feb. 9, 1966.

$500 Testimony of William Melvin Sexton, Feb. 8, 1966, *Activities* HUAC, Part 4, 3184; Testimony Robert Milton Creel, Feb. 9, 1966, *Activities,* HUAC, Part 4, 3272–73.

"card carrying" May, *Informant,* 235.

state orders John H. Hawkins to Rep. John Buchanan, Feb. 9, 1966, Ralph Roton Exhibit No. 1, HUAC, Part 4, 3203.

uncomfortable Testimony of Ralph Roton, Feb. 8, 1966, *Activities,* HUAC, Part 4, 3200–3205; George Lardner Jr., "Klan Aide Says Alabama Gave Him State Job," *WP,* Feb. 9, 1969, 2.

"Klan Aide says" Testimony of Ralph Roton, Feb. 8, 1966, *Activities,* HUAC, Part 4, 3187–3224.

"I refuse to answer" Testimony of Jesse Benjamin Stoner, Feb. 24, 1966, *Activities,* HUAC, Part 5, 3804–3830.

"The nigger is not" Ibid., 3811.

"The record is not" Ibid., 3828.

22. The Escape

"I began collecting" James Earl Ray, "Who Killed Martin Luther King Jr.? The True Story of the Alleged Assassin (Bethesda, MD: National Press Books, 1993), 50.

"I do read the" "Continued Testimony of James Earl Ray, accompanied by Mr. Mark Lane, counsel of record," Aug. 18, 1978, *Investigation*, HSCA, 95th Cong., vol. 3, 256.

dummy Posner, *Killing the Dream*, 141.

Eugene Thomas "Ex-Mayor of Birmingham to Aid Klansman's Trial," *NYT*, Sept. 20, 1966; "8 Negro Jurors Support Acquittal in Rights Killing," AP, Sept. 28, 1963.

IQ Huie, *Dreamer*, 13.

smoky room "Wallace Assails Two Parties' Chiefs: Steps Up Presidential Drive at Segregationist Meeting," *NYT*, Feb. 18, 1967.

Sheriff Clark There are numerous clippings and FBI reports on Clark's troubled visit to St. Louis in the fall of 1965. A comprehensive take can be found in "St. Louis Metropolitan Area Citizens' Council," St. Louis FBI File 157–582.

States-Item "New Oswald Clue Reported Found," AP, Feb. 19, 1967.

"New Orleans authorities" "LA DA Is Mum on JFK Probe," AP, Feb. 18, 1967.

"Black is white" Gene Roberts, "Business Men Aid Inquiry on 'Plot,'" *NYT*, Feb. 25, 1967.

secret plot Gene Roberts, "Figure in Oswald Inquiry Is Dead in New Orleans," *NYT*, Feb. 23, 1967.

"we have solved" "JFK Assassination 'Solved' by DA Garrison," UPI, Feb. 25, 1967.

"people involved can get" "New Orleans DA Fearless Investigator," AP, Feb. 25, 1967.

"strong supporters" HSCA, 369. Manuel Chait, "Brother Surprised at Arrest: Thinks Ray Could Have Been Hired," *St. Louis Post-Dispatch*, June 9, 1968.

Meet the Press George C. Wallace, *Meet the Press*, NBC, April 23, 1967.

Part V: Stand Up for America, 1967–1968

23. Meet Me in California

"They really liked me" Gene Roberts, "Says George Wallace in Awe: 'They Liked Me,'" *NYT*, Nov. 12, 1967.

taxpayers Dan T. Carter, *The Politics of Rage* (Baton Rouge: Louisiana State University, 2000), 313–316.

"When I first came there" "Compilation of the Statements of James Earl Ray," HSCA, 44–48.

phone records show "Final Report," HSCA, 117. Gerald Posner, *Killing the Dream* (New York: Harcourt Brace & Co., 1999), 194.

ballot petition "Compilation," HSCA, 44–48; MURKIN, Los Angeles Field Office, 44-1574 145–180.

American South African Council "Compilation," HSCA, 38. "Final Report,"
HSCA, 113–116.

"down with Mexicans," MURKIN, 3288.

portable television George McMillan, *The Making of an Assassin: The Life of
James Earl Ray* (Boston: Little Brown, 1972), 285.

"The secret organization" "Rioting Aids Klan," AP, Jan. 2, 1968.

"And then I got into" Martin Luther King Jr., "I've Been to the Mountaintop,"
April 3, 1968, Memphis, TN, transcript accessed http://mlk-kpp01
.stanford.edu/index.php/encyclopeida/documentsentry/ive_been
_to_the_mountaintop/.

"The dream of Dr. Martin" President Lyndon B. Johnson, "Address to the
Nation Upon Proclaiming a Day of Mourning," April 5, 1968, transcript
accessed http://www.pbs.org/wgbh/americanexperience/features
/primary-resources/lbj-mourning.

"South African Airways timetable" "Blakely," vol. 4, HSCA, 116.

24. A Sick White Brother

"when the FBI" Posner, *Killing the Dreamer*, 185–194.

"Friends of Rhodesia," "Final Report," HSCA, 114–116.

"heated discussion" "Final Report," HSCA, 121–124.

another bartender "Final Report," HSCA, 123.

"Everybody was stirred up" "Compilation," HSCA, 40.

"a change is absolutely necessary" Garrow, *Bearing the Cross*, 604.

"I don't have any political aspirations" "Dr. King Won't Be a Politico," *Los
Angeles Herald-Examiner*, March 18, 1968.

Selma Posner, *Killing the Dream*, 219–221.

circles near Ibid. A copy of this map is in the possession of SCRD. See
"Atlanta Map, Matchbook, Note," Evidence 2, SCRD.

fake news report Internal FBI "Federal Bureau of Investigation," vol. 6, *Before
the United States Senate Select Comm. to Study Governmental Operations
with Respect to Intelligence Activities*, 94th Cong., Nov.–Dec. 1975, 46–47.

Room 306 There are so many accounts of Ray's crime and capture that it's
futile to try to cite each one. The best I've found are in Frank, *American
Death*; Huie, *Dreamer*; Posner, *Killing the Dream*; Hampton Sides, *Hellhound on His Trail: The Stalking of Martin Luther King, Jr. and the International Hunt for His Assassin* (New York: Doubleday, 2010).
Also Marc Perrusquia, "Six: 01," *MCA*, April 4, 2013, http://media
.commercialappeal.com/mlk/.

25. Stoner's Visit

riots Ben W. Gilbert and the staff of the *Washington Post, Ten Blocks Away from the White House: An Anatomy of the Washington Riots of 1968* (London: Pall Mall Press, 1968).

"an orgy of public" "The Wake," *The Citizen* (Publication of the White Citizens' Council), May 1968, 2.

"typical of the breakdown" "Face to Face with Murphy Martin," WFAA-TV, April 28, 1968. Accessed in Dan T. Carter Research Files, Manuscript, Archives, and Rare Book Library, Emory University.

"she has won the fight" Carter, *The Politics of Rage*, 314.

Gallup "Poll Reports Wallace Leading in the Deep South," *NYT,* June 19, 1968.

Virginia Plan Ray Jenkins, "George Wallace Figures to Win Even If He Loses," *NYT,* April 7, 1968, SM26; Tom Wicker, "George Wallace: A Gross and Simple Heart," *Harper's,* April 1967, 41-49. "The Wallace Threat," *WP,* Feb. 10, 1968.

Eutaw "A.B.C. Charges Wallace Aid Seized Film of Shelton Greeting," *NYT,* June 28, 1968.

Nazi phrase "Wallace Talk Disrupted at Rally in St. Louis," *UPI,* July 17, 1968.

"inside a barbershop" Jack Nelson, "FBI Probes States Rights Party Link to Violence," *WP,* June 13, 1968.

"He has been a good" National States Rights Party, the *Thunderbolt,* May 1968.

NSRP mailed Edward R. Fields to James Earl Ray, "To Whom It May Concern from Edward R. Fields, re: James Earl Ray Case, June 14, 1968," MLK Document 270062, HSCA, Final Report, 381–383.

"As for my personal views" MURKIN, 5212, 4936.

"Art Hanes is a personal friend" "Funds Offered for Defense of James Earl Ray," AP, June 28, 1968.

"acted mad" MURKIN, 5013.

"I don't mind" Martin Waldron, "A Klan Organizer Made Visit to Ray," *NYT,* Oct. 3, 1968.

"Please forgive me" MURKIN, 5193.

August 14 SAC to Director, Aug. 14, 1968, MURKIN 44-1987-M-172. This document refers to the Memphis FBI's MURKIN file number 44-1987. It was discovered through FOIA in the possession of NARA.

"I don't think Hanes" MURKIN, 5196.

"to show cause" This lengthy article is a comprehensive look at Hanes's contempt hearing. "Four Held in Contempt for Ray Case Reports," *MPS,* Sept. 30, 1968.

"serious differences" "Ray's Lawyer Says He May Quit Case," AP, Sept. 28,
      1968.
"Sword of Damocles" "Judge Battle's Decision," MCA, Oct. 1, 1968.
"At 2:30 PM Mr. J. B. Stoner" "Summary of 'A' Block Daily Log," Sept. 27–29,
      1968, Shelby County Sheriff's Department, Daily Activity Reports of
      James Earl Ray, Ray Jail Activity Logs, SCRD.
"A Klan Organizer" Waldron, "A Klan," NYT, Oct. 3, 1968.
"I got a murder" Captain B.J. Smith to Sheriff William Morris, Oct. 18,
      1968, Ray Jail Activity Logs, SCRD.

26. A Blond Latin

"I urged the judge" Byron Shaw, "Are You Sure Who Killed Martin Luther
      King?" Esquire, 165.
"I guess Mr. Hanes is right" Huie, Dreamer, 176.
finest of hotels The author reviewed hotel receipts in OSU's HUIE collection.
      Also, in Huie, Dreamer.
Sirhan Sirhan Robert B. Kaiser, "Conversations in Jail with Sirhan, a Name
      Meaning Wolf," Life, Jan. 16, 1969, 21–24.
Johnny Carson "Conspiracy Seen in King's Death," MCA, Oct. 17, 1968.
black-and-white cover This article is the source for King's quote, as well as
      those related to Ray's time in Canada and his meeting of Raoul. Huie,
      "The Story of James Earl Ray and the Plot to Assassinate Martin Luther
      King: 'I Had Been in Trouble All My Life,'" Look, Nov. 12, 1968.
"The entire article" MURKIN, 5368.
"newspaper reporters" MURKIN, 5434.
"This responds to" MURKIN, 5462.
"I Got Involved Gradually" Huie, "I Got Involved Gradually, and I Didn't
      Know Anyone Was Going to Be Murdered," Look, Nov. 23, 1968.
They Slew the Dreamer MURKIN, 5503.

27. Election Night

money pouring in "Money Comes in by the Cart Full," WP, Oct. 23, 1968.
polls "12-State Area Covered; Nixon Lead Found Cut in the East," NYT,
      Oct. 24, 1968.
"They are on the whole, obscure," "Electors Hold 3d Party Keys," WP, Oct. 20,
      1968.
"if the governor" "Wallace Eyes Sway," AP, July 18, 1964.
"I wouldn't worry" James Earl Ray to William Bradford Huie, Oct. 16, 1968.
      SCRD.
"After supper Ray" "Summary of 'A' Block Daily Log," Nov. 6, 1968, Shelby
      County Sheriff's Department, Daily Activity Reports of James Earl
      Ray, Ray Jail Activity Logs, SCRD.

racial lines "Yung Wie and Hahood, H.R., "Racial Attitudes and the Wallace Vote: A Study of the 1968 Election in Memphis," *Polity*, vol. 3, no. 4, Summer 1974, p. 536.

28. Pink Slip

"Arthur is fighting" Jim Squires, "Memphis Courtroom Drama Unfolds Tuesday," *Nashville Tennessean*, Nov. 10, 1968.

"in the near future" This document is part of the Memphis MURKIN file and was released pursuant to FOIA. SAC Memphis to Director, AIRTEL, 18 Aug. 1968, FBI File 44-1987-Sec-M-179A.

"Cornbread" Arthur J. Hanes, "For Conspiracy," *Look*, April 15, 1969, 113.

the slug broke into pieces Frank, *American Death*, 138.

"A six-year-old kid" Martin Waldron, "Ex-Attorney Links Ray to Rifles for Cuban Exiles," *NYT*, April 2, 1968.

"Due to some disagreements" "A Letter from Ray," *MCA*, Nov. 13, 1968.

"I expect you" Frank, *American Death*, 336.

Life "Life Reports Negotiations for Hanes' Story Underway," *MCA*, Nov. 17, 1968; James Earl Ray to Arthur J. Hanes, undated (most likely Nov. 17, 1968), Ray Correspondence, SCRD.

"typical of a certain breed" Roy B. Hamilton, "Hanes Fires Back Reply to Foreman," *MPS*, Dec. 14, 1968.

Jerry Ray MURKIN, 44853. Jerry Ray to James Earl Ray, Sept. 21, 1968, Ray Correspondence, SCRD.

"fees" "Judge Battle Grants Delay," *MPS*, Nov. 13, 1968.

"Your honor," Transcript, Tennessee v. Ray, No. 16645, Nov. 12, 1968.

"It is the state's position" Transcript, Tennessee v. Ray, No. 16645, Nov. 12, 1968.

"the diatribe" "Judge Battle Grants Delay," *MPS*, Nov. 13, 1968.

"They shall remain" Transcript, Tennessee v. Ray, No. 16645, Nov. 12, 1968.

"They can keep" "Ray's Ex-Lawyer Suggests He Was Hired for Racial Aspect," *NYT*, Nov. 16, 1968.

"A pall hangs" Charles Edmundson, "Foreman Concerned of Brand as Traitor," *MCA*, Nov. 14, 1968.

Part VI: Waiting for Raoul, 1969

29. Tramps

Canada's national television William Bradford Huie and Hanes, Arthur J., Interview by Gordon Donaldson, *CBC News Magazine*, CBC, Nov. 12, 1968.

"conspiracy between black and white persons" "Black-white Plot Got King, Says Huie," AP, Dec. 2, 1968.

pictures from New York MURKIN, 5629.

Wise "Interview with Marvin L. Wise," FD-302, FBI File 89A-DL-60165-40, March 6, 1992; "Interview of Marvin Lynn Wise," HSCA, JFK Collection, Nov. 14, 1977; Ray La Fontaine and Mary La Fontaine, "First Look at Dallas' JFK Files: Evidence on Oswald Picture, Arrested 'Bums,'" *Houston Post*, Feb. 9, 1992, 1.

Jaubert Peter Kihss, "Photos Cited by Research Group in Kennedy Death," *NYT*, May 24, 1968.

"The sharp, pointed nose" "Picture Parallel: Theory of 'Double' in Assassinations," *San Francisco Chronicle*, May 6, 1968, 1, 26.

"seeking the identity" Kihss, "Photos Cited," *NYT*, May 24, 1968.

"Mr. Foreman described" "Continued Testimony of James Earl Ray," HUAC, Vol. 2, 272.

Louis Lomax Louis E. Lomax Papers, 82–30 Box 12, Special Collections, University of Nevada–Reno. This archive contains some original drafts from a series of "investigative" articles that Louis Lomax wrote for the North American Newspaper Alliance. Most of Lomax's bogus MURKIN claims and fascinating life story have been ignored in this book, except to note that Lomax was the first to argue a New Orleans–based conspiracy. His series influenced Huie and angered the FBI.

Clay Shaw "Clay Shaw Trial Slated for Jan. 21," *UPI*, Dec. 11, 1968.

"all accomplished by" "Garrison Feels Deaths Are Linked," *Reuters*, Dec. 18, 1968.

Monteleone Huie, *Dreamer*, 60–81.

Le Bunny Lounge Ibid.

"If you are in New Orleans" Devin McKinney, "An American Cuss," *The Oxford American*, issue 57, 2007, 104–111.

Mexico Ibid.

30. The Bay of Hubris

dialed up Huie, *Dreamer*, 112; Birmingham MURKIN 44-1740-2121.

"When I stood" Huie, *Dreamer*, 112–113.

"has decided to" MURKIN, 5490.

retired army colonel Birmingham MURKIN 44-1740-2118. The author recovered this file through FOIA. It is now part of NARA's MURKIN collection.

The Bay of Pigs Albert C. Persons, *Bay of Pigs* (Birmingham, AL: Swalley Printing Co., 1968), republished by McFarland in 1990.

Asa Carter Birmingham MURKIN 44-1740-2118.

"My slogan is not" "King Threatens to Camp Near the White House," UPI, Nov. 4, 1967.

Hayes Aircraft Trest, *Wings of Denial*, 30–35.

General Reid Doster Warren Trest and Donald Dodd, *Wings of Denial: The Alabama Air National Guard's Covert Role at the Bay of Pigs* (Montgomery, AL: New South Books, 2001), 16.

"Cannot attach sufficient" Mark Fineman and Dolly Mascarenas, "Bay of Pigs: The Secret Death of Pete Ray," *LAT,* March 15, 1998.

Chicago American Albert C. Persons "US Fliers Dead at the Bay of Pigs," *Birmingham Examiner,* Feb. 3, 1963; Albert C. Persons, "Inside Story of Cuban Invasion," *Chicago American,* March 7, 1963.

"The flight that cost them" President John F. Kennedy, 51st Press Conference, March 6, 1963. Accessed at www.youtube.com/watch?v=4yhSzjmNjjI.

"drunkenness and sex orgies" Statement of Rep. William L. Dickinson, "March on Montgomery—The Untold Story," 89 Cong. Rec., vol. 111, No. 57, March 30, 1965, 6113–6114; "Congressman Dickinson Exposes Selma March," the *Thunderbolt,* May 1965, Issue 57.

harmless pictures Albert Persons, *Sex and Civil Rights,* 1. Also, William L. Dickinson Congressional Papers, 89-04-06, Archives and Special Collections, Auburn University–Montgomery.

"the best-selling magazine" Huie, "The Linking Threat of Racial Death," *NYHT,* Aug. 22, 1965.

"Black Knight" Persons, *Sex and Civil Rights,* 2–3.

Selma Raped James J. Clark, *I Saw Selma Raped: The Jim Clark Story,* (Birmingham, AL: Selma Enterprises/Sizemore Agency, 1966). Albert Persons incorporated this short-lived publishing concern with a Birmingham friend named Gary Sizemore. Clark later admitted that someone else wrote the book.

Riot! Riot! Riot! Albert C. Persons, *Riot! Riot! Riot!* (Birmingham, AL: Esco Publishers, 1965).

riot control unit "State Guard's Riot Status Detailed Here," *Tuscaloosa News,* Nov. 8, 1967.

voted 5–4 "Dr. King Loses Plea; Faces Five Days in Jail," *NYT,* June 12, 1967.

"rabble rousers" "State Guard's Riot Status Detailed Here," *Tuscaloosa News,* Nov. 8, 1967.

murder weapon MURKIN, 408.

best of friends Arthur Hanes Jr. (son), in discussions with author, May–June 2010.

liquor James Bennett, "Air Guard Hauling of Whiskey Probed," *BPH,* Jan. 16, 1965, 1.

state plane "Summary of Information Concerning Ku Klux Klan and Civil Rights Activity in Various Areas of the South from the Period May to May 31, 1965," Philip R. Manuel to Francis J. McNamara, July 28, 1965, Box 41, "Records from the 1965 Investigation of the Ku Klux Klan," HUAC, NARA.

Waldron Martin Waldron, "Ray's Ex-Lawyer Suggests He Was Hired for
Racial Aspect," *NYT,* Nov. 16, 1968.

Richard Helms "Subject: Arthur Jackson Hanes," Director of Security to
Mrs. Elizabeth Dunlevy, November 20, 1968, CIA, Record Series 104-
10117-10304, Record Series JFK, Agency File Number 80T01357A,
JFK Assassination System Identification Form, NARA, College Park.

Thomas McDowell "Memorandum for the Record" Deputy Director of
Security, 15 Oct. 1968, CIA, Subject "Hanes, Arthur J.," Record
Number: 104-10117-10304, Record Series: JFK, Agency File Number:
80T01357A, JFK Assassination System Identification Form, NARA,
College Park.

"Arthur Jackson Hanes is a" Ibid.

"Confidential Correspondents' List" Arthur J. Hanes, personnel file, FBI file
67-HQ-17592.

31. An Educated Bluff

"You are hereby" Clerk of the Court J.A. Blackwell, Grand Jury Summons
for William Bradford Huie, State of Tennessee, January 1969, Attorney
General File, SCRD.

Room 1108 "Memorandum of Conversation Held with William Bradford
Huie," Feb. 5, 1969, Attorney General File, SCRD.

"Did Ray leave" "William B. Huie Summon to Bring All Documents Concerning Slaying of King," Attorney General File, SCRD.

"Ray and his brothers" "Memorandum of Conversation Held with William
Bradford Huie," Feb. 5, 1969, Attorney General File, SCRD.

one cigarette Footnote 57, United States Department of Justice, *Investigation
of Recent Allegations Regarding the Assassination of Martin Luther King,
Jr.,* June 2000. Accessed at www.justice.gov/crt/about/crm/mlk/mlk
notes.php.

"Mr. Huie further" Ibid.

"He then related" Ibid.

hovered over his shoulder Robert K. Dwyer to Robert Jensen, Feb. 5, 1969,
Attorney General File, SCRD.

32. A Simple Story

deposition started The entire exchange that follows comes from Huie's grand
jury deposition. "Statement Taken in the Grand Jury Room on February
7, 1969, from William Bradford Huie at 10:55 AM Concerning a Possible
Conspiracy in the Assassination of Dr. Martin Luther King," Attorney
General File, SCRD.

surrendered Charles Edmundson, "Judge Laments Task After Citing
    Author," *MCA*, Feb. 8, 1969.

"I sent Mr. Huie" Edmundson, "Judge Laments," *MCA*, Feb. 8, 1969.

"The Shelby County" "No Indictments," *MPS*, Feb. 11, 1969.

"I think the attorney general" James Earl Ray to Hugh Stanton, Jan. 20, 1969,
    Prosecutor's File, SCRD. *Huntsville* Final Report, HSCA, 257.

33. Guilty, Not Racist

"I am appalled" Percy Foreman to Judge Preston Battle, Nov. 23, 1968,
    Attorney General, SCRD.

"Now, you know," Huie, *Dreamer*, 207.

Mustang James Earl Ray to Judge W. Preston Battle, et. al., Nov. 12, 1968,
    Ray Correspondence, SCRD.

public defender "Ray Ruled a Pauper; Public Defender to Aid Lawyer," *NYT*,
    Dec. 19, 1968.

"is still and will remain " James Earl Ray to Hugh Stanton, Jan. 20, 1969,
    Prosecutor's File, SCRD.

paid Hanes Percy Foreman to Michael Eugene, Feb. 14, 1969, Prosecutor's
    File, SCRD.

Renfro Hays "Statement of Renfro Hayes," Jan. 31, 1969, Prosecutor's File,
    SCRD.

"The only records" Percy Foreman to Michael Eugene, Jan. 31, 1969, Prosecu-
    tor's File, SCRD.

"that a blond male" "Report on Investigation of Ray Case," Feb. 6, 1969,
    Prosecutor's File, SCRD.

"the above mentioned hotels" "Report on Investigation of Ray Case," Feb. 6,
    1969, Prosecutor's File, SCRD.

"After getting up" "Summary of 'A' Block Daily Log for February 13–14,"
    Daily Activity Reports of James Earl Ray, Ray Jail Activity Logs,
    SCRD.

"I write this letter" Percy Foreman to James Earl Ray, Feb. 13, 1969, Prosecu-
    tor's File, SCRD.

"At 9:50 AM" "Summary of 'A' Block Daily Log for February 13–14," Daily
    Activity Reports of James Earl Ray, Ray Jail Activity Logs, SCRD.

"You has asked" James Earl Ray to Percy Foreman, Feb. 18, 1969, Prosecu-
    tor's File, SCRD.

Harry Wachtel Bernard Gavzer, "Ray Guilty Plea Decision Result of Nego-
    tiations," AP, March 15, 1969.

"material facts" "Proposed Stipulation . . . ," undated, Tennessee v. Ray,
    Attorney General File, SCRD.

fifty-six assertions "Proposed Stipulations," Attorney General File, SCRD.

"I don't want the Wallace part" James Earl Ray to Percy Foreman, undated, Attorney General File, SCRD.

34. The Last Supper

"developments" "Hearing for Ray Coming Monday," *MPS*, March 3, 1969.

The journalists This account of Ray's guilty plea is based on the following press reports: "Racism Motive Is Cited as Ray Pleads Guilty, Gets 99-Year Sentence," *MCA*, March 11, 1969, 1; Martin Waldron, "Ray Admits Guilt in Dr. King Death, Suggests a Plot," *NYT*, March 11, 1969; "Ray Case Ends—But Doubt Lingers," *MPS*, March 11, 1969, 1.

"rough-hewn courtroom" "Ray Case Ends—But Doubt Lingers," *MPS*, March 11, 1969, 13.

"James Earl Ray, stand" All statements by Foreman, Canale, and Ray come from "Voir Dire of Defendant on Waiver and Order," Tennessee v. Ray, March 10, 1969.

suddenly spoke "Voir Dire," Tennessee v. Ray, March 10, 1969. Waldon, "Ray Admits," *NYT*, March 11, 1969.

cartoon "More Should Be Told," *MCA*, March 11, 1969, 6.

Eastland "Toward Ray Case Truth," *MCA*, March 13, 1969, 4; Sen. James O. Eastland, Senate Internal Security Subcommittee, NARA (Name Files, Series 1, Boxes 89–90).

Coretta Scott King "Ray: 99 Years—and a Victory," *Newsweek*, March 24, 1969, 29–31.

$165,000 Percy Foreman to James Earl Ray, March 9, 1969, Public Defender File, SCRD.

Carlo Ponti Huie to James Earl Ray, March 7, 1969, Public Defender File, SCRD.

conceded doubts Bernard Cavzer, "Full Truth In Ray Case Still Mystery To Judge," AP, March 17, 1969.

"I wish to inform" James Earl Ray to Hon. Judge W. Preston Battle, March 13, 1969, Public Defender File, SCRD.

heart attack Charles Edmundson, "Ray Case Provided Classicist a Climactic Role," *MCA*, April 1, 1969, 1.

Part VII: Though It Hath No Tongue, 1969–1986

35. Bushman

The final Look *article* All quotes from *Look* come from: Huie, "Why James Earl Ray Murdered Dr. King," *Look*, April 15, 1969, 102–112.

payout "MEMORANDUM OF AGREEMENT," William Bradford Huie and Cowles Communications, Oct. 7, 1968, Attorney General File, SCRD. Ray v. Rose, 535 F.2d 936 (6th Cir. 1976), 969.

repaid Bob Ward, "William Bradford Huie Paid for Their Sins," *Writer's Digest*, September 1974, 16–22; "Plea Spoiled Book, Huie Testifies," *BN*, Oct. 7, 1974.

The Strange Case Clay Blair Jr. *The Strange Case of James Earl Ray* (New York: Bantam Books, 1969).

"If, in the dead" Percy Foreman, "Against Conspiracy," *Look*, April 15, 1969, 112.

"Twenty feet below" Arthur J. Hanes, "For Conspiracy," *Look*, April 15, 1969, 113.

"a very nice letter" Robert Kellett, "New Legal Role Takes Shape in Ray Case," *MCA*, March 22, 1969.

Huntley-Brinkley Report "James Earl Ray; Dr. Martin Luther King-Victim CR-Conspiracy," Memorandum, Birmingham MURKIN, 44-1740-2122.

Today show "Discussion of James Earl Ray Case," Memorandum, April 1, 1969, FBI 94-HQ4 SUB-6450, 35, NARA College Park, Maryland.

36. The Bushy Knoll

Russell X. Thompson Frank, *American Death*, 146–150; William Pepper, *Orders to Kill* (New York: Carol and Graf, 1965), 100–104.

Thompson immediately contacted "Penitentiary Number on Radio That Ray Left Behind Was Overlooked After Assassination of Dr. King," AP, March 18, 1969; "Ray Asks a Review of His Guilty Plea," *NYT*, March 20, 1969. "Rights Group Has No Play to Support a Ray Inquiry," *NYT*, March 21, 1969, 36; "Gunman Says Man Called 'Pete' Assassinated Dr. M.L. King Jr.," UPI, July 25, 1974.

Hoover was angered MURKIN, 44-38861, 5684.

"Thompson also advised" MURKIN, 44-38861, 5864.

"I suppose you James Earl Ray to J. B. Stoner, March 11, 1969, Public Defender File, SCRD.

"In the spring of" "Testimony of Jerry Ray," HSCA, vol. 7, 454.

identical statement Waldron, "Ex-Attorney Links Ray," *NYT*, April 2, 1969.

bugged the telephone "UNKNOWN SUBJECT: ARTHUR J. HANES-VICTIM INTERCEPTION OF COMMUNICATIONS," July 30, 1969, FBI File 139-3430 is Arthur Jackson Hanes Sr.'s FBI file.

turmoil "Power Struggle for Klan Control Speeds Its Decline," *WP*, Oct. 9, 1969, H2.

"airtel" MURKIN, 5828–5829.
"The Bureau is" MURKIN, 5829.
sixth floor MURKIN 5832.
two theories MURKIN 5832; MURKIN, 3833.

37. Belated Justice

"It's just a start" "Ex-Klansman Indicted," UPI, Sept. 27, 1977.
"It's ridiculously high" "Bomb Bonds 'High'" AP, Oct. 7, 1977.
St. Francis "Person in attendance at meeting in Colonel Al Lingo's room at St. Francis Motel September 29, 1963," Albert Burton Boutwell Papers, File #264.5.7, BPL.
his endorsement "Baxley Says Wallace Supports Him Out of Concern of Utility," AP, Sept. 23, 1978.
a jury of nine whites "Chambliss Trial Outcome Watched by the World," AP, Nov. 17, 1977.
Elizabeth Cobbs "Niece Quizzed in Bomb Case," AP, Nov. 16, 1977.
"rough talk" "Case Goes to Jury in Birmingham in '63 Church Bombing Fatal to 4," *NYT*, Nov. 18, 1977; Chambliss Trial Outcome Watched by the World," AP, Nov. 17, 1977.
"God knows, your honor" B. Drummond Ayres Jr., "Alabamian Guilty in '63 Church Blast That Killed 4 Girls; Ex-Klansman Gets Life Term," *NYT*, Nov. 19, 1977.
"What a shame" Ayres Jr., "Alabamian Guilty," *NYT*, Nov. 19, 1977.
"fucking brains out" "Chambliss' Lawyer Motions for a New Trial," *BN*, March 3, 1978. Clipping found online in BPL's Hill Ferguson Papers, 56.6.
"scapegoat" "Hanes Argues for Chambliss," *BPH*, April 6, 1979. Clipping found online in BPL's Hill Ferguson Papers, 56.6.
Hanes and Connor "Correspondence: Robert E. Chambliss to Flora Chambliss, May 1, 1969 to June 28, 1969," File 1969.1.2, Robert E. Chambliss Papers, BPL.
different church bombing Wayne King, "Indictments Recall Terror of Birmingham Sunday in 1963," *NYT*, Oct. 4, 1977.
"He insisted that I" Gary Sease, "Blasts Suspect Stoner Says He Was Asked to Get King Killed," AP, Sept. 28, 1977.
executive session Final Report, HSCA, 382–383.
"Nevertheless, in its review" Ibid.
conviction "Segregationist Stoner Is Convicted in '58 and Gets 10 Years," AP, May 15, 1980.

38. The Grapevine

Brushy Mountain Leon Daniel, "James Earl Ray Among Six Prison Escapees," *UPI*, June 11, 1977.

Playboy "Earl Ray Fails Polygraph," AP, Aug. 9, 1977.

bloodhounds "Ray Captured, Tennessee Tells US: Take Him Over," AP, June 14, 1977.

novel lead W. Pate McMichael, "The Plot to Kill a King," *St. Louis Magazine*, Jan. 2007.

St. Louis detectives Sergeant Robert Downey's extensive file on the St. Louis Art Museum Robbery of January 1978. The author possesses copies of Downey's collection of investigative reports.

"Byers talked freely" St. Louis to Director, "Re St. Louis Tel Call to Bureau, March 13, 1979," March 13, 1979, St. Louis FBI File 62-5097.

played bridge Marc Perrusquia, "Ray Expected Pay for Killing King, Investigators Conclude," *MCA*, March 23, 1998, 1.

White Citizens' Council "St. Louis Metropolitan Area Citizens' Council," St. Louis FBI File 157-582.

"It's not exactly" St. Louis FBI File 157-582, 22.

bankrolled Final Report, HSCA, 368–369.

Rotary Club McCuen Gill, *The St. Louis Story: Library of American Lives* (St. Louis, MO: Historical Record, Association, 1952), vol. 1–2, 784. Gene Roberts, "Says George Wallace in Awe: 'They Liked Me,'" *NYT*, Nov. 12, 1967.

"unofficial" Huie, *Dreamer*, 177.

Meet the Press George C. Wallace, *Meet the Press*, NBC, April 23, 1967.

"He and I are both" Final Report, HSCA, 369.

plethora of segregationist Final Report, HSCA, 364–368.

New York Times "Report by a Missouri Man Suggests Plotters Sought Murder of Dr. King," *NYT*, July 26, 1978, A1.

local judge Final Report, HSCA, 361–362. "Testimony of Murray L. Randall, special judge, St. Louis, Mo.," *Investigation*, 95th Cong., Nov. 27, 1978, vol. 7, HSCA, 204–237.

two anonymous sources Final Report, HSCA, 363.

"The conspiratorial" "Narration of Gene Johnson, deputy chief counsel," Nov. 29, 1978, *Investigation*, HSCA, 95th Cong., vol. 7, 174–175.

Wolf Hollow All the dialogue for Byers's testimony comes from "Testimony of Russell George Byers," Nov. 27, 1978, *Investigation*, 95th Cong., vol. 7, HSCA, 177–203.

"Cooley's gang" MURKIN, 3645.

Alexander Eist "Testimony of Alexander Eist, retired, Metropolitan Police Force, London, England," Nov. 9, 1978, *Investigation*, 95th Cong., vol. 4, HSCA, 10–76.

Rhodesia "Narration by G. Robert Blakey, on possible criminal motive of James Earl Ray and playing of tape," Nov. 10, 1978, *Investigation*, 95th Cong., vol. 4, HSCA 111–121.

Bank of Alton Drew Pearson and Jack Anderson, "Conspiracy Theory Exploded in King Assassination Case," *Washington Merry-Go-Round*, July 31, 1968.

four shots Wendall Rawls Jr., "House Unit Believes Kennedy and King Were Plot Victims," *NYT*, July 17, 1979, A1; Final Report, HSCA, 83–85.

39. Walking It Back

"no holds were barred" "Report on the Department of Justice Task Force to Review the FBI Martin Luther King, Jr., Security and Assassination Investigations," Department of Justice, Jan. 11, 1977, 1–6.

Internal FBI "Federal Bureau of Investigation," vol. 6, *Before the United States Senate Select Comm. to Study Governmental Operations with Respect to Intelligence Activities*, 94th Cong., Nov.–Dec. 1975, 46–47.

Stanley Levison David J. Garrow, "The FBI and Martin Luther King," *Atlantic Monthly*, July/August 2002, 80–88.

"uproarious party" Drew Pearson, "Kennedy, Despite Denials, Ordered FBI Wiretapping," *Washington Merry-Go-Round*, May 24, 1968; Jack Anderson, "Hoover Employed Dirty Tricks on King," *Washington Merry-Go-Round*, Nov. 27, 1975.

threatening letters "Final Report," Book III, April 23, 1976, *Before the United States Senate Select Comm. to Study Governmental Operations with Respect to Intelligence Activities*, 94th Cong. Beverly Gage, "What an Uncensored Letter to M.L.K. Reveals," *NYT*, Nov. 11, 2014. The most notorious letter can accessed at http://mobile.nytimes.com/2014/11/16/magazine/what-an-uncensored-letter-to-mlk-reveals.html?_r=2&referrer=.

enjoined Ray v. Rose, 392 F.Supp. 601 (6th Cir. 1975), 607–608.

salacious title Huie, *Did the FBI Kill Martin Luther King?* (Nashville, TN: Thomas Nelson, 1977).

"In all I must have" Huie, *Did the FBI*, 211–212.

Atlanta Magazine Huie, "James Earl Ray: The Final Wail of a Lonely Loser," *Atlanta Magazine*, January 1979, 35–37.

"An 'investigating'" Huie, "The One and Only," *Skeptic*, vol. 18 March/April 1977, 25–27, 56–57.

interrogation "Report of HSCA Interview with William Bradford Huie, April 10, 1978, Hartselle, Alabama," MLK Exhibit F-613, April 10, 1978, *Investigation*, 95th Cong., HSCA vol. 7, 439–445.

Asa Carter Final Report, HSCA, 658.

"Forrest Carter" Dan T. Carter, "The Transformation of a Klansman," *NYT*, Oct. 4, 1991.

"He mentioned that" "Subject: UNSUBS; BOMBING BETH ISRAEL CON-GREGATION SYNAGOGUE, 5315 OLD CANTON ROAD, JACK-SON, MISSISSIPPI, 9/18/67," Airtel, SAC Jackson to SAC Birmingham, July 18, 1968, Birmingham FBI File 174-117, FBI File 100-4561-105.

Hanes Everything about Huie's relationship with Hanes comes from "Report of HSCA Interview," HSCA vol. 7, 439–445; Report of HSCA Interview with William Bradford Huie, April 10, 1978, Hartselle, Alabama," MLK Exhibit F-613, April 10, 1978, *Investigation*, 95th Cong., HSCA vol. 7, 439–445.

40. The Klan?

a subpoena Final Report, HSCA, 379–380.

queue Ibid.

Klansman George Wilson Ibid.

"two documents" Ibid.

Source A Ibid.

Source B Ibid.

"The committee was" Ibid.

eyebrows Marc Perrusquia, "Ray Expected Pay for Killing King, Investigators Conclude," *MCA*, March 23, 1998, 1. John Birch Society, *White Book of the John Birch Society*, 1963.

met secretly Jack Nelson and Nicholas C. Chriss, "Radical Rightists Play Key Roles in Wallace Drive," *LAT*, Sept. 17, 1968, 1.

personal invitations Ibid.

Floyd Kitchen Jules Witcover, "George Wallace Isn't Kidding," *Reporter*, Feb. 23, 1967, 23; "The Extreme Right Invasion of the 1968 Campaign," Anti-Defamation League of B'Nai B'rith, October 1968, vol. 18, No. 3, 474.

"national staff" Witcover, "George Wallace," ADL, vol. 18, No. 3, 474.

two miles Both Floyd G. Kitchen and Carol Ray lived in Maplewood, Missouri. Kitchen sent out both Citizens' Council and American Independent Party literature from a Maplewood address.

"can't help" Floyd G. Kitchen to W. Pate McMichael, April 6, 2010, in possession of the author; Floyd G. Kitchen to W. Pate McMichael, April 22, 2010, in possession of the author.

41. Full Circle

Huie died "William Bradford Huie, 76, Writer and Crusader for Civil Rights, Dies," *WP*, Nov. 24, 1986, B6.

"Castleton discovers" Lil Kilpatrick, "Huie's Novel Debunks 'Kennedy Myth,'" *Decatur* (Alabama) *Daily*, April 6, 1980.

"General Reed" "The Adversary," Box 12, Folder 95, 101, p. 67–140, HUIE. Also see "The Adversary-Notes," Box 83, Folder 105.

"Art Hanes got in touch" Huie, interview, *Eyes on the Prize.*

"I went in to see" "Huie's Deposition," Cornelia Wallace v. G. Wallace . . . , Box 42, Folder 450, HUIE.

screenplay Ibid.

Cornelia "Motions regarding Cornelia Wallace v. G. Wallace . . . ," Box 40, Folder 447–449, HUIE.

Epilogue

"I'll buy anybody" Ernest B. Furgurson, "Birmingham Now: Hanes Unrepentant But Resigned," the *Baltimore Sun*, March 10, 1983.

"mock trial" Guilt or Innocence: Trial of James Earl Ray, produced by Jack Saltman, directed by Clive Halls (Los Angeles: Home Box Office, April 4, 1993), VHS, 179 min.

no basis "Death Scene of Dr. King is Changed," *MPS*, Aug. 7, 1968.

Ramparts William Pepper, "The Children of Vietnam," *Ramparts*, January 1967, 45–68.

Riverside Martin Luther King Jr., "Beyond Vietnam," delivered April 4, 1967, at Riverside Church, New York City.

first sources Pepper, *Orders to Kill*, 136–137.

BBC Pepper, *Orders*, 160–165.

first book James Earl Ray, *Who Killed Martin Luther King? The True Story by the Alleged Assassin* (Washington, DC: National Press Books, 1992).

Alpha 184 Stephen G. Tompkins, "Army Feared King," *MCA*, March 21, 1993.

"On the order" Pepper, *Orders*, 417–421.

Turning Point "Who Shot Martin Luther King Jr.?" *Turning Point*, ABC News, June 19, 1997.

confronted "Ray Tells Son He Didn't Kill Father," CNN, March 27, 1997.

final investigation United States Department of Justice, *Investigation of Recent Allegations Regarding the Assassination of Martin Luther King, Jr.*, June 2000.

Lloyd Jowers Trial Transcript, Coretta Scott King v. Lloyd Jowers, Circuit Court of Shelby County, 13th Judicial District, State of Tennessee, No.

97242, Dec. 8, 1999. Accessed at www.thekingcenter.org/civil-case
-king-family-versus-jowers.

Grabow "VI: Raoul and His Alleged Participation in the Assassination,"
Recent Allegations, DOJ.

Wilson Ibid.

"Part of the evidence", Trial Transcript, King v. Jowers, 2619.

family tradition Ibid.,780–809.

whitewash "Art Hanes Jr.: Son of Segregationist Birmingham Mayor Says
Dad Privately Tried to Integrate," *BN*, Feb. 20, 2013. Accessed at http://
blog.al.com/spotnews/2013/02/art_hanes_jr_son_of_segregatio.html.

SELECTED BIBLIOGRAPHY

Arsenault, Raymond. *Freedom Riders: 1961 and the Struggle for Racial Justice*. New York: Oxford University Press, 2006.

Bass, Jack. *Taming the Storm: The Life and Times of Frank M. Johnson, Jr. and the South's Fight over Civil Rights*. New York: Doubleday, 1993.

Bernstein, Irving. *Promises Kept: John F. Kennedy's New Frontier*. New York: Oxford University Press, 1991.

Branch, Taylor. *At Canaan's Edge: America in the King Years, 1965–1968*. New York: Simon & Schuster, 2006.

———. *Pillar of Fire: America in the King Years, 1963–1965*. New York: Simon & Schuster, 1999.

Carter, Dan. T. *Politics of Rage: George Wallace, Origins of the New Conservatism, the Transformation of American Politics*. Second Edition. Baton Rouge: Louisiana State University, 2000.

Clark, E. Culpepper. *The Schoolhouse Door: Segregation's Last Stand at the University of Alabama*. New York: Oxford University Press, 1995.

Clark, James J. *I Saw Selma Raped: The Jim Clark Story*. Birmingham: Selma Enterprises/Sizemore Agency, 1966.

Dorman, Michael. *We Shall Overcome*. New York: Delacorte, 1964.

Epstein, Edward Jay. *Inquest: The Warren Commission and the Establishment of Truth*. New York: The Viking Press, 1966.

Eskew, Glenn. *But for Birmingham: The Local and National Movements in the Civil Rights Struggle*. Chapel Hill: The University of North Carolina Press, 1997.

Frederick, Jeffery. *Stand Up for Alabama: George C. Wallace*. Tuscaloosa: University of Alabama Press, 2007.

Frank, Gerold. *An American Death*. New York: Doubleday, 1972.

Garrow, David J. *Bearing the Cross: Martin Luther King, Jr., and the Southern Christian Leadership Conference.* New York: HarperCollins, 1986.

———. *Protest at Selma: Martin Luther King, Jr. and the Voting Rights Act of 1965.* New Haven: Yale University Press, 1978.

Gordon, J.A. *Nightriders: The Inside Story of the Liuzzo Killing.* Birmingham: BRALGO Publications, 1966.

Hanes, James Oscar. *Aggressive Evangelism.* Nashville: Cokesbury Press, 1935.

———. *Five Years on the Firing Line.* Nashville: House M.E. Church, 1913.

Huie, William Bradford. *Did the FBI Kill Martin Luther King?* Nashville: Thomas Nelson, 1977.

———. *He Slew the Dreamer.* New York: Delacorte Press, 1970.

———. *Mud on the Stars.* New York: L.B. Fisher Publishing, 1942.

———. *Mud on the Stars.* Tuscaloosa: University of Alabama Press, 1996.

———. *Ruby McCollum: Woman in a Suwannee Jail.* New York: E.P. Dutton, 1956.

———. *The Execution of Private Slovik.* New York: Duell, Sloan & Pearce, 1954.

———. *The Klansman.* New York: Delacorte, 1967.

———. *The Revolt of Mamie Stover.* New York: Duell, Sloan & Pearce, 1951.

———. *Three Lives for Mississippi.* Oxford, MS: University of Mississippi Press, 2000.

Jones, William Grover. *The Wallace Story.* Northport, AL: American Colonial Printing, 1966.

King, Martin Luther, Jr. *A Call to Conscience: The Landmark Speeches of Dr. Martin Luther King, Jr.* New York: Hachette, 2001.

May, Gary. *The Informant: The FBI, the Ku Klux Klan, and the Murder of Viola Liuzzo.* New Haven, CT: Yale University Press, 2005.

McMillan, George. *The Making of an Assassin: The Life of James Earl Ray.* Boston: Little Brown, 1972.

McMillen, Neil R. *The Citizens' Councils: Organized Resistance to the Second Reconstruction 1954–64.* Champaign: University of Illinois Press, 1994.

McWhorter, Diane. *Carry Me Home: Birmingham, Alabama: The Climactic Battle of the Civil Rights Revolution.* New York: Simon & Schuster, 2002.

Mikell, Robert M. *Selma.* Charlotte, NC: Citadel Press, 1965.

Newton, Michael. *A Case of Conspiracy: James Earl Ray and the Assassination of Martin Luther King, Jr.* Los Angeles: Holloway House Publishing, 1980.

Nicholas, Michael Cooper. *"Cities Are What Men Make Them": Birmingham, Alabama, Faces the Civil Rights Movement, 1963.* Providence, RI: Brown University, 1974.

Nunnelly, William A. *Bull Connor*. Tuscaloosa: University of Alabama Press, 1991.

Persons, Albert C. *Bay of Pigs*. Birmingham, AL: Swalley Printing Co., 1968.

———. *Riot! Riot! Riot!* Birmingham, AL: Esco Publishers, 1965.

———. *Sex and Civil Rights: The True Selma Story*. Birmingham, AL: Esco Publishers, 1965.

Pepper, William. *Orders to Kill*. New York: Carol and Graf, 1965.

Posner, Gerald. *Killing the Dream*. New York: Harcourt Brace & Co., 1999.

Pride, Richard Allen. *The Political Use of Racial Narratives: School Desegregation in Mobile, Alabama, 1954–1967*. Champaign: The University of Illinois Press, 2002.

Raines, Howell. *My Soul Is Rested: Movement Days in the Deep South Remembered*. New York: Penguin Books, 1983.

Roberts, Gene, and Hank Klibanoff. *The Race Beat: The Press, the Civil Rights Struggle, and the Awakening of the Nation*. New York: Knopf, 2006.

Rowe, Gary Thomas. *My Undercover Years with the FBI*. New York: Bantam, 1976.

Sides, Hampton. *Hellhound on His Trail: The Stalking of Martin Luther King, Jr. and the International Hunt for His Assassin*. New York: Doubleday, 2010.

Simonelli, Frederick James. *American Fuehrer: George Lincoln Rockwell and the American Nazi Party*, Champaign,: University of Illinois Press, 1999.

Sims, Patsy. *The Klan*. Second Edition. Lexington: The University of Kentucky Press, 2006.

Stanton, Mary. *From Selma to Sorrow: The Life and Death of Viola Liuzzo*. Athens: University of Georgia Press, 2000.

Trest, Warren, and Donald Dodd. *Wings of Denial: The Alabama Air National Guard's Covert Role at the Bay of Pigs*. Montgomery, AL: New South Books, 2001.

Webb, Clive. *Rabble Rousers: The American Far Right in the Civil Rights Era*. Athens: University of Georgia Press, 2010.

Willis, Gary, and Ovid Demaris. *Jack Ruby*. New York: The New American Library, 1967.

Wright, Simeon, with Herb Boyd. *Simeon's Story: An Eyewitness Account of the Kidnapping of Emmett Till*. Chicago: Chicago Review Press, 2010.

INDEX

Aaron, Judge Edward, xiii, 50–51, 70, 177
Adams, Clifford Leroy, 44–45
Adams, Hal W., 45
Albany, Georgia, 65–66
American Independent Party, 148, 217, 243, 244, 257
American Mercury (magazine), 39–40, 41, 43
Appell, Donald, 141

Baker, Leo, 198
Battle, W. Preston
  death of, 222
  Foreman defending Ray, 212, 219–22
  gag order, 23–25, 27, 29, 31–32, 167–68, 169, 172, 184–85, 195, 209–10
  Hanes fired, 181, 183, 184–85
  Huie involvement, 33–35, 169, 192, 210
Baughn, Hubert, 40
Baxley, Bill, 235, 236
Bay of Pigs invasion, 148, 193, 194, 196–98, 201, 202, 203, 206, 207, 258–59, 264
Beasley, James, 207
Benevetta, Tony, 228–30
Bevel, James, 66, 98, 142

Birmingham, Alabama
  Bay of Pigs, 197–98, 201–2, 203, 206, 259, 264
  as "Bombingham," xiii, 50, 66, 68, 71, 74, 75–76, 135, 142, 238
  Green Beret unit, 264–66
  Hanes as mayor, xiii, 9, 10, 11, 12, 52, 56–66, 68–69, 140, 197, 202, 261, 270
  integration, 59–63, 73–76
  King and, 63, 66–69, 200
  Mother's Day Riot, 57–58, 128–29
  16th Street Church, xiii, 66, 75–80, 134, 135, 142, 235–38
Birmingham Trust National Bank, 140, 149, 173, 247
Bonebrake, George, 14, 183, 213, 262
Boutwell, Albert, 65, 74
Brady, Tom, 46
Bremer, Arthur, 236
Breslin, Jimmy, 111, 114
Brewer, Bessie, 161, 195, 227, 262
Brewster, Willie, 130
Browder v. Gayle (1956), 131
Brown, Ned, 120
Brown v. Board of Education (1954), 46, 47
Bryant, Carolyn, 47, 48, 49

Bryant, Roy, 47, 48
Buckley, William F., Jr., 43
Burke, Emory, 81
"bushman" theory, 180, 213, 226–
    27, 230, 261, 262–63, 264
Butler, Robert, 14–15
Byers, Russell, 242–43, 244–46
Byrd, Robert, 176

Cagle, Charles, 79
Caldwell, Earl, 180, 262–63
Canale, Phil, 30, 183, 205–7, 209,
    215–16, 217, 220
Carson, Johnny, 170–71
Carter, Asa Earl, 50, 70, 101, 177,
    197, 239, 252–53, 257
Carter, Harold "Cornbread," 180,
    213, 227, 231
Chalmers, Lester V., Jr., 140–41
Chambliss, Robert "Dynamite,"
    79–80, 84, 235–38
Champagne, Donald, 262
Chaney, James, 87–90
Charlton, Louise, 106
church bombings, xiii, 50, 66,
    75–80, 134, 135, 142, 235–38
CIA (Central Intelligence Agency),
    55, 197–98, 202–3, 264
Civil Rights Act (1964), 87, 243
Clark, Jim, 96–100, 111, 148, 199,
    243, 257
Clark, Ramsey, 12, 17, 18–19, 31
Clinton, Bill, 266, 269–70
Cloud, John, 99–100
Cobbs, Elizabeth, 236–37
Cole, Nat King, 50
Collins, Addie Mae, 75
Communist conspiracy
    Democratic National Convention,
        35
    FBI aiding Communism, 82
    Hanes about Ray, 26–27, 29, 30,
        31
    King as Communist, 66, 72, 142,
        158, 226, 249–50
    Niggerism as, 123

Oswald affiliation, 29, 148
    Wallace on assassinations, 164
Connor, Eugene "Bull," xiii, 12,
    56–58, 60, 62, 64, 65, 66–69,
    75, 238
Cooper, Annie Lee, 97
Creel, Robert, 107, 122, 123, 136,
    137

Daniels, Jon, 124, 125, 129
Del Monte, Bo, 157–58
DeMere, McCarthy, 20, 21
Democratic National Convention
    (1968), 35
Dickinson, William, 198
Doar, John, 131
Donaldson, Sam, 164
Dorman, Michael, 120, 121, 126
Doster, Reid, 197, 199–201, 206,
    209
Downey, Robert, 242
Dulles, Allen, 89
Dwyer, Robert, 184

Eastland, James, 222
Eaton, William, 106, 111, 114, 123,
    131, 136
Eisenhower, Dwight, 43, 44, 131
Eist, Alexander, 247
Engram, Everett, 125
Eugene, Michael, 7–10, 15, 19, 183,
    212–13

FBI (Federal Bureau of Investigation)
    Byers report, 242–43, 245
    church bombing, 78, 83–84
    Hanes as Special Agent, 10, 11,
        55, 202, 203, 234, 264
    Hanes on gunrunning, 232–34
    Huie Look articles, 171–72
    King harassment, 249–50, 262
    Mississippi civil rights workers,
        88–93
    Ray extradition, 14, 17, 18–21
    Ray manhunt, xii, 27–28
    source material, xii

"Ten Most Wanted Fugitives" list, 157, 162
Thompson's Benevetta, 229–30
Wilson and Mustang, 267–68
See also Hoover, J. Edgar; Rowe, Gary Thomas
Ferrie, David, 148, 193, 269
Fields, Edward R., 81, 166
Flowers, Richmond, 113, 201
Floyd, Bart, 50, 51
Foreman, Percy, 182–83, 184, 192, 211–22, 226, 228, 267
Forrest, Nathan Bedford, 94–95
Frank, Gerold, xii, 182
Freedom Riders, 57, 100, 128, 130
Freedom Summer (1964), 87

gag order, 23–25, 27–30, 167, 169, 195
   contempt committee, 31–32, 167–68, 172, 184–85, 209–10
Galt, Eric S., 2, 23, 173
Garrison, Jim, 3, 148–49, 189–90, 191, 193, 231, 268, 269
Gaston Motel (Birmingham), 68, 71
Godfrey, Donald, 135
Goldwater, Barry, 176
Goodman, Andrew, 87–90
Grabow, Glenda, 267
Gray, Wade, 198
Grooms, Hobart, 59–60
Guilt or Innocence: The Trial of James Earl Ray (HBO), 261–63

Hall, John, 79
Hanes, Art, Jr., 11, 13, 23, 53, 59, 179, 181, 184, 235, 236, 237, 238, 270–71
Hanes, Arthur J. (Art), 53–56
   as Birmingham mayor, xiii, 9, 10, 11, 12, 52, 56–66, 68–69, 140, 197, 202, 261, 270
   church bombing, 76, 79
   as CIA asset, 55, 202–3, 264
   death threats, 22, 26, 238
   as FBI Special Agent, 10, 11, 55, 202, 203, 234, 264
   Hayes Aircraft, 55, 195, 197, 201, 202, 256
   as Klan attorney, xiii, 9, 18, 36, 131–32, 140, 166, 179, 231–32, 234, 235–38, 255–56, 264
   Liuzzo murder, 127–30, 131–32, 141
   Montgomery to Selma, 102
   Murphy death, 124
   Raoul conspiracy, xiii, 213, 230
   Ray in London, 8–13, 15–17, 18–19, 33, 165, 166, 212–13, 259
   Ray in Memphis, 21–23, 29–32, 179–85, 210, 228, 230, 231, 232–34
   Ray publishing deal, 33–35, 169–70, 195, 210, 212, 226–27, 253, 259
   Shelton and, 18, 179–80, 236
   Stoner versus, 166, 167–68, 169–70
   as Wallace supporter, 88, 176, 233, 236, 256, 270
   White Citizens' Council, 72–73
Hanes, Eleanor, 53, 179, 181
Hanes, Jimmy Oscar, 52–53, 59
Hayes Aircraft, 55, 56, 67, 195, 197, 201, 202, 256
Hayneville, Alabama
   Daniels murder, 124, 125, 129
   Liuzzo murder, 110–16, 127–30
Hays, Renfro, 180, 212
Helms, Richard, 202
He Slew the Dreamer (Huie), 225, 250, 259
Hoover, J. Edgar
   church bombing, 78, 80
   on Hanes, 11, 12–13, 18–19, 128, 232
   on Huie, 88–89, 119
   Liuzzo murder, 105
   Ray extradition, 17, 18–19
   Reader's Digest story, 27–29
   See also FBI (Federal Bureau of Investigation)

Hotel Albert (Selma), 95
House Select Committee on Assassinations (HSCA), 241–48, 252–57
House Un-American Activities Committee (HUAC), 119, 133–45, 156
Hudson, Bill, 67
Huie, Lois, 49
Huie, Ruth, 41, 49
Huie, William Bradford
  background, xiii–xiv, 39–45, 51
  Bay of Pigs, 196–98, 206, 207, 258–59
  church bombing, 77–78
  Daniels murder, 124
  death threats, 126, 131
  Hanes firing, 182–83
  King friendship, 49–50, 250–51
  King slaying testimony, 204–10
  Liuzzo murder, 110–11, 119–22, 123, 125–26
  Mississippi civil rights workers, 88–93
  Raoul conspiracy, xiii–xv, 171–72, 173, 189, 192, 206, 208, 209, 225, 259
  Ray publishing deal, 33–35, 169–74, 195–96, 199, 211–13, 222, 225, 253, 259
  Till story, xiii, 46–49
  Wallace peacemaking, 260
  writing by, xiv–xv, 34, 39–40, 41, 42, 43–44, 45, 48–49, 51, 77, 90, 109, 121, 130, 171, 174, 196, 225, 250–54, 258, 259
Humphrey, Hubert, 175, 177–78
Hunt, E. Howard, 268
Hunter-Gault, Charlayne, 261
Hurston, Zora Neale, 44–45

Jackson, Jesse, 264
Jackson, Jimmie Lee, 97–98
Jacksonville, Florida, 135–38
Jaubert, Sergio, 191–92
Jeffers, Lew, 56, 67

Johnson, Frank M., 101, 131–32
Johnson, Lyndon, 87–88, 90, 100–101, 105, 139, 162, 176
Johnson, Paul, 90
Johnston, Paul, 121–22, 125
Jones, Solomon, 180, 226–27, 230
Jowers, Lloyd, 266–67, 269–70

Katzenbach, Nicholas, 105, 121
Kauffmann, John, 244, 245–46
KBI. See Klan Bureau of Investigation
Kennedy, John F.
  Alabama, 67, 68, 72, 75, 80, 176
  assassination, xi, 148–49, 189–91, 193, 207, 209, 248, 267, 270
  Bay of Pigs, 198
  Connor at inauguration, 56
  Huie interview, 42
Kennedy, Joseph, Sr., 41
Kennedy, Richard, 119, 120, 121
Kennedy, Robert, 1, 67, 71, 170, 193, 221, 249
King, Coretta Scott, 215–16, 222, 250, 266
King, Dexter, 266, 267
King, Martin Luther, Jr.
  in Albany, Georgia, 65–66
  antiwar speech, 263
  assassination, xi, 1, 159–61, 163, 165, 193, 220, 232, 238–39, 242, 245, 246, 259, 263, 265, 267, 269–70
  assassination of John F. Kennedy, xi
  Birmingham, 63, 66–69, 200
  on church bombing, 76, 78
  as Communist, 66, 72, 142, 158, 226, 249–50
  on death penalty, 216
  death threats, xi, 68, 71, 94, 160–61, 227, 245, 250
  FBI harassment of, 249–50, 262
  Huie friendship, 49–50, 250–51
  on Klan convictions, 132
  in Los Angeles, 158–59

March on Washington, 72,
140–41
in Memphis, 160–61
Nobel Peace Prize, 94, 246
Selma, 94–98, 100–103
Three Lives for Mississippi foreword, 171, 251
King, Tom, 57, 58
King v. Jowers (1999), 269–70
Kitchen, Floyd, 257
Klan Bureau of Investigation (KBI),
68, 72, 107, 141–42
Klokan Committee, 136–38
Ku Klux Klan
attorney Hanes, xiii, 9, 18, 36,
131–32, 140, 166, 179, 231–32,
234, 235–38, 255–56, 264
attorney Stoner, 36, 80–83, 102,
130, 135, 136–37, 140, 144–45,
238–39
church bombings, xiii, 50, 66,
75–76, 134, 135, 142, 235
convictions against, 130–32, 145,
237–38, 239
first imperial wizard, 95
HUAC investigations, 119, 133–
45, 156
Klokan Committee, 136–38
Liuzzo murder, 111, 113, 114, 141
NSRP and, 102, 134, 135, 136, 166
Original Ku Klux Klan of the
Confederacy, 50–51, 70
United Klans of America, xiii, 9,
18, 57, 68, 137, 141, 143–44
Wallace and, v, 70, 71, 73–74, 75,
78, 88, 110, 120, 130, 143, 145,
147, 156, 256–57
"White Man's Defense Fund," 140,
149, 165, 173
See also Murphy, Matthew Hob-
son, Jr.; National States Rights
Party (NSRP); Rowe, Gary
Thomas

Lane, Mark, xiv, 264
Langston, Tommy, 57, 128

Latimer, James M., 229
Lawson, James, 247
Layton, Larry, 242
Lee, George W., 47
Levison, Stanley, 249
Lewis, Clayton, 89
Lewis, John, 100
Liberto, Frank, 267, 269
Lingo, Al, 71, 78, 79, 96, 97, 201,
236
Liuzzo, Viola, 11, 12, 104–8, 112–
16, 127–30, 131, 140, 141, 198
Lomax, Louis, 155, 192–93
Longines Chronicles (TV), 42–43
Lorraine Motel (Memphis), xi, 160,
161, 165, 180, 195–96, 220,
262, 265
Lowery, Joseph, 227

MacArthur, Douglas, 23, 54
Maddox, Lester, 243
Maguire, J. Russell, 43
Manuel, Philip, 133–38
Marcello, Carlos, 193, 269
Marshall, Burke, 67
Martin, Marie, 154–55, 216
McCarthy, Joseph R., 42
McCollum, Ruby, 44–45
McDowell, Thomas, 202
McMillan, George, 83
McNair, Chris, 77
McNair, Denise, 75, 77–78, 237
McNair, Maxine, 77
Memphis, Tennessee
King assassination, xi, 1–2, 160–
61, 163, 165, 213, 271
King v. Jowers, 269
Lorraine Motel, xi, 160, 161, 165,
180, 195–96, 220, 262, 265
Ray from London, 20–23, 30, 32
trial venue, 17–18, 179–80, 184,
211, 212, 215, 261
Mencken, H. L., 39–40, 43
Metz, George, 91–92
Milam, Juanita, 49
Milam, J. W., 47, 48

Miles College, 62–63
Morris, William (sheriff), 20–21, 23,
    30, 31, 36, 167, 181, 182
Morris, William Hugh, 239
Mother's Day Riot, 57–58, 128–29
Moton, Leroy, 104–5, 112, 128, 198
Murphy, Matthew Hobson, Jr.
    church bombing, 79–80, 83, 84,
        236
    death of, 122–24, 125
    Klan activities, 102, 135, 136–37,
        201
    Liuzzo murder, 106–7, 110, 111–
        16, 121, 140, 141

National States Rights Party
    (NSRP), 36
    Brewster murder, 130
    Hanes and, 73
    King attacked by, 95
    Klan and, 102, 134, 135, 136, 166
    Stoner and, 36, 80–83, 95, 130,
        165
    Wallace honored by, 75
"Never," 52, 56, 74, 96, 111
New Orleans
    Garrison activity, 3, 148, 189, 193
    Raoul connection, 171–72, 193–
        94, 209, 262, 269
    Ray in, 2, 155, 159, 192–94, 207,
        216, 270
    White Citizens' Council of Amer-
        ica, 147
Night Riders (Klan), 113
Nixon, Richard, 1, 175–76, 177–78,
    268

O'Hara, Richard, 243, 245
O'Leary, Jeremiah, 27–29
Oswald, Lee Harvey, xiv, 16, 29,
    30, 148–49, 190, 193, 194, 207,
    209, 248, 267

Patriotic Legal Fund, 165
Pepper, William, 263–67, 269
Persons, Albert, 196–99

Persons, Larry, 196–97
Pettus Bridge, 99–103, 159
Pitts, Lucius, 62–63
Ponti, Carlo, 222, 225
Pool, Joe, 143–44
Poor People's Campaign, 158
Posner, Gerald, xii
Pritchett, Laurie, 65
Project C, 64–69, 74, 75, 77–78,
    120, 200

Randall, Murry, 245
Raoul
    conspiracy creation, xiii, 181,
        185
    Hanes on, 213, 230
    Huie on, 171–72, 173, 189, 192,
        206, 208, 209, 225
    as Raul, 267–70
    Ray on, 193, 262
    Thompson on, 228–30
Ray, Carol, 243, 257
Ray, Jack, 3, 8, 17, 148, 177, 182,
    218, 243, 244, 247
Ray, James Earl
    background, 2, 8, 247
    Birmingham, 149, 159, 160, 195,
        199, 200–201, 262
    Brushy Mountain penitentiary,
        240–41, 246, 262
    Dexter King and, 266
    Foreman as attorney, 182–83, 184,
        192, 211–22, 226, 228
    guilty plea, 204–5, 214–17, 219–
        22, 225, 230, 261, 269
    Hanes fired, 179–85, 210
    Huie publishing contract, 33–35,
        169–74, 210, 222
    King assassination, 159–62
    London arrest, 1, 7–10, 14–19,
        162, 165
    in Los Angeles, 149, 153, 154–55,
        157–59
    media portrayal, xi, 1–3, 13, 35
    Memphis from London, 20–23,
        30, 32

Missouri State Penitentiary, 146–
49, 244
New Orleans, 2, 155, 159, 192–
94, 207, 216, 270
Pepper as attorney, 261–66
plastic surgery, 157, 174
Rhodesia, 157, 162, 247
as Sneyd, 1, 8, 10, 13, 15, 17, 162,
213
Stoner as attorney, 36, 165–67,
168, 169–70, 231
as Wallace supporter, 154–55,
157–58, 167, 177–78, 205–6,
216–17, 244
Ray, Jerry, 3, 8, 167, 177, 182–83,
206, 208, 210, 218, 247
Ray, Thomas "Pete," 198
Reader's Digest, 27–29, 30
Reeb, James, 124
Robertson, Carole, 75
Rockwell, George Lincoln, 43
Rosecrans, William, Jr., 135–38
Roton, Ralph, 107, 141
Rowe, Gary Thomas
arrest, 105, 106–8
HUAC testimony, 133–38
Huie offer, 119–20, 121–22,
125–26
testimony, 109–10, 113–15, 128–
30, 131
Ruby, Jack, xiv, 30, 209, 267
Russell, Jane, 42

Salisbury, Harrison, 52
Schwerner, Michael, 87–90
Selma, Alabama
Civil War, 94–95
Hanes and Luizzo murder, 11, 12
marches, 94–103, 131
Montgomery, Alabama march,
99–103, 131
Sexton, Melvin, 255, 256
Shamburger, Riley, 198
Shanahan, Neil, 105, 107–8, 115,
262
Shaw, Clay, 189–90, 193, 194

Shelton, Robert K.
Hanes and, 18, 179–80, 236
House investigations, 136–37,
139–40, 143, 145, 255
Klan activities, 68, 79, 102, 110
Liuzzo murder, 106–7, 111, 114,
134–35
as Wallace supporter, 145, 156,
164, 257
Sheppard v. Maxwell (1966), 24,
31
Shores, Arthur, 74
Shuttlesworth, Fred, 61, 74, 238
Shuttlesworth, Ruby, 61
Sides, Hampton, xii
Sirhan, Sirhan, 170, 221
Sixteenth Street Baptist Church,
xiii, 66, 75–80, 134, 135, 142,
235–38
Slovik, Eddie, 43–44
Sneyd, Raymond George, 1, 8, 10,
13, 15, 17, 162, 213
Snow, Henry, 232–33
Stanton, Hugh, 212
Stein, Charles, 155, 159, 192, 207,
216
Stein, Rita, 155, 159, 216
Stephens, Charles Quitman, 180,
191
St. Louis, Missouri
Grapevine Tavern, 257
Ray home, 8, 14, 153, 164
Sutherland plot, xv, 242–44, 245
Wallace presidential candidacy,
148, 153, 164, 243–44,
Stokes, Louis, 245
Stoner, J. B.
church bombing, 238–39
HUAC investigation, 135, 136–37,
144–45
on King, 95, 102
as NSRP figurehead, 36, 80–83,
130, 140, 165
as Ray attorney, 36, 165–67, 168,
169–70, 231
as Wallace supporter, 165

Strange, Hubert, 130
Sullivan, Joseph, 89, 91, 92, 93
Sullivan, William, 249
Sutherland, John H., xv, 243–44, 245–46, 256, 257

Taylor, Macy, 227, 232
Thagard, T. Werth, 112, 114, 115
They Slew the Dreamer (Huie), xiv–xv, 34, 174, 196, 225, 251
Thomas, Eugene, 106, 114, 123, 131, 136
Thompson, Russell X., 228–31
Three Lives for Mississippi (Huie), 109, 121, 171, 251
Thunderbolt (NSRP), 81, 83, 111, 144–45
Till, Emmett, xiii, 47–48, 49
Tompkins, Stephen, 264–66, 269
tramps, 190–92, 194, 209, 265, 268
Turner, William, 191

United Klans of America, xiii, 9, 18, 57, 68, 137, 141, 143–44

Vinson, Fred, Jr., 9
voting rights, 47, 87, 94, 95, 97, 98, 101, 124, 131

Wachtel, Harry, 215–16
Waggoner, Jabo, 60, 64, 65
Waldron, Martin, 202
Wallace, Cornelia, 260
Wallace, George Corley
  electors as, 176
  Gallup polls, 163, 164
  as governor of Alabama, 70–75, 78, 79, 99, 101–2, 103, 143–44, 154, 201, 236

  Hanes as supporter, 88, 176, 233, 236, 256, 270
  Huie peacemaking, 260
  Judge Johnson versus, 132
  on King assassination, 163–64
  Klan and, v, 70, 71, 73–74, 75, 78, 88, 110, 120, 130, 143, 145, 147, 156, 256–57
  presidential candidacy, v, 88, 123, 145, 147–48, 149, 153–54, 155, 164, 175–76, 177–78, 236, 243–44, 257
  Ray as supporter, 154–55, 157–58, 167, 177–78, 205–6, 216–17, 244
  Shelton as supporter, 145, 156, 164, 257
  Stoner as supporter, 165
Wallace, Lurleen, 154, 164, 257
Wallace, Wade, 78–79
Warren, Earl, 24
Weenick, Lawrence, 245
Wesley, Cynthia, 75
White Citizens' Council, xiii, 46, 56, 72, 128, 147, 163, 243, 256
"White Man's Defense Fund," 140, 149, 165, 173
Wilkins, Collie Leroy, 104–5, 106, 111, 114, 116, 123, 128, 129, 131, 136–37
Wilson, Donald, 267–69, 270
Wilson, George, 255–56
Wise, Marvin, 190–91
Wood, Don, 195

Young, Andrew, 265, 267

Zachary, N. E., 262